MODERN HUMANITIES RESEARCH ASSOCIATION
TUDOR AND STUART TRANSLATIONS
VOLUME 27

GENERAL EDITORS
ANDREW HADFIELD
NEIL RHODES

PETRARCH'S *TRIUMPHI* IN THE BRITISH ISLES

MODERN HUMANITIES RESEARCH ASSOCIATION
TUDOR AND STUART TRANSLATIONS

General Editors
Andrew Hadfield (University of Sussex)
Neil Rhodes (University of St Andrews)

Associate Editors
Guyda Armstrong (University of Manchester)
Fred Schurink (University of Manchester)
Louise Wilson (Liverpool Hope University)

Advisory Board
Warren Boutcher (Queen Mary, University of London);
Colin Burrow (All Souls College, Oxford);
A. E. B. Coldiron (Florida State University)
Patricia Demers (University of Alberta)
José Maria Pérez Fernández (University of Granada)
Robert S. Miola (Loyola College, Maryland)
Alessandra Petrina (University of Padua)
Anne Lake Prescott (Barnard College, Columbia University)
Quentin Skinner (Queen Mary, London)
Alan Stewart (Columbia University)

texts.mhra.org.uk

Petrarch's *Triumphi* in the British Isles

Edited by Alessandra Petrina

Modern Humanities Research Association
Tudor and Stuart Translations 27
2020

Published by

*The Modern Humanities Research Association
Salisbury House
Station Road
Cambridge CB1 2LA
United Kingdom*

© Modern Humanities Research Association 2020

Alessandra Petrina has asserted her right under the Copyright, Designs and Patents Act 1988 to be identified as the author of this work. Parts of this work may be reproduced as permitted under legal provisions for fair dealing (or fair use) for the purposes of research, private study, criticism, or review, or when a relevant collective licensing agreement is in place. All other reproduction requires the written permission of the copyright holder who may be contacted at rights@mhra.org.uk.

First published 2020

*ISBN 978-1-78188-882-7 (HB)
ISBN 978-1-78188-881-0 (PB)*

CONTENTS

Preface		ix
Acknowledgements		xi
List of abbreviations		xiii
List of illustrations		xiii
1.	Introduction	1
	1.1 The early dissemination of the *Triumphi* in Europe	4
	1.2 Petrarch in early modern England	9
	1.3 The *Triumphi*	16
	1.4 The dissemination of the *Triumphi* in the British Isles	21
	1.5 Early translations of the *Triumphi*	27
	1.6 The English translations	35
	1.6.1 Henry Howard, Earl of Surrey	36
	1.6.2 Henry Parker, Lord Morley	37
	1.6.3 William Fowler	40
	1.6.4 'E. D.'	47
	1.6.5 Mary Sidney, Countess of Pembroke	47
	1.6.6 John Florio	51
	1.6.7 The translation attributed to Elizabeth I	52
	1.6.8 Anna Hume	55
	1.7 Conclusion	58
2.	William Fowler's translation of Petrarch's *Triumphi*	63
	2.1 Text	68
3.	Translating the *Triumphus Mortis*	160
	3.1 Henry Parker, Lord Morley	160
	3.1.1 Text	161
	3.2 'E. D.'	175
	3.2.1 Text	175
	3.3 Mary Sidney, Countess of Pembroke	176
	3.3.1 Text	177
	3.4 Anna Hume	188
	3.4.1 Text	189
4.	Other Petrarchs: Fragmentary translations of the *Triumphi*	202
	4.1 Henry Howard, Earl of Surrey, 'Such wayward ways hath love'	202
	4.1.1 Text	203
	4.2 John Florio, *Second Frutes*	205

	4.2.1	Text	205
	4.3	The translation attributed to Elizabeth I	206
	4.3.1	Text	207
5.	Further reading		211
6.	Bibliography		213
	6.1	Manuscript sources	213
	6.2	Printed sources	213
	6.2.1	Editions and translations of Petrarch's works	213
	6.2.2	Other printed sources	214
	6.3	Studies	217
Index			228

GENERAL EDITORS' FOREWORD

The aim of the *MHRA Tudor & Stuart Translations* is to create a representative library of works translated into English during the early modern period for the use of scholars, students and the wider public. The series will include both substantial single works and selections of texts from major authors, with the emphasis being on the works that were most familiar to early modern readers. The texts themselves will be newly edited with substantial introductions, notes, and glossaries, and will be published both in print and online.

The series aims to restore to view a major part of English Renaissance literature which has become relatively inaccessible and to present these texts as literary works in their own right. For that reason it will follow the same principle of modernisation adopted by other scholarly editions of canonical literature from the period. The series will have a similar scope to that of the original *Tudor Translations* published early in the last century, and while the great majority of the works presented will be from the sixteenth century, like the original series it will not be rigidly bound by the end-date of 1603. There will, however, be a very different range of texts with new and substantial scholarly apparatus.

The *MHRA Tudor & Stuart Translations* will extend our understanding of the English Renaissance through its representation of the process of cultural transmission from the classical to the early modern world and the process of cultural exchange within the early modern world.

Andrew Hadfield
Neil Rhodes

PREFACE

Unlike Petrarch's *Canzoniere*, his *Triumphi* saw two complete and a number of partial translations into English in the sixteenth and early seventeenth centuries:

Complete translations:

Henry Parker, Lord Morley (composed during reign of Henry VIII?, printed in 1555);

William Fowler (completed in 1587).

Partial translations:

Henry Howard, Earl of Surrey: *Triumphus Cupidinis*, III. 151-87 (1540s);
E. D.: *Triumphus Mortis*, I. 79-100 (printed in 1585);
Mary Sidney, Countess of Pembroke: *Triumphus Mortis* (1590s);
John Florio: *Triumphus Pudicitie*, 76-90, 174 (printed in 1591);
Elizabeth I(?): *Triumphus Eternitatis*, 1-80 (date uncertain);
Anna Hume: *Triumphus Amoris, Pudicitie, Mortis* (printed in 1644).

The present edition attempts to offer as wide a range as possible of these translations, and to reconstruct the dissemination of the *Triumphi* in the British Isles in the early modern period. Chapter 1 is therefore an introductory chapter discussing the influence Petrarch's works had in the late medieval and early modern period, focussing on the *Triumphi*, and looking at book circulation and ownership, as well as quotations, allusions, and re-purposings of the topic in paintings and tapestries. I also discuss the various translators, setting their work against their respective contexts, and analysing their characteristics in terms of language, style, and metrical and lexical choices.

Chapter 2 presents a modern annotated edition of William Fowler's translation. I have chosen to edit this version since the other complete translation, by Henry Parker, Lord Morley, is already available in an excellent, comparatively recent edition.[1] Fowler's translation does appear in the complete edition of Fowler's works published by the Scottish Text Society between 1914 and 1940;[2] the three volumes constitute an invaluable asset for any student of Fowler's literary output, or indeed for any student of the Italian influence on Scottish literature in the early modern period. But there was the necessity of an updated and more easily available edition of this text, which could set it against the

---

[1] *Tryumphes of Fraunces Petrarcke. Translated by Lord Morley*, ed. by D. D. Carnicelli (Cambridge: Harvard University Press, 1971).
[2] *The Works of William Fowler, Secretary to Queen Anne, Wife of James VI*, ed. by Henry W. Meikle (Edinburgh: Blackwood, 1914, 1936, 1940).

background of the English and Scottish discovery of Petrarch's Italian poems. Following the usage of the MHRA Tudor and Stuart Translations series, I have presented the text with modernised spelling and punctuation, providing a full set of footnotes which are meant to help the reader not only with difficult, antiquated, or no longer used words and phrases, but also with obscure historical or literary allusions, or notable translation choices.

The other translations are presented in chapters 3 and 4. In the case of Morley and Hume, I have chosen the third triumph (the *Triumphus Mortis*) and inserted it in chapter 3 together with the translations of the same section undertaken by Mary Sidney and 'E. D.' (in the latter case, only a very short fragment was actually translated). I have chosen to focus on this particular triumph not only because it appears to have met the interest of a number of writers, including Mary Sidney, possibly the most gifted translator of this group, but because, as I hope to show in the Introduction, it represents a real innovation even in Petrarch's experimental handling of the triumphal material. In the various translations it encountered more specifically English and Scottish poetic traditions, such as the *danse macabre*, or the *ubi sunt* poem. All remaining translators (Henry Howard Earl of Surrey, John Florio and the translator identified with Elizabeth I) are presented in chapter 4, and their versions edited in their entirety, in order to show the range and diversity of the efforts of writers dealing with Petrarch's challenging work, who occasionally inserted their translations into other works (as in the case of Surrey and Florio) or, as in the passage from *Triumphus Eternitatis* whose translation is attributed to Queen Elizabeth, chose an excerpt detaching it from its original context and offering it as an individual meditation on time and eternity. A list of suggestions for further reading completes the book.

For all references to Petrarch's original version the modern edition I use is the one edited by Marco Ariani in 1988.[3] Since the editorial history of the *Triumphi* is confused and complex, and early modern printed editions sometimes differ considerably from the modern text, I have also offered a short survey of the early modern editions and their impact in the Introduction; all editions specifically referred to are also listed in the Bibliography. All quotations in languages other than English are translated in the footnotes; translations are mine unless otherwise indicated. Throughout the texts, I have followed the practice of marking with an apostrophe the elided 'v' in 'over' and 'even', and the elided 'k' in 'taken'. I have also added accents to indicate syllables that would be elided in modern pronunciation but that are required by the metre (as in 'piercèd'). While all edited texts are presented with modernised spelling and punctuation, a diplomatic transcription of the manuscripts and early printed editions I have used is available on the University of Padua website, at this address: <https://www.disll.unipd.it/ricerca/pubblicazioni-open-access>.

---

[3] *Triumphi*, ed. by Marco Ariani (Milan: Mursia, 1988).

ACKNOWLEDGEMENTS

Writing the acknowledgements page is a most pleasant task, as a book draws to its completion. To me it feels like having a party at which a great number of friends, young and old, are invited — and I will never be able to say how grateful I am to you all.

I wish to thank, first of all, the librarians and staff at the National Library of Scotland and Edinburgh University Library; the British Library; the Bodleian Library; the Inner Temple Library (special thanks are due to Michael Frost); Cambridge University Library; Bayerische Staatsbibliothek; and York Minster Library. Thanks to His Grace, the Duke of Norfolk, who allowed me to visit the Archives at Arundel Castle and study the Arundel Harington manuscript, and to the helpful and supportive staff of the Archives. For the permission to edit William Fowler's translation of the *Triumphi*, and to reproduce some images from MS Drummond De.1.10 and from MS Hawthornden 2063, I would like to thank, respectively, Edinburgh University Library Special Collections and the National Library of Scotland. For the permission to publish an edited version of Mary Sidney's translation of Petrarch's *Triumphus Mortis*, extant in manuscript (Inner Temple Library, Petyt MS 538.43), I would like to thank the Masters of the Bench of the Inner Temple. The cover image is by courtesy of the Italian 'Ministero per i beni e le attività culturali e per il Turismo'; the image cannot be further reproduced.

Sally Mapstone first suggested I undertake the study of William Fowler's translations of Italian works: her scholarship, friendship and encouragement have shaped much of my work. Julia Boffey and Tony Edwards encouraged me to persevere in the study of English translations of Petrarch, and supported me in moments of self-doubt. Andrew Hadfield and Neil Rhodes were all that general editors should be: their learning and friendship have accompanied me constantly. I also wish to thank the anonymous reader at the MHRA for insightful comments and invaluable suggestions, and Simon F. Davies for his impeccable copy-editing.

My colleagues and friends at the Dipartimento di Studi Linguistici e Letterari, Università degli Studi di Padova have created a perfect working and thinking environment. I wish to thank, in particular, Sergio Bozzola, Rocco Coronato, Ivano Paccagnella, Elisabetta Selmi; Franco Tomasi, who has put his immense knowledge at my disposal with characteristic, self-effacing kindness; Angelica Vedelago and Camilla Caporicci, who have kindly put aside their own concerns to engage with me on discussions of early modern translation and all things Petrarchan; and Allison Steenson, who has offered her expertise on early modern manuscripts and metrical issues, and has helped me solve some of the thornier problems connected with William Fowler's translation, as well as providing me with reproductions of an immense number of manuscripts. Thanks also to my attentive and forbearing students.

I have had the opportunity of presenting early drafts of some sections at a number of conferences, and of discussing my hypotheses with attentive and receptive audiences; for this I wish to thank Almási Zsolt, Tamás Karáth and their colleagues of the Pazmany University in Budapest; Massimo Sturiale and Giovanni Iamartino, who organized a conference on Elizabethan translation in Ragusa, in the course of which I had the chance of discussing the Petrarch translations with the late Robert Cummings; Donatella Montini and Iolanda Plescia of the Sapienza University in Rome; Ian Johnson, Giulio Pertile and Claudia Rossignoli, who were generous hosts more than once at the University of St Andrews; Helen Hackett and Alexander Sampson, who organized the Early Modern Exchanges conference in London; Giuliana Iannaccaro and all my friends at IASEMS; and Brenda Hosington and Marie-Alice Belle at the Université de Montreal. In the course of these and other conferences, in discussions, email exchanges and casual meetings, I have also had occasion to be profoundly grateful to Guyda Armstrong, Maurizio Ascari, Carlo Bajetta, Priscilla Bawcutt, Warren Boutcher, William Carroll, Kent Cartwright, Nick Havely, Domenico Lovascio, Alasdair MacDonald, David Norbrook, Donatella Pallotti, Brian Richardson, John Roe, Gabriela Schmidt, Fred Schurink, Emanuel Stelzer, Laura Tosi, and Christiania Whitehead. Giovanni Petrina has solved my problems with Petrarch's Latin, Stefano and Laura have hunted some sources for me, and together with the rest of my family they have accompanied me in this long journey. Oscar Meana has helped me with French passages and moments of despair: dedicating my work to him expresses only a tiny portion of my gratitude and love.

LIST OF ABBREVIATIONS

AHM *The Arundel Harington Manuscript of Tudor Poetry*, ed. by Ruth Hughey (Columbus: The Ohio State University Press, 1960)
Ariani Francesco Petrarca, *Triumphi*, ed. by Marco Ariani (Milan: Mursia, 1988)
DOST *Dictionary of the Older Scottish Tongue*, in *DSL: Dictionary of the Scots Language* <https://dsl.ac.uk>
EEBO *Early English Books Online* <https://search.proquest.com/eebo>
MED *Middle English Dictionary* <https://quod.lib.umich.edu/m/middle-english-dictionary/dictionary>
Meikle *The Works of William Fowler, Secretary to Queen Anne, Wife of James VI*, ed. by Henry W. Meikle, 3 vols (Edinburgh: Blackwood, 1914, 1936, 1940)
ODNB *Oxford Dictionary of National Biography* <https://www.oxforddnb.com>
OED *Oxford English Dictionary* <https://www.oed.com>
PERI *Petrarch Exegesis in Renaissance Italy* <https://petrarch.mml.ox.ac.uk>
TFP *Tryumphes of Fraunces Petrarcke: Translated by Lord Morley*, ed. by D. D. Carnicelli (Cambridge: Harvard University Press, 1971)

LIST OF ILLUSTRATIONS

Cover illustration: Andrea del Sarto (1486–1530), *Ritratto di donna col 'petrarchino'* (detail), *c*. 1528 (Florence, Galleria delle Statue e delle Pitture degli Uffizi, inv. 1890 n. 783)

Page 61 Frontispiece of William Fowler's translation (Edinburgh, Edinburgh University Library Special Collections, MS Drummond De.1.10, fol. 1r)

Page 66 Opening page of William Fowler's translation of the *Triumphus Amoris* (Edinburgh, Edinburgh University Library Special Collections, MS Drummond De.1.10, fol. 6r)

Page 67 Opening page of William Fowler's translation of the *Triumphus Amoris* (Edinburgh, National Library of Scotland, MS Hawthornden 2063, fol. 39r)

INTRODUCTION

'One saies of *Petrarche* for all: A thousand strappadas coulde not compell him to confesse, what some interpreters will make him saie he ment.' Thus John Florio, in the first edition of his dictionary *A Worlde of Wordes* (1598). Modern commentators or scholars of Petrarch will wryly recognize their own predicament in this description of the Italian poet's impenetrability under the veil of a most alluring smoothness. Florio then goes on, 'And a Judicious gentleman of this lande will uphold, that none in England understands him thoroughly'.[1]

It would be interesting to know who this 'Judicious gentleman' was, and whether Florio was proposing his own evaluation of the shortcomings of English translators and commentators, or simply voicing a belief shared by the early modern English community of readers. The mystery that is Petrarch continues to the modern day, and if we trace the progress of his *fortuna* we find a number of paradoxical elements: upon his death, in 1374, this very prolific writer left a substantial corpus of poems, prose works and letters in Latin, which marked his fame in the century following his death; today they have all but disappeared from memory, and are exclusively the domain of specialists. This is particularly true of the poem on which he staked his future fame, *Africa*. On the other hand, his most famous work at the present time is the collection of Italian poems now known as the *Canzoniere*, which the poet referred to as *Rerum Vulgarium Fragmenta* ('fragments in the vernacular'); in late medieval and early modern Europe, this collection was normally taken into consideration together with the *Triumphi*, the other Petrarchan masterpiece in the vernacular. Together, the two works became not only the first Petrarchan text, but also the first in Italian to be printed, in 1470, and remain strongly linked in readers' consciousness throughout the sixteenth century;[2] yet over the past century the fame of the *Canzoniere* has almost eclipsed the *Triumphi*, and now Petrarch is known almost solely as the author of the former.

The reception of Petrarch in English culture mirrors this situation. When we think of Petrarch in late medieval English literature, we are faced with two phenomena. On the one hand, there is the early fifteenth-century English translation of *De remediis utriusque fortunae*, possibly the first Petrarchan Latin text to be translated into English, and a text that enjoyed widespread circulation

---

[1] John Florio, *A Worlde of Wordes* (London: Blount, 1598), sig. A4r.
[2] [*Princeps* of *Rerum Vulgarium Fragmenta* and *Triumphi*] incipit: A Pie decolli ove labella vesta (Venice: Vindelinus de Spira, 1470).

in late medieval Europe;[3] on the other, we have Geoffrey Chaucer, who, apart from inserting a translation of one of Petrarch's Italian sonnets into his *Troilus and Criseyde*, almost certainly used his Latin version of the story of Griselda for his *Clerk's Tale*, explicitly invoking Petrarch's shadow in the Prologue. Chaucer might also have been influenced by the *Triumphi* in the writing of his *House of Fame*, though there is much uncertainty on this point.[4] Yet if it is problematic to gauge the influence of Petrarch in England, it is even more problematic to attempt to do so through Chaucer, who represents a unique case of close connection with contemporary Italian writing.[5] This uniqueness is registered not only by modern scholarship, but also by early modern intellectuals: Philip Sidney, in his *Defence of Poesy*, 'marveled that Chaucer "in that misty time could see so clearly"'.[6] As we chart the dissemination and influence of Petrarch's works in medieval and early modern England, it may be more accurate to say that there are two Petrarchs, one Latin and one Italian, each claiming a distinct place in the English literary imagination between the fourteenth and the sixteenth centuries: fifteenth-century English humanists, from John Tiptoft to John Lydgate, showed great interest, and in some cases veneration, for Petrarch's Latin works, apparently unaware of the existence of the Italian ones, while poets and translators of the following century were progressively

---

[3] Cambridge, Cambridge University Library, MS Ii.VI.39, fols 177v–88v. See Francesco Petrarca, *A Dialogue between Reason and Adversity: A Late Middle English Version of Petrarch's De Remediis*, ed. by F. N. M. Diekstra (Assen: Van Gorcum, 1968).

[4] J. A. W. Bennett, *Chaucer's Book of Fame: An Exposition of 'The House of Fame'* (Oxford: Clarendon Press, 1968), pp. 108–10. However, rather than with the *Triumphus Fame*, Bennett finds more analogies with the *Triumphus Temporis*. His claim is based on a similar use of images, such as the sun participating in the dissolution of human fame; he also notes, citing Brusendorff, that the Clerk of Oxford's apostrophe to the 'stormy people, unsad and evere untrewe' depends on lines 133–34 of the *Triumphus Temporis*. For an analysis of the theme of Fame in Petrarch, and implicitly in Chaucer, see also Piero Boitani, *Chaucer and the Imaginary World of Fame* (Cambridge: D. S. Brewer, 1984), pp. 103–24. Nicholas Mann detects the influence of *De remediis utriusque fortunae* (especially the dialogue *De alchimia*, I. 111) in the alchemist's portrait in the Canon's Yeoman's Tale ('Il Petrarca e gli inizi del Rinascimento inglese', *La Cultura*, 15 (1977), 3–18 (p. 4)).

[5] Ironically, Chaucer was to be vindicated as superior to either Petrarch or Boccaccio a couple of centuries later. On fol. 1r of his copy of Lodovico Domenichi's *Facetie, motti, et burle* Gabriel Harvey writes: 'Classicis auctoribus addo Bartasium, ob divinum furorem: Rabelaisium ob humanum: Chaucerum ob mixtum. Malo Chaucerum quam Petrarcham: Boccatium, aut Ariostum: Rabelaisium, quam Aretinum' ('To the classical authors I add Du Bartas on account of his divine frenzy, Rabelais on account of his humanity, Chaucer for a mixture of the two. I prefer Chaucer to Petrarch, Boccaccio and Ariosto; and Rabelais to Aretino'). See Virginia F. Stern, *Gabriel Harvey: His Life, Marginalia and Library* (Oxford: Clarendon Press, 1979), p. 175 (I have amended Stern's translation). Interestingly, Harvey had read and appreciated Petrarch's *Triumphi*: see Eleanor Relle, 'Some New Marginalia and Poems of Gabriel Harvey', *The Review of English Studies*, 23 (1972), 401-16 (pp. 411-12).

[6] Richard Waswo, 'The Petrarchan Tradition as a Dialectic of Limits', *Studies in the Literary Imagination*, 11 (1978), 1-16 (p. 8).

more attracted to the Italian works. In his *Fall of Princes*, written in the 1430s, John Lydgate even offers a list that includes most of Petrarch's Latin production, while making no reference to the *Triumphi* or the *Canzoniere*:

> Writyng of old, with lettres aureat,
> Labour of poetis doth hihli magnefie,
> Record on Petrak, in Rome laureat,
> Which of too Fortunys wrot the remedie,
> Certeyn Ecloogis and his Cosmographie,
> And a gret conflict, which men may reede and see,
> Of his querellis withynne hymsilff secre.
>
> He wrot sevene Psalmys of gret repentaunce,
> And in his Affrik comendid Scipioun,
> And wrot a book of his ignoraunce
> Bi a maner of excusacioun,
> And sette a notable compilacioun
> Upon the lyff[e] called solitarye,
> To which this world is froward and contrarie.
>
> And thus be writyng he gat hymsilff a name
> Perpetuelli to been in remembraunce,
> Set and registred in the Hous of Fame,
> And made Epistles of ful hih substaunce
> Callid Sine Titulo; and mor hymsilff tavaunce,
> Of famous women he wrot thexcellence,
> Gresilde preferryng for hir grete pacience.[7]

The hypothesis that the century after Petrarch's death saw a more decided interest in his Latin works is confirmed by a census of the surviving manuscripts. The comprehensive survey of Petrarch manuscripts in British libraries undertaken in 1975 by Nicholas Mann (who counted over 250 manuscripts, of which forty, all containing Latin works, had been composed or copied in England between the fourteenth and the fifteenth centuries)[8] supports the impression that both *Canzoniere* and *Triumphi*, though their popularity had been growing in Italy and to a lesser extent in Europe since the later decades of the fifteenth century, were unknown in the British Isles until the late 1520s, when Sir Thomas Wyatt returned from his ambassadorial mission to the papal court.[9] The belated

---

[7] *Lydgate's Fall of Princes*, ed. by Henry Bergen (London: Oxford University Press, 1924-27), book IV, lines 106-26.
[8] Nicholas Mann, 'Petrarch Manuscripts in the British Isles', *Italia Medioevale e Umanistica*, 18 (1975), 139-509. For a quick overview, see Mann, 'Petrarch and Humanism: The Paradox of Posterity', in *Francesco Petrarca: Citizen of the World*, ed. by Aldo S. Bernardo (Padua and Albany: Antenore and State University of New York Press, 1980), pp. 287-99.
[9] The one exception I have been able to find might be Jacob Locher, who in the introduction to Alexander Barclay's translation of Sebastian Brant's *The Shyp of Folys of*

English reaction to Petrarch's Italian works thus strengthens the traditional critical dichotomy: the two Petrarchs, Latin and Italian (and, by implication, medieval and humanist) appear very difficult to reconcile, and although of course the Latin works of Petrarch survived the Middle Ages and were read in early modern Europe, they were progressively relegated to second place once the Italian poems were brought to the fore.[10] Petrarch himself appears to have been conscious of embodying a dichotomy, and speaks of himself as 'velut in confinio duorum popularum constitutus ac simul ante retroque prospiciens' ('Set as if on the border between two people, and able to look forward as well as backward').[11] It is perhaps upon this sense of a divided self that we can base our understanding of the enormous and multifaceted influence the Italian writer exercised upon European literature over the centuries.

1.1 The early dissemination of the *Triumphi* in Europe

Prior to the invention of printing the Italian works were circulated in manuscript in Europe (if not in the British Isles), perhaps with a slight preference for the *Triumphi* over the *Canzoniere*: writing in 1943, Ernest Wilkins noted that 'of 213 fourteenth- and fifteenth-century manuscripts listed by Narducci as containing one or both of the two works, some 85 contained the Triumphs alone, some 79 contain both Triumphs and *Canzoniere*, and only some 49 contain the *Canzoniere* alone'.[12] Over seventy years later, new manuscript findings have substantially increased the number, but also significantly changed the proportions: the *PERI* database, still undergoing revision, includes in its census 277 manuscripts containing the *Triumphi*, as well as three lost manuscripts; of these, 193 appear to contain both texts, and seventy-five the *Triumphi* alone, while the number of manuscripts containing the *Canzoniere* alone is much harder to specify, since a very high number of codices contains a greater or smaller selection of the poems.[13] It is a generalization, though one that contains

the Worlde (1509) refers to Philippus Beroaldus's Latin version of Petrarch's Italian poems. See Jackson Campbell Boswell and Gordon McMurry Braden, *Petrarch's English Laurels, 1475–1700* (Farnham: Ashgate, 2012), no. 9, pp. 15–16.

[10] As Gordon Braden notes, 'Petrarch's Latin and vernacular works moved through western Europe on different schedules, with tenuous links to one another; they were printed together only in the Basel *Opera* of 1554 and 1581' (*Petrarchan Love and the Continental Renaissance* (New Haven: Yale University Press, 1999), p. 62).

[11] Francesco Petrarca, *Rerum memorandarum libri*, ed. by Marco Poletti (Florence: Le Lettere, 2014), I. 19. 4, p. 54.

[12] Ernest H. Wilkins, 'The Fifteenth-Century Editions of the Italian Poems of Petrarch', *Modern Philology*, 40 (1943), 225–39 (p. 225). He is referring to Enrico Narducci's catalogues of Petrarch's manuscripts, compiled in 1874.

[13] See *Petrarch's Exegesis in Renaissance Italy* (PERI), prepared by Giacomo Comiati and Lorenzo Sacchini with Francesco Venturi (overseen by Simon Gilson and Federica Pich) <https://petrarch.mml.ox.ac.uk/> (accessed 15 October 2019). The database is currently the

a good deal of truth, to say that Petrarch's Italian works were canonized thanks to Pietro Bembo's *Prose della volgar lingua*, first published in 1525; as noted above, the printing of the poems themselves had begun much earlier, in 1470.

In Italy, and by implication in Europe, the vernacular works were subjected to different interpretations by successive generations of readers and commentators; this tells us more about the different ages' responses to the poet than about his own intentions. The earliest commentary was written in the 1420s and attributed to Antonio da Tempo in Padua; this was followed by that of Francesco Filelfo (working only on the first 136 sonnets of the *Canzoniere*), who dedicated his work to Filippo Maria Visconti in 1446; Filelfo's commentary was completed by Hieronimo Squarzafico, who published it in Venice in 1484. These early readings, combined in what William Kennedy calls 'the Antonio-Filelfo-Squarzafico commentaries with their view of Petrarch as a Ghibelline monarchist',[14] became *Petrarcha con doi commenti*, a work which went through at least nine separate editions between 1503 and 1523.[15] Pietro Bembo responded by proposing a reading centred on the Medici values of republicanism. Bembo had already supervised the first edition printed by Aldus Manutius of *Canzoniere* and *Triumphi*, with the title *Le cose volgari di messer Francesco Petrarcha* (1501). It was not annotated,[16] but it was proposed as an explicit construction of a classic, prepared with the canonical rules of a critical edition (Bembo was working with the autograph manuscripts in his possession).[17] From this early work he developed a more articulated reflection, culminating in his publication of the *Prose*. Other commentators, such as Giovanni Andrea Gesualdo and Bernardino Daniello,[18] were more interested in the rhetorical analysis of the poems; and a group of commentators — including Fausto da Longiano in 1532 and Antonio Brucioli in 1548[19] — authorized 'a more radical, less predictable

---

best tool available for work on the early dissemination of Petrarch's texts. For an overview of the early editions of Petrarch, see also Guyda Armstrong, 'Re-materialising the Incunable Petrarch: Ernest Hatch Wilkins and the Politics of Bibliographical Description', *Italian Studies*, 75 (2020), 55-70.

[14] William J. Kennedy, 'Petrarchan Poetics', in *The Cambridge History of Literary Criticism, III: The Renaissance*, ed. by Glyn P. Norton (Cambridge: Cambridge University Press, 1999), pp. 119-26 (p. 120).

[15] The first edition is *Petrarcha con doi commenti* (Venice: Albertino da Lissona, 1503). See William J. Kennedy, *Authorizing Petrarch* (Ithaca: Cornell University Press, 1994), p. 2.

[16] Kennedy, 'Petrarchan Poetics', p. 120.

[17] Stefano Jossa, 'Bembo and Italian Petrarchism', in *The Cambridge Companion to Petrarch*, ed. by Albert Russell Ascoli and Unn Falkeid (Cambridge: Cambridge University Press, 2015), pp. 191-200.

[18] *Il Petrarcha con l'espositione di m. Giovanni Andrea Gesualdo* (Venice: Giovanni Antonio Niccolini da Sabbio, 1533); *Sonetti, canzoni, e triomphi di messer Francesco Petrarcha con la spositione di Bernardino Daniello* (Venice: Giovanni Antonio Niccolini da Sabbio, 1541).

[19] *Il Petrarcha col commento di m. Sebastiano Fausto da Longiano* (Venice: Francesco Bindoni and Maffeo Pasini, 1532); *Sonetti canzoni e Triomphi di m. Francesco Petrarca con*

view than the others, of a Petrarch imbued with Protestant Reformist ideals', representing the poet as 'proto-Protestant, disdainful of scholastic clichés, teeming with references to Saint Augustine and the Scriptures, and adept in satirizing the Avignon papacy'.[20] The reading of Petrarch as proto-Protestant is based on a very restricted number of texts: sonnets 136 to 138 of the *Canzoniere* (the anti-papacy sonnets), and the *Liber sine nomine*, Petrarch's most polemical work. The latter was occasionally used and paraphrased in Protestant circles; in 1555, during the Council of Trent, Petrus Paulus Vergerius the younger, a papal nuncio who had converted to the Lutheran cause, published it with a preface that made its anti-Catholic interpretation explicit.[21] The anti-papacy sonnets enjoyed great popularity in England, being among the most frequently translated.[22] Another commentator, Bernardo Ilicino, wrote a commentary on the *Triumphi* alone, which appeared in at least twenty-three editions between 1475 and 1522,[23] and is believed by some scholars to be the basis of important subsequent commentaries, from Gesualdo to Vellutello to Leopardi.[24] The great *fortuna* the *Triumphi* enjoyed between the late fifteenth and sixteenth centuries has made producing a modern, philologically informed edition today a rather daunting task, and even critical editions tend to perpetuate a text that has been determined by early modern editors and commentators.[25]

By the second quarter of the sixteenth century the enhanced interest in the Italian Petrarch was supported by two recently published books: the joint edition of *Canzoniere* and *Triumphi* by Alessandro Vellutello,[26] which appeared

---

breve dichiaratione e annotatione di Antonio Brucioli (Venice: Antonio Brucioli, 1548).

[20] Kennedy, *Authorizing Petrarch*, p. 3. On other, minor commentaries preceding Vellutello's, see Gino Belloni, *Laura tra Petrarca e Bembo: studi sul commento umanistico-rinascimentale* (Padua: Antenore, 1992), pp. 58–62.

[21] Robert Coogan, 'Petrarch's *Liber Sine Nomine* and a Vision of Rome in the Reformation', *Renaissance and Reformation / Renaissance et Réforme*, 7 (1983), 1–12 (p. 5).

[22] Boswell and Braden, p. 4.

[23] [*Triumphi* with Ilicino's commentary and RVF 1–136 with Filelfo's commentary] incipit: AD Illustrissimum Mutinae Ducem Divum Borsium estensem Ber-nardi glicini Medicinae ac philosophiae discipuli in triumphorum. CL[arissimi] P[oetae] Fra[ncisci] Petrarce expositio incipit (Bologna: Hannibal Malpiglius, 1475–1476). RVF, the acronym for *Rerum Vulgarium Fragmenta*, refers to the name used by Petrarch for the collection now better known as the *Canzoniere*. See Angela Pozone, 'Un commentatore quattrocentesco del Petrarca: Bernardo Ilicino', *Atti della Accademia Pontaniana*, 23 (1974), 371–90 (p. 371). See also the *PERI* database.

[24] D. D. Carnicelli, 'Bernardo Illicino and the Renaissance Commentaries on Petrarch's *Trionfi*', *Romance Philology*, 23 (1969), 57–64.

[25] As noted by Amilcare A. Iannucci, who notes that there are over 300 known manuscripts of the *Triumphi*, concluding: 'the vulgate text may be flawed, but in terms of the *Triumphs*' reception in the Renaissance, it is the one that counts'; 'Foreword', in *Petrarch's 'Triumphs': Allegory and Spectacle*, ed. by Konrad Eisenbichler and Amilcare A. Iannucci (Ottawa: Dovehouse, 1988), pp. xi–xv (p. xii).

[26] First published as *Le volgari opere del Petrarcha con la espositione di Alessandro Vellutello*

for the first time in 1525 and was reprinted, in various forms, no less that fifty-two times in the sixteenth century,[27] enjoying great popularity across Europe, including England; and Bembo's *Prose della Volgar Lingua*, first published in the same year. Bembo's election of Petrarch as the model of Italian poetry (while Boccaccio was the model of prose) sanctioned the definitive supremacy of Petrarch's Italian poetry over his Latin prose, and set a model that quickly became standard for European lyric poets.[28] His endorsement of Petrarch as the supreme example of poetry in the Italian vernacular also offered a substantial contribution to the construction of this poet as a modern classic. At the same time, in the edition he prepared for Manutius in 1501, Bembo had explicitly proposed a biographical reading: 'promoting a division into a first part written during Laura's life and a second written after her death, Bembo endorsed the reading of Petrarch's masterpiece as an autobiographical narrative containing a spiritual journey from earthly to divine love'.[29] Vellutello's edition decidedly developed this interpretation, transforming the two works into an autobiographical unit, re-ordering the sequence of the *rime sparse*, inserting a biographical note on both the poet and Laura and even a map of Vaucluse, thus canonizing Petrarch's love progress through his poetry and transforming the poetic corpus into a (romantic) narrative. The success this edition enjoyed can be measured not only by the twenty-three printings between 1525 and 1584,[30] but also by concomitant events such as the 1527 celebrations for the wedding between François I's son and Caterina de Medici, which took place in Lyon and included the 'discovery' of Laura's tomb, while French and Italian court poets exalted the King as a new *Franciscus*.[31]

Vellutello's paratextual material placed the *Canzoniere* 'squarely in the centre of Petrarch's literary career',[32] perhaps to the detriment of the *Triumphi*, and accompanied the development of the reception of Petrarch's Italian poetry, which saw the *Triumphi* slowly but inexorably supplanted by the earlier work. The difference in their reception may also help us understand the structural difference between the two works, which conditioned their development in

(Venice: Giovanni Antonio Nicolini da Sabbio, 1525).
[27] As attested by the *PERI* database.
[28] Pietro Bembo, *Prose della volgar lingua*, in *Prose e Rime*, ed. by Carlo Dionisotti (Turin: UTET, 1966), pp. 175-78.
[29] Jossa, p. 193.
[30] Jossa, p. 195.
[31] See Brian Richardson, *Print Culture in Renaissance Italy: The Editor and the Vernacular Text 1470-1700* (Cambridge: Cambridge University Press, 1994), pp. 77-78. I wish to thank Franco Tomasi for discussing this point with me.
[32] William J. Kennedy, 'Versions of a Career: Petrarch and his Renaissance Commentators', in *European Literary Careers: The Author from Antiquity to the Renaissance*, ed. by Patrick Cheney and Frederick A. de Armas (Toronto: University of Toronto Press, 2002), pp. 146-64 (p. 158).

the work of translators and imitators. As a sequence composed of potentially autonomous units (whether sonnets or other lyric forms), the *Canzoniere* allowed a literary fruition that depended on its fragmentary nature;[33] this encouraged the proliferation of many imitations, transformations and parodies in the work of early modern English poets. The very flexible structure of the *Canzoniere* made it an obvious text to use for adaptation or *transcreation*,[34] rather than straightforward translation. The *Triumphi* is generally perceived as a much more unified work, which may be the result of misreading, since as we know the work never reached a fully complete and harmonious form in its creator's eyes. Petrarch himself did not leave many traces concerning his own planning and structuring; as recent editors have noted, this might be due to his own dissatisfaction with an ever-unresolved construction.[35] The allusions we do have, in his letters or postils, speak of restlessness and discontent: in a letter to Boccaccio, for instance, he notes his intention of beginning a great work ('magnum eo in genere opus inceperam', 'I started working on a great enterprise'),[36] but also notes his hesitation, and his consciousness of his hubristic intentions; the postils often mark his fluctuating attitude: 'mane dum hoc scribo et ista percurro, fastidio potius quam studio' ('As I write this and go through it in the morning, annoyed rather than interested').[37] Even more striking is his wry comment in a letter to the Archbishop of Genoa: 'Certus labor, fructus incertus' ('The effort is assured, the result uncertain').[38]

No such uncertainty appears in Vellutello's presentation of Petrarch's works. In the introduction to the *Triumphi*, he noted that 'quantunque l'una da l'altra opera sia diversa, nondimeno, ciascuna per se stessa, quasi come di sua perfettione mancasse, resteria ignuda' ('Though the two works are different from each other, yet each on its own, as if lacking in perfection, would be naked'), and he also, somewhat ominously, promised the reader 'che io emenderò molti luoghi ne l'opera' ('I shall emend this work in many places').[39] This, together with the re-ordering of the *Canzoniere*, was part of his effort to present Petrarch's Italian opus as one work, and though modern philology would not agree with Vellutello's sometimes intrusive re-ordering, there is little doubt that

---

[33] Francesco Guardiani, 'The Literary Impact of the *Trionfi* in the Renaissance', in *Petrarch's 'Triumphs'*, ed. by Eisenblicher and Iannucci, pp. 259–68 (p. 259).
[34] This useful term is proposed by Derrick McClure in his 'Translation and Transcreation in the Castalian Period', *Studies in Scottish Literature*, 26 (1991), 185–98.
[35] Marco Ariani, 'Introduzione', in Ariani, p. 5.
[36] *Rerum senilium Libri IV–VII*, ed. by Elvira Nota (Paris: Les Belles Lettres, 2003), v. 2, pp. 139–41.
[37] *Postilla* to line 73 of *Triumphus Cupidinis*, I, 12 September 1358. Quoted in Ariani, p. 6.
[38] *Rerum familiarum Libri XVI–XIX*, ed. by Ugo Dotti (Paris: Les Belles Lettres, 2005), XIX. 16, p. 383.
[39] *Il Petrarcha. Con l'espositione d'Alessandro Vellutello di novo ristampato con le figure ai triomphi* (Venice: Gabriel Giolito, 1547), p. 161r.

this was the Petrarch sixteenth-century European readers were most familiar with. The miraculous fusion of narration and lyrical contemplation is central to the appreciation, reception and extraordinary fame of Petrarch's Italian works — both in the *Canzoniere*, with its splendidly oxymoronic existence as a sonnet sequence, and in the *Triumphi*, more traditionally seen as an epic poem, following the model of Dante's *Commedia* also in the choice of *terza rima*,[40] but like the *Commedia* leaving ample space for philosophical contemplation. Already in 1563 Antonio Minturno, writing his *Arte Poetica*, would implicitly set the *Triumphi*, together with Dante's poem and Virgil's *Aeneid*, as one of the three masterpieces of epic poetry.[41] Although later in the sixteenth century other commentaries on the poems appeared (sometimes more influential ones from the scholarly point of view), there is no doubt that Vellutello's work and the immense popularity it enjoyed determined an autobiographical approach that influenced a number of translations, adaptations, rewritings and parodies. It also made for constant appropriation and re-creation of Laura, who took on a quasi-historical reality that authorized her being given, in a number of instances, a voice of her own.

1.2 Petrarch in early modern England

A full analysis of the dissemination of the Italian works of Petrarch in England may have been hampered by the fact that too often Petrarch has been identified solely with the *Canzoniere*, his sonnet sequence, which is today by far the most famous of his works. It is true that it was a major influence on early modern European lyric poetry, both in literature and in music (just as the *Triumphi*, though to a lesser extent, influenced literature and the visual arts); on the other hand, given the structure of the sonnet sequence, it was much more obvious for translators, poets and musicians to copy, adapt or imitate a single sonnet or *canzone* than the whole work. Some sonnets in particular (such as 'Solo e pensoso' or 'Zefiro torna') enjoyed great popularity, possibly at the expense of other sections.[42] This situation has led to critical statements such as, 'in Renaissance England Petrarch was a name rather than a book [...] But if it was a name, it was a name beyond all others'.[43] This reduction of Petrarch to a name

---

[40] *Terza rima* is an Italian metrical form, consisting of sets of three hendecasyllabic lines in which the middle line of each set rhymes with the first and last of the following one (*aba, bcb, cdc*, etc.). Made famous by Dante's *Commedia*, it also appears in Boccaccio's *Amorosa Visione*.

[41] Antonio Minturno, *L'Arte Poetica* (Venice: Giovanni Antonio Valvassori, 1564), pp. 36-38 and 393-94.

[42] For the *Canzoniere*, the edition used throughout is *Canzoniere*, ed. by Gianfranco Contini (Turin: Einaudi, 1975).

[43] George Watson, *The English Petrarchans: A Critical Bibliography of the Canzoniere* (London: The Warburg Institute, 1967), p. 3.

(a phenomenon similar to what has been observed of the early English reception of Machiavelli) is only possible if one does not take into account the response to the *Triumphi*, translations of which have been frequently underestimated or ignored, to the point that it has recently been stated that 'Elizabethan poets generally avoided close translations of Petrarch'.[44]

This profound misunderstanding of the reception of Petrarch's Italian poetry is related to the present vogue for the *Canzoniere*, to the detriment — even the consignment to oblivion — of any other of his works. It has been asserted that Richard Tottel's publication of *Songes and Sonettes* in 1557 marked 'the turning-point in English Petrarchism';[45] after Chaucer's experiments and allusions, the first English translation of the 'Italian' Petrarch is identified with the corpus of twenty-seven sonnets translated by Thomas Wyatt, possibly as a result of his journey to Italy in 1527. The fame of the early English versions of Petrarch's sonnets, and the subsequent imitations, adaptations and parodies, may have clouded the issue as concerns the reception of the Italian poet, leading to an overestimation of the influence of the *Canzoniere* and an underestimation of the *Triumphi*. Yet, unlike the *Canzoniere*, the latter work was translated in its entirety on at least two different occasions in the sixteenth century, and its fame remained enduring and pervasive. Robert Coogan traces the development of Petrarchism in England in greater detail:

> By the last quarter of the fifteenth century, his Latin prose has an honoured place at Oxford and Cambridge. By the middle of the sixteenth century, the *Trionfi* have added a new dimension to Petrarch's image. Although he remains the humanist who shook the dust from the classics and the philosopher who ponders life and death, time and eternity, he becomes also the poet who has the Lady Laura at his side. At the end of the century, the *Canzoniere* firmly establish [sic] the cult of Petrarch.[46]

In the first stages of this transition from the Latin to the Italian Petrarch Thomas Wyatt played a major role. After his return from Italy in 1528, Wyatt presented Catherine of Aragon with a New Year's gift, a translation of Plutarch's *De tranquillitate et securitate animi* (the intermediary text being the Latin translation by Guillaume Budé).[47] Yet originally he had entertained

---

[44] Joshua Scodel, 'Lyric', in *The Oxford History of Literary Translation in English: Volume 2: 1550–1660*, ed. by Gordon McMurry Braden, Robert Cummings and Stuart Gillespie (Oxford: Oxford University Press, 2010), pp. 212–47 (p. 237).

[45] William A. Sessions, *Henry Howard: The Poet Earl of Surrey: A Life* (Oxford: Oxford University Press, 1999), p. 188.

[46] Robert Coogan, 'Petrarch's "Trionfi" and the English Renaissance', *Studies in Philology*, 67 (1960), 306–27 (p. 307). The first complete translation of the *Canzoniere* is dated 1879: see Kennedy's reconstruction in *The Collected Works of Mary Sidney, Countess of Pembroke: Volume 1: Poems, Translations and Correspondence*, ed. by Margaret P. Hannay, Noel J. Kinnamon and Michael G. Brennan (Oxford: Clarendon Press, 1998), p. 259, n. 20.

[47] Colin Burrow, 'Wyatt, Sir Thomas (c. 1503–1542)', *ODNB*. See also Susan Brigden and

a different project: he translated Plutarch only because he had 'baulked at the stiffer task of translating Petrarch's *De remediis utriusque fortunae*', as the queen had requested.[48] The decision might surprise us, since *De remediis* had already been translated in late medieval England. In the dedicatory letter to the queen prefacing his translation Wyatt explains his decision, beginning with a straightforward apology for not obeying her request:

> The boke of Fraunces Petrarch of the remedy of yll fortune at the commaundement of your highnesse I assayd as my power wolde serve me to make into our englyssh. And after I had made a prose of nyne or ten Dialogues the labour began to seme tedious by superfluous often rehersyng of one thyng, which tho peraventure in the latyn shalbe laudable by plentuous diversite of the spekyng of it (for I wyll nat that my Jugement shall disalowe in any thyng so aproved an auctor) yet for lacke of suche diversyte in our tong it shulde want a great dele of the grace. Altho as me semeth and as sayth this Plutarch the plentuousnesse and faire diversyte of langage shulde nat so moch be desyred in suche thynges as the frutes of the advertysmentes of them whiche in my opinyon this sayde Plutarch hath handsomly gadred togyder without tedyousnesse of length contaynyng the hole effect of that your hyghnes desyred of Petrarch in his lytell boke which he wrate to one of his frendes of the Quiete of mynde nerawhyt erryng from the purpose of the sayd Petrarch.[49]

It is a rather extraordinary passage: the absent Petrarch, rather than the present Plutarch, is foremost in the writer's mind. Wyatt is obviously negotiating an awkward refusal to comply with the queen's request, and adroitly turns it into a critique of Petrarch's expository method.[50] The fault seems initially to reside with 'our englyssh', which has nothing comparable to the semantic diversity of Latin; but this is implicitly challenged by the fact that Plutarch had been in fact translated *from Latin*. Wyatt therefore exposes what, at the end of the passage, is perceived as Petrarch's prolixity and love of *variatio* for its own sake (the 'tedyousnesse of length'), in contrast with Plutarch's *frutes*. He adds an interesting caveat: 'I wyll nat that my jugement shall disalowe in any thyng so aproved an auctor', an aside (anticipated by *peraventure* in the previous line) underlining individual taste which, in this case, appears to run counter

---

Jonathan Woolfson, 'Thomas Wyatt in Italy', *Renaissance Quarterly*, 58 (2005), 464–511.
[48] Burrow, 'Wyatt, Sir Thomas', *ODNB*. Greg Walker offers a different, and fascinating, interpretation of Wyatt's decision in *Writing under Tyranny: English Literature and the Henrician Reformation* (Oxford: Oxford University Press, 2005), pp. 284–85.
[49] Thomas Wyatt, *Tho. wyatis translatyon of Plutarckes boke, of the quyete of mynde* (London: Richard Pynson, 1528), sig. A2. See *The Complete Works of Sir Thomas Wyatt the Elder: Volume I: Prose*, ed. by Jason Powell (Oxford: Oxford University Press, 2016), pp. 1–41. A modern edition of Wyatt's translation is Fred Schurink (ed.), *Plutarch in English, 1528–1603*, 2 vols (London: Modern Humanities Research Association, forthcoming), i.
[50] On the political implications of Wyatt's gesture, see *The Complete Works of Sir Thomas Wyatt*, p. 7.

to received opinion; in the end, Plutarch may offer the same matter with less tediousness.

Wyatt cautiously criticizes Petrarch's Latin prose just as he was discovering his Italian lyric poetry. The dichotomy between the two Petrarchs, the Latin/medieval and the Italian/humanist, seems to have been solved by the translator with a decided preference for the latter, a preference that would influence the course of English lyric poetry, although the Latin Petrarch does not disappear completely: *De remediis utriusque fortunae* would be translated once more, in 1579, by Thomas Twyne, and mentioned in later works; Samuel Daniel would translate *De vita solitaria* around 1610.[51] It is also notable that Wyatt should discuss the comparative merits of Petrarch and Plutarch in linguistic terms, addressing his considerations to a queen whose Latin might be better than her English. Language is a constant preoccupation underlining the efforts of the English and Scottish translators of Petrarch, and is often mentioned in prefatory material. This is not in itself surprising: in an age in which translation was a fundamental tool for language learning,[52] the choice of authors to translate could primarily be dictated by their linguistic or stylistic qualities. Even in prefacing his 1553 translation of such a controversial book as Niccolò Machiavelli's *Prince* into French, Guillaume Cappel would list among Machiavelli's qualities 'un bon moien de proceder, un stile propre a la matiere, une connoissance des histoires, une experience asseurée' ('a good way to proceed, a style which is appropriate to the matter, a knowledge of history, an assured experience');[53] the linguistic excellence of the original could also be an excuse for translating an otherwise dubious text. In the case of sixteenth-century English writers, this preoccupation was reinforced by a perceived inferiority on the part of the target language, as already shown in Wyatt's dedicatory letter: unlike French (a language which would naturally meet the requirements set by classical or canonical texts), English was still perceived to be inadequate. Late medieval writers would occasionally make use of this topos, as in the case of Geoffrey Chaucer, who refers to the 'naked words' of English in his *Treatise on the Astrolabe*;[54] but even more interesting is the discussion

---

[51] Francesco Petrarca, *Phisicke against fortune, aswell prosperous, as aduerse conteyned in two books* [...] *now first Englished by Thomas Twyne* (London: Richard Watkyns, 1579). For the continuing influence of *De remediis* on the English sixteenth century, see Robert Coogan, 'Petrarch's Latin Prose and the English Renaissance', *Studies in Philology*, 68 (1971), 270–91. On Daniel's translation, see Jessica Stoll, 'Petrarch's *De vita solitaria*: Samuel Daniel's Translation c. 1610', *Modern Language Review*, 109 (2014), 313–32.
[52] Jason Lawrence, 'Who the devil taught thee so much Italian?' *Italian Language Learning and Literary Imitation in Early Modern England* (Manchester: Manchester University Press, 2005), pp. 45–54.
[53] Niccolò Machiavelli, *Le Prince de Nicolas Machiavelle secretaire et citoien de Florence. Traduit d'Italien en Françoys Par Guillaume Cappel* (Paris: Charles Estienne, 1553), sig. IIIv.
[54] Geoffrey Chaucer, *A Treatise on the Astrolabe*, in *The Riverside Chaucer: Third Edition*,

of the value of English as the language of translation from Latin, appearing in John Trevisa's *Dialogue between a Lord and a Clerk* (probably completed in 1387), prefacing his translation of Ranulph Higden's *Polychronicon*. The Clerk's observation that 'Þe Latyn ys boÞe good and fayr', and thus needs no translation into an inferior language, prompts from the Lord a spirited defence ('what haÞ Englysch trespased Þat hyt myȝt noȝt be translated into Englysch?'),[55] which is followed by a fascinating canon of medieval English literature, starting from King Alfred — a canon entirely based upon translation. The objective difficulty of translation (as the source text is generally chosen for the beauty of its language and style) is compounded by the perceived shortcomings of English; but in order to overcome exactly these shortcomings, English has to make use of translation, enriching its vocabulary and refining its syntax through borrowings, calques and imitation.

It is a matter of debate whether this perception would be sharpened by the meeting of the early modern English translators with Petrarch, but this meeting took place once Pietro Bembo's famous dictum had proclaimed him the master of Italian poetry, an indisputable example to be imitated; on the other hand, the philosophical profundity of the *Triumphi* would justify the undertaking of a translation. Thanks to his Latin works, Petrarch had already made his appearance in a number of late medieval English texts exalting the beauties of classical authors, or had been grouped with Dante and Boccaccio in a celebration of the supremacy of the Italian *tre corone*; in either language he would be considered a model of style. Establishing a canon of English literature meant establishing one's literary ancestors, but very often in the case of English we find antiquity discarded in favour of modern excellence, as in this passage from George Puttenham's *Art of English Poesy*, in which Wyatt and Surrey are commended because

> having traveled into Italy and there tasted the sweet and stately measures and style of the Italian poesy, as novices newly crept out of the schools of Dante, Ariosto, and Petrarch, they greatly polished our rude and homely manner of vulgar poesy from what it had been before, and for that cause may justly be said the first reformers of our English meter and style.[56]

Here the chosen authorities are vernacular writers of no antiquity, whose influence on contemporary English writing may be controversial; the definitive version of Ariosto's *Orlando Furioso* appeared only in 1532, so it is doubtful whether Wyatt and Surrey might have been influenced by this poem (although

ed. by Larry D. Benson (Oxford: Oxford University Press, 1987), pp. 661–83 (p. 662).
[55] John Trevisa, *Dialogue between a Lord and a Clerk*, in *A Book of Middle English: Third Edition*, ed. by J. A. Burrow and Thorlac Turville-Petre (Oxford: Blackwell, 2005), pp. 235–42 (pp. 239–40).
[56] George Puttenham, *The Art of English Poesy*, ed. by Frank Whigham and Wayne A. Rebhorn (Ithaca: Cornell University Press, 2007), p. 148.

Surrey incorporated a translation of a passage from Ariosto into one of his poems). A few pages later the same English poets are once again praised because 'their conceits were lofty, their styles stately, their conveyance cleanly, their terms proper, their meter sweet and well-proportioned, in all imitating very naturally and studiously their master Francis Petrarch'.[57] Yet, writing in 1589, Puttenham considers Petrarch only the author of the *Canzoniere* — there is no mention of the *Triumphi* or of the Latin works in his treatise. The role of the *Triumphi* is more marginal and difficult to define than either the *Canzoniere* or the Latin works: it is a text that enjoyed a striking but short-lived popularity within a restricted circle.

The influence of Petrarch is also intersected by a thorny question: the shaping of the English reception of Italian culture. Italian language learning was a vogue that interested almost exclusively the upper classes and courtly circles in early modern England, even if Italian culture was alluded to and exploited in more popular forms such as the theatre.[58] Intellectuals such as Gabriel Harvey would add Italian and French to the languages they already knew, Latin and Greek, in an attempt to emulate courtiers and perhaps be accepted by them; as Gabriel Harvey notes, 'Quomodo Comes Leicestrensis, Dominus Hattonus, Eques Sidneius, multique praeclari Aulici nostrates fluentissime loquuntur Linguam Italicam. Cur non Axiophilus eadem iam iamque dexteritate?' ('How fluently the Earl of Leicester, Master Hatton, Sir Philip Sidney and many of our renowned nobles speak the Italian language. Why couldn't Axiophilus speak it with the same dexterity?').[59] The same Harvey, in his correspondence with Edmund Spenser, would lament the rising importance of French and Italian to the detriment of Latin and Greek, even in a bastion of classical learning such as Cambridge:

> *Matchiavell* a great man: *Castilio* of no small reputation: *Petrarch*, and *Boccace* in every mans mouth: *Galateo* and *Guazzo* never so happy: over many acquainted with *Unico Aretino*: The French and Italian when so highly regarded of schollers? The Latine and Greeke, when so lightly?[60]

His own predicament is an instance of the growing importance of what

---

[57] Puttenham, p. 150.

[58] Michael Wyatt, *The Italian Encounter with Tudor England: A Cultural Politics of Translation* (Cambridge: Cambridge University Press, 2005); Lawrence. Warren Boutcher explores Florio's striving for upward social mobility through his linguistic ability in '"A French Dexterity, & an Italian Confidence": New Documents on John Florio, Learned Strangers and Protestant Humanist Study of Modern Languages in Renaissance England from c. 1547 to c. 1625', *Reformation*, 2 (1997), 39–109.

[59] This marginal note appears on sig. Aiiir of Harvey's copy of John Florio's *First Fruites* (Axiophilus is Harvey's pseudonym). See Stern, p. 156.

[60] Gabriel Harvey, *The Works of Gabriel Harvey, D. C. L.*, ed. by Alexander B. Grosart, 3 vols (London: The Huth Library, 1884), I, p. 69.

Warren Boutcher felicitously calls the pragmatic humanist.[61] Writers like William Thomas and John Florio used this cultural fashion to produce their dictionaries or other works meant to help learners of Italian, with the result that during the reign of Elizabeth the Italian language seemed to be reaching the same popularity as French.[62] Books like Castiglione's *Libro del Cortegiano* were printed (by John Wolfe, in 1588) in parallel columns, Italian, French and English: a publication that offered the latest advice on courtly fashion in all three courtly languages.

Inevitably, the Italian that was being received was a literary language, moulded by the authors listed by John Florio in his dictionary: a language learned for reading rather than for use, and shaped according to prescription rather than description. Although Florio's dictionary included words belonging to regional varieties, in the absence of a universally recognised standard Italian, English readers would accept the Italian written text as a linguistic model, especially if it had been canonized and made authoritative as Petrarch's work was. William Thomas, in his *Historie of Italie*, would link the choice of good Italian to courtly speech ('in maner all gentilmen dooe speake the courtisane'),[63] without proposing a systematic distinction between what was prescribed by Bembo and what one could learn in everyday intercourse with native speakers.[64] The fact that London did have a community of Italian native speakers, mostly belonging to the merchant class, with some religious or political refugees, created a strange short-circuit: while this Italian-speaking community was mainly interested in learning English for very practical reasons, Italian language learning was an elite achievement, conflating linguistic research and social aspirations. Bayerlipp has persuasively suggested that John Florio might have been aware of this dichotomy to the point of envisaging a double audience for his works ('In Florio's *Firste Fruites*, his first book on the Italian language published in 1578, he included rules for Italians on English pronunciation, therefore addressing a double audience'), maintaining in his *Worlde of Wordes* a more conservative diction: 'the two books were intended for different readerships, the dialogue book for speakers of Italian, the dictionary for readers

---

[61] Boutcher, 'French Dexterity', p. 52.
[62] Susanne Bayerlipp, '"All gentilmen dooe speake the courtisane": Negotiations of the Italian *Questione della lingua* in William Thomas and the Florios', in *Elizabethan Translation and Literary Culture*, ed. by Gabriela Schmidt (Berlin: Walter de Gruyter, 2013), pp. 147–65 (p. 148).
[63] William Thomas, *The historie of Italie* (London: Thomas Bertelet, 1549), p. 3v.
[64] 'Although the models Thomas used in his grammar and dictionary followed Bembo's linguistic purism and therefore an antiquated norm, Thomas, on the other hand, seems especially fascinated by contemporary speech and its supraregional uniformity' (Bayerlipp, p. 155). Bayerlipp explains Thomas's use of the word *courtisane* by noting that 'rather than to Bembo's antiquated Tuscan, he is here referring to the kind of language Castiglione promotes so ardently in his *Libro del cortegiano*' (p. 155).

of Italian literature'.[65] Within this context, the authors proposed by Florio in his dictionary as his sources also became the best possible models for correct and elegant use. Petrarch's excellence as a master of eloquence was attested not only by Bembo: he had been celebrated by Leonardo Bruni in 1436 in his *Lives of Dante and Petrarch*, and by Erasmus in his *Ciceronianus*.[66] But Petrarch, unlike Castiglione or Machiavelli, did not propose language as a clear if sophisticated vehicle of communication: his Italian was for the very few, given its lyrical structure and its metrical complexity, but also its semantic compression and philosophical profundity. At the same time, the Petrarchan challenge also prompted original solutions and creative deviations from the original.

1.3 The *Triumphi*

Probably composed in the last few months of Petrarch's life, unfinished or never fully revised, the *Triumphi* still puzzle editors and scholars.[67] The very structure of the work demanded of the ever-introspective poet further reflection on his life and on the impulses (particularly carnal love and ambition) that he had fought in his quest for spiritual elevation: the *Triumphus Cupidinis*, or triumph of earthly love, which opens the sequence, is followed and defeated by the *Triumphus Pudicitie*; in its turn, chastity is defeated by death in the *Triumphus Mortis*; then follows the *Triumphus Fame*, Petrarch's last celebration of worldly glory. Fame is defeated by time in the *Triumphus Temporis*, before they all bow to eternity in the final *Triumphus Eternitatis*. Each force vanquishes the previous one, in a vertical progression, 'like a ladder that the poet-persona climbs',[68] and the apotheosis sees eternity subsume everything in a timeless contemplation of God, which can be reached only by an effort of discipline through which the mind turns upon itself absolutely: the iconological significance of the centre turns the literary triumph into a representation of meditation,[69] reflecting a personal and idiosyncratic experience rather than offering a representation of an everyman.[70] This discipline is also the reader's: the conscientious progress

---

[65] Bayerlipp, pp. 160–61.
[66] Braden, p. 61.
[67] Ariani, p. 5.
[68] Fabio Finotti, 'The Poem of Memory: *Trumphi*', in *Petrarch: A Critical Guide to the Complete Works*, ed. by Victoria Kirkham and Armando Maggi (Chicago: The University of Chicago Press, 2009), pp. 63-83 (p. 63).
[69] Alastair Fowler underlines the significance of the representation of cosmic centrality in *Triumphal Forms: Structural Patterns in Elizabethan Poetry* (Cambridge: Cambridge University Press, 1970), pp. 23-27.
[70] Marie Axton, 'Lord Morley's Tryumphes of Petrarcke: Reading Spectacles', in *'Triumphs of English': Henry Parker, Lord Morley: Translator to the Tudor Court. New Essays in Interpretation*, ed. by Marie Axton and James P. Carley (London: The British Library, 2000), pp. 171-200 (pp. 171-72).

through the apparently endless lists of names, particularly evident in the *Triumphi Cupidinis* and *Fame* and often requiring, given Petrarch's penchant for obscure allusion, a determined exegetical effort, is rewarded in the first part of the poem by the unexpected and poignant glimpse into Petrarch's dream of domestic love (*Triumphus Mortis*) and then, in the last two triumphs, by a severe and salutary meditation on the transitory nature of human experience. The various triumphs are of unequal length, divided into a varying number of chapters. As with the *Canzoniere*, it is also possible to read each triumph, and indeed each chapter, as a self-standing unit.

The effort on the part of a number of translators to imitate complex metrical elements such as *terza rima* attests to the fact that, unlike what happened with other Italian works circulating in early modern England, translators were keen to explore the form and style as well as the content of Petrarch's poems, and to look at metre as a fruitful challenge (as they did with the sonnet form in the *Canzoniere*). Another aspect of the *Triumphi* which might have appealed to the early modern translator is erudition. This may surprise us, as we tend to link the display of erudition to a medieval (thus by definition *passé*) attitude, and since in English literature we associate erudition with excruciatingly long and learned lists such as those in Lydgate's *Fall of Princes*; yet there is no doubt that a reading of the *Triumphi* (especially the *Triumphus Cupidinis* and *Triumphus Fame*) would open up a vista of classical lore, of pre-Christian mythology and history. English lyrical poetry in its early modern development would then find its own voice eschewing those elements in Petrarch that point directly at classical erudition: a striking instance is Surrey's translation of 'Zefiro torna' ('The Soote Season'), in which all the classical allusions of the original are substituted by an elaborate but carefully naturalistic description of a homely landscape. On the other hand, the *Triumphi* were often read, in England as well as in the rest of Europe, as a repository of figures and images to be explored with humanist curiosity.

Erudition is one of the elements marking the liminality of the *Triumphi*, posed tantalizingly between medieval and Renaissance cultural attitudes. This work is one of the most ambitious of the Petrarchan canon, offering 'a broad-based, integrated, and overarching assessment of its author's complex cultural, historical, ethical, and ideological preoccupations'.[71] It also presents the apparent paradox of being written in Italian, thus underlining its strong connection with the nascent tradition of literary writing in the Italian vernacular and with the *Divina Commedia* in particular; some sections, especially in the *Triumphus Eternitatis*, and the choice of *terza rima* mark

---

[71] Zygmunt G. Barański, 'The Triumphi', in *The Cambridge Companion to Petrarch*, ed. by Albert Russell Ascoli and Unn Falkeid (Cambridge: Cambridge University Press, 2015), pp. 74–84 (p. 74).

this work as a direct riposte to Dante's masterpiece. The other great model is probably Giovanni Boccaccio's *Amorosa visione*, a work in its turn greatly indebted to Dante.[72] In the *Triumphi*, the 'synthesis of classical and vernacular elements'[73] embraces epic and Christian themes, allegory, dream vision and lyric poetry, thus offering a variant on the motif of the *summa* or *speculum* that had enjoyed such popularity in late medieval literature. The same link between past and present is offered by the structure of the vision, which often deploys lists or enumerations, presenting the reader with a long procession of witnesses to the power of love, chastity or time. Although very often Petrarch is taken as the one and only source for triumphal forms in the European Renaissance, his own work owed structural debts to a number of antecedents: the primary model is the Roman triumph, discussed in his coronation oration,[74] but he could also rely on more recent examples, inscribed within the form of the medieval dream vision, such as the *Roman de la rose* or, to come back to Dante, the procession in the final four cantos of Dante's *Purgatorio*.[75] The procession appearing in the first chapter of the *Triumphus Cupidinis* might also have been influenced by Aeneas's dream in book VI of the *Aeneid*.[76] All these examples show that, rather than the initiator of a genre, Petrarch should be seen as a writer who brought the genre to perfection and radically transformed it, using a well-established form to subvert it and make it into the vehicle not of historical roll-calling, but of philosophical meditation, as many English translators were quick to realize. Petrarch himself was aware of the novelty of this enterprise, as can be seen in a letter to Boccaccio, in which he underlines the necessity of 'inaccessa tentare', attempting what had not been tried before.[77]

If we consider the reception of the *Triumphi* and *Canzoniere* as part of the same phenomenon, we are forced to rethink our notion of English Petrarchism. The clichés of the beautiful woman with an icy heart, or of the masochistic male contemplating his distant beloved, are no longer satisfactory, since the

---

[72] Vittore Branca, *Boccaccio Medievale* (Florence: Sansoni, 1956), p. 186. See also Martin Eisner, 'Petrarch Reading Boccaccio: Revisiting the Genesis of the *Triumphi*', in *Petrarch and the Textual Origins of Interpretation*, ed. by Teodolinda Barolini and H. Wayne Storey (Leiden: Brill, 2007), pp. 131–46. On the relation between *Amorosa Visione* and *Commedia* see Guyda Armstrong, 'Boccaccio and Dante', in *The Cambridge Companion to Boccaccio*, ed. by Guyda Armstrong, Rhiannon Daniels and Stephen J. Milner (Cambridge: Cambridge University Press, 2015), pp. 121–38 (pp. 134–35).
[73] Barański, p. 74.
[74] The text of the oration can be found in Carlo Godi, 'La "collatio laureationis" del Petrarca nelle due redazioni', *Studi Petrarcheschi*, 5 (1988), 1–58.
[75] Giuseppe Mazzotta, *The Worlds of Petrarch* (Durham, NC: Duke University Press, 1993), pp. 98–99. On the relationship between *Triumphi* and *Roman de la rose*, see Carlo Calcaterra, *Nella selva del Petrarca* (Bologna: Cappelli, 1942), pp. 155–61.
[76] Mazzotta, p. 101.
[77] *Rerum familiarum Libri XX–XXII*, ed. by Vittorio Rossi and Ugo Dotti (Paris: Les Belles Lettres, 2015), XXII. 2, p. 284.

Triumphi sublimate this basic posture into a more articulate and complex form of meditation. Gary Waller speaks of Petrarchism as 'a suggestive mixture of poetic workshop and psychological encounter session [...] a psycho-erotic model in which ideological and social tensions were acted out':[78] there is no doubt that the formal model offered by Petrarch (especially as concerns the sonnet, but also in epic poetry and the triumphal form) fundamentally modified poetry in England, probably playing a role in the definitive abandonment of rhyme royal (a much practiced form for courtly poetry between Chaucer and Shakespeare) in favour of the sonnet as a short form that could encourage semantic and logical compression, and display 'much excellently ordered in a smal roome'.[79] Yet his influence goes beyond these formal characteristics; nor can we reduce the Petrarchan perspective solely to a male gaze, or to an exercise in solipsistic psychologizing. It may be argued that the *Triumphi* were especially appealing to a number of female translators, from Mary Sidney to Anna Hume, since they found here an all-encompassing attitude that they could appropriate and interpret as autonomously as their male counterparts, using the form to activate not only psychological introspection but also religious or political reflection (which was, after all, far from absent in the original). Even the centrality of the self, so predominant in the *Canzoniere* (and so easy to associate with Petrarch's rather obsessive self-expression), appears in the *Triumphi* to give way to a reflection involving all humanity, annihilating, in a passage of dazzling clarity in the last *Triumphus*, all differences of time and space. It is not surprising, therefore, that the translation of the *Triumphus Eternitatis* attributed to Elizabeth I could be read against a Boethian background, or that Anna Hume could use her translation activity to reflect on Protestantism.

In keeping with Petrarch's vision of himself as *humanista*, we can inscribe his literary effort within what William Kennedy calls 'a shared sense of experience and application, calling and vocation, conveyed through an emergent sense of profession and a still unformed sense of professionalism'.[80] From this perspective, Petrarch offered sixteenth-century English poets a sophisticated tool with which they seem to have been previously unacquainted; through translation and imitation first, then by finding a way of distancing themselves from such a cumbrous model, they were offered the opportunity to hone and develop their craft. This new sense of poetry as a profession and a social vocation engenders new questions about the role of poetry. Kennedy notes that professionalism often expressed itself in the form of membership of a group — whether an *accademia* or, in more modern terms, a literary salon. This

---

[78] Gary F. Waller, *The Sidney Family Romance: Mary Wroth, William Herbert, and the Early Modern Construction of Gender* (Detroit: Wayne State University Press, 1993), p. 136.
[79] Samuel Daniel, *A Defence of Ryme* (London: Edward Blount, 1603), sig. F8r.
[80] William J. Kennedy, *Petrarchism at Work: Contextual Economies in the Age of Shakespeare* (Ithaca: Cornell University Press, 2016), p. 6.

membership raises the question of the status of the amateur:

> Such groups may welcome amateurs as well as professionals, but while the former participate in order to acquire a veneer of culture and sophistication as a social asset, the latter aim to learn from, collaborate with, and compete against their peers. The group acts as a surrogate guild (in the Renaissance there were no guilds for poets, though there were for musicians and visual artists), enabling its participants to benefit from a social, cultural, and economic trust available to members of late medieval artisan associations and early modern trade companies.[81]

The definition of the literary group as a surrogate guild is striking, but the clear-cut distinction between amateur and professional may generate some misunderstanding. This distinction may work quite well within literary genres obviously meant for public fruition, such as drama, the essay, the pamphlet or possibly epic poetry, but in an age in which printing was still finding its scope, lyric poetry tends to remain a form confined to specific social or intellectual spheres, marked not by professionalism but by status. Philip Sidney is the example that immediately springs to mind when we think of amateur poetry at its highest level, and indeed he seems conscious of the issue as he speaks of 'decadent sports',[82] and maintains in his *Astrophil and Stella* an attitude very much at variance with his celebration of the poet in *A Defence of Poesy*. The emergence from the patronage system was a slow and gradual process, and found in the development of printing in Europe a means to identify writing with professionalism that had been unknown before, triggering a connection between the act of writing and a wide audience that was the equivalent of the stage or the concert hall for the playwright/actor or musician. Faced with this new challenge, European poets found in Petrarch an ideal starting point for the development of their craft; the difficulty of the task induced reflection on the activity of translation but also enhanced the desire to translate and to rethink the boundaries between past and present, classical and vernacular, as shown in this passage from Joachim du Bellay's *Deffence et Illustration de la Langue Françoyse*:

> qu'on me lyse un Demosthene et Homere Latins, un Ciceron et Vergile Françoys, pour voir s'ilz vous engendreront telles affections, voyre ainsi qu'un Prothée vous transformeront en diverses sortes, comme vous sentez, lysant ces aucteurs en leurs langues. Il vous semblera passer de l'ardente montaigne d'Aethne sur le froid sommet du Caucase. Et ce que je dy des langues Latine et Greque se doit reciproquement dire de tous les vulgaires, dont j'allegueray seulement un Petrarque, du quel j'ose bien dire, que si Homere et Virgile renaissans avoint enterpris de le traduyre, ilz ne

---

[81] Kennedy, *Petrarchism at Work*, p. 7.
[82] Jason Scott-Warren, *Early Modern English Literature* (Cambridge: Polity Press, 2005), pp. 66–70.

le pouroint rendre avecques la mesme grace et nayfveté qu'il est en son vulgaire Toscan.

(Just read a Latin Demosthenes and Homer, a French Cicero and Virgil to see if they will beget such emotions in you — will, indeed, transform you like a Proteus into differing kinds — as you feel reading those authors in their own languages. Going from the original to the translation, you will seem to pass from the burning mountain of Etna to the cold summit of the Caucasus. And what I say of the Latin and Greek languages can be equally said of all the vulgar tongues, of which I will cite only Petrarch, of whom I dare say that if a reborn Homer and Virgil undertook to translate him, they could not render him with the same grace and freshness that he has in his native Tuscan.)[83]

Translation, a flexible activity, strongly dependent on the shape and genre of the original, was also the primary training ground for early modern poetic voices in England, whether as a highly professional activity or a private pursuit. Engaging with Petrarch's Italian poems, English writers could find a literary identity.

1.4 The dissemination of the *Triumphi* in the British Isles

While before the age of printing the *Triumphi* enjoyed greater fame than the *Canzoniere*, to judge from the number of extant manuscripts, from the second half of the fifteenth century the European (though perhaps not the English) fame of *Canzoniere* and *Triumphi* proceeded at an analogous pace.[84] Undoubtedly the *Triumphi* left a stronger trace in sixteenth-century English reading and writing than we recognize: Roger Ascham acidly wrote that Italianate English youths 'have in more reverence, the triumphes of Petrarche: than the genesis of Moses',[85] and Walter Raleigh alluded to the *Triumphi* in 'A Vision upon this conceipt of the *Faery Queene*', envisioning Spenser taking the place of Petrarch as the heir of Homer — a very Petrarchan conceit.[86] In the dedicatory letter to his poem *Amyntas* (1585), Thomas Watson also evoked Petrarch's *Triumphi*,

---

[83] Text and translation are taken from Joachim du Bellay, *The Regrets with The Antiquities of Rome, Three Latin Elegies, and The Defense and Enrichment of the French Language*, ed. and trans. by Richard Helgerson (Philadelphia: University of Pennsylvania Press, 2006), pp. 334–35.
[84] See the relevant entries in the *PERI* database.
[85] Roger Ascham, *The Scholemaster*, in *English Works*, ed. by William Aldis Wright (Cambridge: Cambridge University Press, 1904), pp. 171–302 (p. 232).
[86] Edmund Spenser, *The Poetical Works*, ed. by J. C. Smith and E. de Selincourt (London: Oxford University Press, 1912), p. 409. For a brief assessment, see Heather Campbell, 'Petrarch's *I Trionfi* in the English Renaissance' (unpublished D.Phil. thesis, York University, Ontario, 1990), pp. 16–20.

along with Homer and Virgil's epic poems.[87] Most importantly, though some of the translations, adaptations or parodies of individual sonnets from the *Canzoniere*, from Chaucer onwards, have attained unique literary status, there seems to have been no comprehensive view of this sonnet sequence,[88] while English writers did grapple with the complex and sometimes creaking machinery of the *Triumphi*, following the example set by French translators and imitators between the end of the fifteenth century and the early sixteenth.

The earliest allusion to the poem in England may be found in a letter written by Edmund Bonner, afterwards Bishop of London, to Thomas Cromwell in April 1530, while he was probably preparing for the mission to Rome he undertook in 1542:

> wher ye willing to make me a good Ytalion promise unto me, longe agon, the Triumphes of Petrarche in the Ytalion tonge. I hartely pray you at this tyme by this beyrer, Mr. Augustine his servant, to sende me the said Boke with some other at your devotion; and especially, if it please you, the boke called Cortigiano in Ytalion.[89]

A few years later, Henry Parker, Lord Morley (the first translator of the *Triumphi*), would recommend to the same Thomas Cromwell, in a letter, Machiavelli's *Principe* and *Discorsi* as 'surely a good thing for your Lordship and for our Sovereign Lord in Council'.[90] There may be an even earlier, indirect allusion in the book of Latin poetry given by the Italian poet Johannes Michael Nagonius to Henry VII in 1496: here the king was portrayed 'as an epic hero whose most impressive deeds were yet to come. Based on the imagery of Petrarch's highly popular *Trionfi*, the frontispiece shows Henry riding in a triumphal car drawn by two white horses'.[91] By the first quarter of the sixteenth century, copies of Petrarch's works could be found at court: the list of books at Richmond Palace compiled in February 1535 includes a manuscript with the *Historia Griseldis* in the French translation by Philippe de Mézières (now British Library, MS Royal 19 C.vii).[92] Catherine of Aragon owned *De Remediis* in the Castilian translation by Francisco de Madrid, published in Zaragoza in

---

[87] Thomas Watson, *The Complete Works: Volume 1*, ed. by Dana F. Sutton (Lewiston: The Edwin Mellen Press, 1996), pp. 286–87.
[88] One possible exception is Thomas Watson's translation of (the whole?) *Canzoniere* in Latin. Unfortunately, this has survived only 'as excerpts in other of his works' (Albert Chatterley, 'Watson, Thomas (1555/6–1592)', *ODNB*).
[89] *Original Letters, Illustrative of English History: Third Series, Volume II*, ed. by Henry Ellis (London: Richard Bentley, 1846), p. 178.
[90] The letter is printed as item 285 in *Letters and Papers, Foreign and Domestic, of the Reign of Henry VIII*, vol. xiv, part 1, ed. by James Gairdner and R. H. Brodie (London: Eyre and Spottiswoode, 1864), p. 111.
[91] James P. Carley, *The Books of Henry VIII and his Wives* (London: The British Library, 2004), p. 44. The book is now York Minster Library, MS XVI.N.2.
[92] Carley, *The Books of Henry VIII and his Wives*, pp. 22–23.

1518 (her request to Wyatt to translate it into English suggests that this version might have served her as a language-learning tool). She also had a copy of *Los seys triunfos*, the Castilian translation of the *Triumphi* by Antonio de Obregon, published in Logroño by Arnao Guillen de Brocar in 1512 (now British Library, C.63.i.10); both volumes still present the HR monogram, standing for *Henricus Rex*.[93] The same monogram could be found in other Italian books, according to the inventory of the Upper Library in Westminster of 1542: 'Bocase de casibus illustrium virorum in frenche' (Boccaccio's *De Casibus* in Premierfait's translation, now British Library, Royal 20 C.IV) and 'Cent Novelles de Messire Boccasio in lingua Italica' (*Decameron*, Venice, 1510).[94] It appeared also in a book catalogued as 'Triumphes of Petrarch in Italian' (now British Library, C.83.e.11), a reprint of the version with a commentary by Bernardo Ilicino, originally printed in Bologna in 1475/6 (this edition was printed in Milan by Giovanni Angelo Scinzenzeler, in 1512, with the title *Opere del preclarissimo Poeta Miser Francesco Petrarcha*). Catherine Parr owned a copy of *Canzoniere* and *Triumphi* in the Venice edition by Alessandro Vellutello (1544).[95]

In other instances we find Petrarch associated with aristocratic circles: a copy of 'petrark, in Italion', as well as a 'tryumph of petrark' is listed in the inventory, made in 1556, of the goods of Sir William More (a gentleman of Loseley, in Surrey), together with other books in the same language.[96] Sir Thomas Smith, principal secretary of state to King Edward VI and Queen Elizabeth, and a keen linguist, possessed a number of Italian works, including unspecified 'Dantes' and 'Petrarcha', as well as 'Il *Petrarcha* cum Com.', as shown by the catalogue of his library compiled in August 1566.[97] The 1609 Lumley Catalogue, made after Lord Lumley's death and describing possibly 'the largest private library of the Elizabethan period',[98] includes a number of Petrarchan items: among the Theologi, the *Psalmi paenitentiales*; among the Historici, the *Vitae virorum illustrium Roman: imperatorum, rhetorum, grammaticorum, sophistarum et c.*

---

[93] Carley, *The Books of Henry VIII and his Wives*, p. 121.
[94] James P. Carley, 'Marks in Books and the Libraries of Henry VIII', *Papers of the Bibliographical Society of America*, 91 (1997), 583-606 (p. 603). The inventory is transcribed in James P. Carley, *The Libraries of Henry VIII* (London: The British Library, 2000), pp. 30-226, and includes 1450 items.
[95] Carley, *The Books of Henry VIII and his Wives*, p. 138. The book is now British Library, C.27.e.19.
[96] John Evans, 'Extracts from the Private Account Book of Sir William More', *Archaeologia: or, Miscellaneous Tracts Relating to Antiquity*, 36 (1855), 284-310 (p. 291).
[97] The catalogue is printed in John Strype, *The Life of the Learned Sir Thomas Smith K^t. Doctor of the Civil Law; Principal Secretary of State to King Edward the Sixth, and Queen Elizabeth* (London: Roper, 1698), pp. 139-47.
[98] Sears Jayne and Francis R. Johnson, eds, *The Lumley Library: The Catalogue of 1609* (London: The Trustees of the British Museum, 1956), p. 1. The catalogue is preserved in Cambridge, Trinity College Library (MS o.4.38); there is another manuscript copy in London, British Library (MS Additional 36659, fols 222-23, 363).

(an edition of the *Vitae* printed in Basel in 1563); among the Artes Liberales et Philosophi, *Francisci Petrarchae opera* (Basel, 1581), and *Francis Petrarkes triumphes englished by Henrie Parker lorde Morley, anglice* (1565); described as a 'Liber manuscriptus, varios tractatus continens' (now British Library, Royal 8.B.vi) there is also *Franciscus Petrarcha super historiam Walteri Marchionis et Griseldis uxoris eius*. Other allusions are more ambiguous: Warren Boutcher discusses a sonnet by Henry Constable, from his 1594 sequence *Diana*, titled 'To his Mistresse upon occasion of a Petrarch he gave her, shewing her the Reason why the Italian commentres dissent so much in the Exposition thereof', and adds: 'this shows that copies of Petrarch were available — indeed common enough to be given as gifts — and that English readers like Constable had seen enough of them to form an opinion on how their interpretations differed'.[99]

Petrarch appeared also in university and ecclesiastical libraries: the Cambridge University inventories include a 'List of books in the 1589 inventory of Abraham Tilman (CUI 1589–1592)', where we find 'Petrarke in Italian', which might of course refer to either or both *Canzoniere* and *Triumphi*, but probably to both.[100] According to its 1605 catalogue, the Bodleian Library owned a copy of the 1581 Basel edition of Petrarch's works, a copy of the Vellutello (1545), one of the Gesualdo (1553), and one of the Filelfo (1515) editions of *Canzoniere* and *Triumphi*, as well as the *Secretum* in an Italian version (Siena, 1517).[101] The seventeenth-century catalogue of Syon Library includes, under the heading 'Franc. *Petrarcha*', a copy of the 1581 Basel edition of his works, as well as other volumes.[102]

In Scotland, the library of the young James VI, as early as 1573, included a 'Petrarche in Ital.' (as well as 'Lyves of Petrarq in Ital.'), which may indicate any one of the numerous editions including both *Triumphi* and *Canzoniere*;[103] in the library of Mary Queen of Scots we find 'The morall Triumphis of Petrark in Italiane', which may be the same book.[104] Among the books owned by Adam Bothwell, bishop of Orkney (1527–1593), there was 'Il Petrarche

---

[99] Warren Boutcher, 'Humanism and Literature in Late Tudor England: Translation, the Continental Book and the Case of Montaigne's *Essais*', in *Reassessing Tudor Humanism*, ed. by Jonathan Woolfson (Basingstoke: Palgrave Macmillan, 2002), pp. 242–68 (pp. 257–58).
[100] Sears Jayne, *Library Catalogues of the English Renaissance: Reissue with New Preface and Notes* (Godalming: St Paul's Bibliographies, 1983), p. 187.
[101] *Catalogus librorum bibliothecae publicae quam vir ornatissimus Thomas Bodleius eques auratus in Academia Oxoniensi nuper instituit [...] authore Thomas James ibidem bibliothecario* (Oxford: Joseph Barnes, 1605), pp. 368 and 622.
[102] J[oannes] S[pencer], *Catalogus Universalis librorum omnium in Bibliotheca Collegii Sionii apud Londinenses* (London: Robert Leybourn, 1650), p. 112.
[103] George F. Warner, *The Library of James VI: 1573–1583: From a Manuscript in the Hand of Peter Young, his Tutor* (Edinburgh: Constable, 1893), p. xxxii.
[104] Julian Sharman, *The Library of Mary Queen of Scots* (London: Elliot Stock, 1889), p. 72.

con l'Espositione', probably a copy of Vellutello.[105] The library of William Drummond of Hawthornden included a volume containing Petrarch's *Africa* and *Epistolae* (item 356), a book described as 'Le Petrarque en rime françoise avecq ses commentaires, traduit par Philippe de Maldeghem [...] 8° Brussels, R. Velpius, 1600. Bought in Paris, 1608' (item 1133; a French version of the *Canzoniere*), 'Il Petrarca di nuovo ristampato et diligentemente corretto. 24° Venice, N. Misserino, 1596' (item 1261), the 'Chronica delle vite de Pontefici et Imperatori romani' (item 1262), and the manuscript of William Fowler's translation of the *Triumphi*, now in Edinburgh University Library.[106]

Inventories, library catalogues, wills and other archival documents give us only very partial insights, and this survey is no exception. Any conclusion drawn from these findings is bound to be provisional: with this caveat, it seems that the Italian Petrarch found its focus of interest among court writers, appealing more to an aristocratic or elitist audience than, for instance, the work of Machiavelli. In the case of the latter (who also had implicit or explicit censorship to contend with) we find proof of ownership among university students, and allusions even in popular literature such as the pamphlet or the drama — a phenomenon that is much more limited in the case of Petrarch.[107] The allusions made to the *Triumphi* by Ascham and Raleigh speak of a courtly audience. Thomas Churchyard in his *Pleasant conceite*, a short poem presented as a New Year's gift to Queen Elizabeth in 1593, alludes to 'tryumphs [...] for Lady *Lawraes* sake'.[108] In *The Blazon of Jealousie* (1615), a translation from Benedetto Varchi, Robert Tofte inserted translations from a number of sonnets from the *Canzoniere*, and also a few lines from the *Triumphus Eternitatis*.[109] Thomas Kyd's *Householder's Philosophy*, a translation of Torquato Tasso's *Padre di famiglia* published in 1588, may contain an incorrect quotation from *Triumphus Eternitatis*.[110] Ben Jonson owned a copy of the 1581 Basel edition of Petrarch's *Opera omnia*, which might be the only (partially) Italian work he

---

[105] Duncan Shaw, 'Adam Bothwell, a Conserver of the Renaissance in Scotland', in *The Renaissance and Reformation in Scotland: Essays in Honour of Gordon Donaldson*, ed. by Ian B. Cowan and Duncan Shaw (Edinburgh: Scottish Academic Press, 1983), pp. 141–69 (p. 160).
[106] Robert H. MacDonald, *The Library of Drummond of Hawthornden* (Edinburgh: Edinburgh University Press, 1971).
[107] Alessandra Petrina, *Machiavelli in the British Isles: Two Early Modern Translations of The Prince* (Farnham: Ashgate, 2009), pp. 14–45.
[108] Thomas Churchyard, *A Pleasant conceite penned in verse* (London: Roger Warde, 1593), sig. A4r.
[109] Robert C. Melzi, 'A Contribution to the History of Petrarchism in England: Robert Tofte and The Blazon of Jealousy', *Rivista di Studi Italiani*, 15 (1997), 1–32 (pp. 14–15).
[110] As noted by Domenico Lovascio in his forthcoming edition of *The Householder's Philosophy*, due to appear in *The Collected Works of Thomas Kyd*, general editor Brian Vickers (Woodbridge: Boydell & Brewer). I wish to thank Domenico for drawing my attention to this point.

owned; the copy, now at the Folger Library, offers no revealing marginalia.[111] The only time Shakespeare mentions Petrarch is in *Romeo and Juliet*, when Mercutio mocks the poet's procession of famous women (and, by implication, an elitist taste), evoking figures that make their appearance in the *Triumphi*:

> Now is he for the numbers that Petrarch flow'd in. Laura to his lady was but a kitchen wench (marry, she had a better love to berhyme her), Dido a dowdy, Cleopatra a gipsy, Helen and Hero hildings and harlots, Thisby a grey eye or so, but not to the purpose. (II. 4. 38–43)[112]

When Shakespeare needs to make a joke on the lovelorn suitor, as he does in *Merry Wives of Windsor* (I. 1. 198–99), he mentions *Tottel's Miscellany*, not Petrarch. The *Miscellany* 'upsets every Petrarchan premise, getting under the skin, the nerves, and the usually safe thinking of conventional Petrarchism':[113] in this, Shakespeare may be responding not to Petrarch but to an English Petrarchism in which the *Triumphi* do not have a place. A beautiful allusion may be found in *Henry IV Part I*. Hotspur's final words may carry an echo the very structure of the *Triumphi*:

> But thoughts, the slaves of life, and life, time's fool,
> And time, that takes survey of all the world,
> Must have a stop[.] (V. 4. 81–83)[114]

Some scholars have used the obvious appeal of Petrarchan motifs to a minority audience as a way of explaining the gap between the first and second wave of Petrarchism; Richard Waswo, for instance, argues that they coincided with the courtly flourishing of Henry VIII and Elizabeth: 'Such a milieu could simply not exist in the midst of the social and political upheavals of the Reformation: the Edwardian protectorates, the Marian persecutions, and the struggles that led to the Elizabethan Settlement'.[115] The articulation of courtly love in poetic form was, since its origins, a restricted game, a *trobar clus*; it became in early modern England an instrument in the negotiation of power, as shown by Thomas Wyatt's sonnet 'Whoso List to Hunt'.

The impression that the reception of Petrarch's *Triumphi* concerns mainly an elite readership is confirmed by the fact that the only printed translation of the

---

[111] Christopher Martin, 'Retrieving Jonson's Petrarch', *Shakespeare Quarterly*, 45 (1994), 89–92.
[112] The edition used is *The Riverside Shakespeare*, ed. by G. Blakemore Evans (Boston: Houghton Mifflin, 1974). Ronald L. Martinez calls the tragedy 'a site of Shakespeare's confrontation with Petrarch and Petrarchism'. See 'Francis, Thou Art Translated: Petrarch Metamorphosed in English, 1380–1595', *Humanist Studies & the Digital Age*, 1 (2011), 80–108 (p. 96).
[113] Kennedy, *Petrarchism at Work*, p. 32.
[114] See Gabriele Erasmi, 'Petrarch's *Trionfi*: The Poetics of Humanism', in *Petrarch's 'Triumphs'*, ed. by Eisenblicher and Iannucci, pp. 161–74 (p. 172).
[115] Waswo, p. 12.

Italian Petrarch in the sixteenth century is Henry Parker, Lord Morley's version of the *Triumphi*, a publication meant for a courtly readership. Such a readership might also have been conversant with Italian, or at least with French, and thus able to read Petrarch in the many editions available in either of those languages. Danielle Clarke notes that 'given the number of times he is mentioned, you would expect a wider dissemination sphere'.[116] But the gap between allusions and traces of actual ownership is inevitably wide, given the ephemerality of books: early modern translations often represent the peak of a more generalized interest.

1.5 Early translations of the *Triumphi*

We can trace increasing dissemination of the *Triumphi* in Europe, which prompted a number of translations, starting with France and Spain. As noted above, at least one copy of the Spanish translation by Antonio de Obregon made its way to England thanks to Catherine of Aragon, but the French versions seem especially significant for English translators. In France the fame and indeed the direct knowledge of the *Triumphi* preceded that of the *Canzoniere*, thus echoing an Italian trend.[117] While the first complete translation of the *Canzoniere* in French, by Vasquin Philieul, appeared in 1548, among the earliest translations we note the French abridgement in verse by Jean Robertet (a friend and guest of Charles d'Orléans), probably written in the second half of the fifteenth century, and an abridgement in prose, generally attributed to Georges de la Forge, datable to the latter quarter of the fifteenth century, and preserved in six manuscripts[118] prior to its first printed edition, in 1514 (it was then reprinted in 1519, 1520 and 1531). The first complete French translation in verse was undertaken by Simon Bourgouyn around 1530; it survives in at least three manuscripts.[119]

Bourgouyn's translation is considered 'the catalyst for the first English translation of the *Trionfi*', undertaken by Lord Morley;[120] this would explain

---

[116] Danielle Clarke, '"Lover's Songs Shall Turne to Holy Psalmes": Mary Sidney and the Transformation of Petrarch', in *Mary Sidney, Countess of Pembroke*, ed. by Margaret P. Hannay (Farnham: Ashgate, 2009), pp. 137–49 (p. 137).

[117] Carlo Pellegrini, 'Il Petrarca nella cultura francese', *Rivista di letterature moderne*, 1 (1946), 75–84 (pp. 75–76); Elina Suomela-Härmä, 'Stratégies de traduction dans la première version française des "Triomphes" de Pétrarque', *Moyen Français*, 51–53 (2002–2003), 547–58 (p. 548).

[118] Suomela-Härmä, 'Stratégies de traduction', p. 548. William Kennedy proposes 1476 as the date for the Robertet translation: see *The Site of Petrarchism: Early Modern National Sentiment in Italy, France, and England* (Baltimore: The Johns Hopkins University Press, 2003), p. 106.

[119] Francesco Simone, *Il Rinascimento francese. Studi e ricerche* (Turin: SEI, 1961), p. 210. The date of composition is debated, with some critics opting for a much earlier date, around 1510.

[120] James P. Carley and Myra D. Orth, '"Plus que assez": Simon Bourgouyn and his French

the allusion, in Morley's dedicatory preface, to the manuscript of a French translation he had had occasion to consult.[121] Bourgouyn's version might also have served, at least by implication, as a model for William Fowler's; we know the latter saw Morley's English translation and at least one French version, since he polemically declares, in his dedicatory epistle, that his intention to translate Petrarch was reinforced by his seeing, in previous versions, that the work was not just translated, but 'magled' (i.e. maimed) and 'dismembered'.[122] Bourgouyn precedes each triumph with a short summary in verse, in which he offers the *sens historique* and *sens moral* of the poem; introducing the *Triumphus mortis*, he writes:

> Sens historique: Icy Laura, pleine d'honneur, ioyeuse
>   Avec ses armes de purité
>   Et sa tres digne enseigne et glorieuse
>   S'en retournoit, d'amour victorieuse,
>   Au lieu auquel elle avoit habité.
> Sens moral: L'homme ioyeux d'avoir suppedité
>   Son appetit avec foy, esperance
>   Et charité qui luy sont asseurance
>   Il s'en retourne en terre le corps nud
>   Qui est le lieu dont premier est venu.
>
> (Historical reading: Here the honourable, joyful Laura, armed with purity and her glorious and worthy ensign, returned, victorious in love, to the place in which she had dwelled. Moral reading: Man, happy to fulfil his longing with faith, hope and charity, which support him, leaves on earth his naked body, as he had originally arrived.)[123]

Though some of the English translators also prefaced each triumph or even each chapter with a short description (as in the case of Anna Hume), Bourgouyn's careful allegorical reading was not imitated in any of the English versions, possibly because it was too close to a late medieval practice of *moralitas* that could easily be associated with Catholicism. At the same time, however, the high moral teaching of the Petrarchan verse is often put forward by translators as the first reason for their enterprise, even if aesthetic or stylistic considerations seem predominant once the translation is actually engaged upon. The interest in moral teachings offers the translator an opportunity to explore metrical, stylistic and lexical challenges. At the same time, for Bourgouyn as for the English translators, the literary exploration of the source text highlights Petrarch's notorious difficulties: the semantic compression of the text, the wealth of classical and historical allusions, the astounding erudition, particularly evident in sections introducing long cortèges of figures

---

Translations from Plutarch, Petrarch and Lucian', *Viator*, 34 (2003), 328–63 (p. 328).
[121] Carley and Orth, p. 333.
[122] Edinburgh University Library, MS Drummond De.1.10, fol. 2v.
[123] Quoted in Simone, p. 204.

INTRODUCTION

from the past, often not directly named but simply referred to. This is one of the most interesting consequences of the passage from the Latin to the Italian Petrarch: the moral weight of his reflections (far more relevant in the *Triumphi* than in the *Canzoniere*) guarantees and almost authorizes the transition from his Latin to his vernacular works; at the same time, readers encounter in the Italian Petrarch the last and most refined representative of a tradition of lyrical poetry that continues and develops the courtly love conventions present in Provençal poetry.[124] Paradoxically, Petrarch's lyric poetry was received in early modern Europe not as the last example of a centuries-old heritage, but as a new, original poetic voice, sparking a new compositional mode. The growing fascination with this modality of writing made the popularity of the *Canzoniere* almost inevitable (ultimately relegating the *Triumphi* to comparative obscurity).

The tendency to explore the moral significance of Petrarch's poems is confirmed by another French translation, which followed Bourgouyn's version. Printed in 1538 by Denis Janot, in Paris, it had been undertaken by Jean Meynier, Baron d'Oppède; it was reprinted in 1545 and 1547, and it also included Marot's version of *canzone* 323.[125] Once again the moral content is highlighted in the preface; moral considerations inform some of the translation choices, occasionally leading Meynier to add lines (sometimes of an explanatory nature) to Petrarch's text. For instance, at the end of the second chapter of the *Triumphus Mortis*, after the passage in which Petrarch asks Laura how much longer he will live (lines 187–90), the French translator adds these lines:

> Incontinent me laissant seul illa [*sic*]
> La hault au ciel tout soubdain s'envolla,
> Malgré la mort ny sa cruelle enuye
> Et toutefoys une eternelle vie,
> Avecq les sainctz et les sainctes elle a.
> O que heureux fuz quand ma muse parla
> De son renom tant par si que par la,
> Et qu'il luy plut de moy ester servye
>   Incontinant.

(On the spot, leaving me, she at once went up to heaven; in spite of death and its cruel torment, she has eternal life among the saints. O, how happy I was when my muse spoke to me of her fame, both on earth and in heaven, and how she was pleased to be served by me, on the spot.)[126]

---

[124] As John Freccero observes, 'Petrarch's poetic achievement, for all of its grandeur, would appear to be decidedly conservative with respect to the Middle Ages. Far from repudiating the verse forms of his predecessors, he brought them to technical perfection and established them as models for future generations of poets'. See 'The Fig Tree and the Laurel: Petrarch's Poetics', *Diacritics*, 5 (1975), 34–40 (p. 34).

[125] Julia Conaway Bondanella, *Petrarch's Visions and Their Renaissance Analogues* (Madrid: José Porrúa Turanzas, 1978), p. 48. This translation is discussed in Simone, pp. 211–20.

[126] Quoted in Simone, p. 215.

These examples show that a possible path towards the analysis of these translations is via their paratexts, which strive to adapt Petrarch's moral, philosophical and religious message to vastly changed intellectual circumstances.

The *Triumphi* also found another channel of dissemination in early modern Europe: not through literary translation, but through a transposition into a different medium, which encouraged the development of a widely different interpretation of the work. Petrarch's sequence celebrated an innovative literary use of a pictorial or ceremonial device. The original decoration of the *Sala virorum illustrium* (now Sala dei Giganti) in the Carrara Palace in Padua was inspired by the poet's own *De viris illustribus*. This work, Petrarch's most important historical collection, presents a series of biographies of characters from Roman history, and though the general structure is quite different, there is an analogy with the *Triumphi* in that both present a survey of emblematic figures, whose historical relevance may also turn them into exempla for the reader. The spectacular function of history is the theme here; the writer would then present in the *Triumphi* the experience of the dream vision as spectacle.[127] The fact that *De viris illustribus* was 'adapted by painters during his lifetime and under his very eyes'[128] is proof of its author's strong awareness of the power of symbolic images. This form of transposition is of course very different from the actual translations. Only the superficial shape of the triumph is being imitated, and the painters' attention focuses on those triumphs whose visual impact is more readily perceivable: love, fame, death.

This phenomenon may have been prompted by the early editions of the poem. No fourteenth-century illuminated manuscript of the poem is extant, the earliest being dated 1414, and containing only one image in the *Triumphus Mortis*;[129] from the mid-fifteenth century onwards we see more illuminated manuscripts, but, as has been observed, they often bear little relation to the text, and tend to rely on conventional images of each successive force standing on a chariot — a detail that Petrarch provides only in the first triumph.[130] In 1488 Bernadinus Rizus of Novara printed, in Venice, an edition in which each section was opened by a full-page woodcut illustrating the respective triumph.[131]

---

[127] Renee Neu Watkins, 'Petrarch and the Black Death: From Fear to Monuments', *Studies in the Renaissance*, 29 (1972), 196–223 (p. 219).
[128] Theodor E. Mommsen, 'Petrarch and the Decoration of the *Sala Virorum Illustrium* in Padua', *Art Bulletin*, 34 (1952), 95–116 (p. 95). On the decoration of the *Sala*, see also Margaret Plant, 'Patronage in the Circle of the Carrara Family: Padua, 1337–1405', in *Patronage, Art and Society in Renaissance Italy*, ed. by F. W. Kent and Patricia Simons (Oxford: Clarendon Press, 1987), pp. 177–99.
[129] Probably composed in Bologna; now Munich, Bayerische Staatsbibliothek, MS Ital. 81.
[130] For a study of the illuminated manuscript tradition of the *Triumphi*, see Ada Labriola, 'Da Padova a Firenze: l'illustrazione dei Trionfi', in *Francesco Petrarca. I Trionfi, Commentario*, ed. by I. Giovanna Rao (Castelvetro di Modena: Artcodex, 2012), pp. 59–115.
[131] [*RVF* with Filelfo's and Squarciafico's commentaries and *Triumphi* with Ilicino's

This was the first printed instance of a long-standing association of this text with a pictorial tradition, evoking Petrarch's poem in woodcuts, paintings, frescoes or tapestries. But the iconography associated with the most prominent figures of the *Triumphi* often deviated from the Petrarchan model, relying on more conventional traditions: one example is the representation of Death as a male figure, especially in northern Europe. We find examples of triumphs in medieval art (for instance, Giotto's frescoes in Assisi), but, as Coogan notes, 'Petrarch's *Trionfi* are organic and dynamic and, consequently, so impressed the imagination of the Renaissance artist that they became the most decisive impetus for the popularity of the genre'.[132] At the same time, however, a number of scholars have remarked on the sameness of the various illustrations of Petrarch's work between the late fourteenth and the late sixteenth centuries.[133]

The very complexity of the *Triumphi* invites adaptation, in their exploration of a number of themes, from love to death to fame, that Petrarch had analysed throughout his literary life. Themes that were familiar to readers of *De remediis utriusque fortunae*, such as 'desire for glory, and contempt for glory; sense of the futility of life; lament over old age, and praises of old age; idealization of Death; Augustinian conception of time, moralistic view of history',[134] were now given a poetic and strongly symbolic representation. The *Triumphi*, a *summa* of Petrarch's Latin writings, constitute the ideal *trait d'union* to overcome the distinction between the medieval and the early modern poet: they use the new language and the new medium to revisit old themes. By working on visual imagination, the triumphal form offers new life and new meditational modes to themes fully explored elsewhere; as attested by Quattrocento and Cinquecento paintings, from Mantegna's triumphal frescoes at Hampton Court, to Piero della Francesca's diptych for Federigo da Montefeltro, to the work by Albrecht Dürer for the Emperor Maximilian, in choosing the triumphal form Petrarch struck at the very core of the Renaissance vision. He did not supply a prototype: this was a felicitous encounter; the moral purpose met the love for erudition and the evocation of the classical past that so fascinated humanist Europe. The *Triumphi*'s nature — 'not so much an allegorical work as an allusive one cast

---

commentary] incipit: Prohemio del prestante Oratore & poeta Messer Francesco Philelpho al illustrissimo & i[n]victi simo principe Philippo Maria Anglo Duca de Milano circa la interpretatione per lui sopra gli sonetti & ca[n]zone de messer Francesco Petrarcha facta (Venice: Bernardinus Rizus Novariensis, 1488).
[132] Coogan, 'Petrarch's "Trionfi"', p. 313; see also Lucia Battaglia Ricci, 'Immaginario Trionfale: Petrarca e la tradizione figurativa', in *I Triumphi di Francesco Petrarca*, ed. by Claudia Berra (Milan: Cisalpino, 1990), pp. 255–98, and J. B. Trapp, *Erasmus, Colet and More: The Early Tudor Humanists and their Books* (London: The British Library, 1991), p. 37.
[133] TFP, p. 38.
[134] Jean Seznec, 'Petrarch and Renaissance Art', in *Francesco Petrarca: Citizen of the World*, ed. by Aldo S. Bernardo (Padua and Albany: Antenore and State University of New York Press, 1980), pp. 133–50 (p. 136).

within an allegorical frame'[135] — is such that they offer themselves readily to translation or adaptation.

At the same time, the reception of the *Triumphi* in the visual arts seems to be partly the result of a misreading. Only the first two triumphs, the *Triumphus Cupidinis* and the *Triumphus Pudicitie*, can be properly called so, in that they employ the traditional iconographical repertory of the procession.[136] In his first *Triumphus* in particular, Petrarch was obviously fascinated by the Roman pageant, and found here an ideal blueprint for his representation of love according to Ovidian lines. This delight with ancient lore is echoed in a complex reworking, both in his writings and in his life, of an element intimately connected with Roman triumphal processions: the laurel crown (Petrarch famously received the poetic coronation in the form of a laurel crown in Rome in 1341, a few years before the composition of the first two *Triumphi*). But as the complex machinery of the *Triumphi* develops, this initial motif is transformed beyond recognition. Starting from the *Triumphus Mortis* Petrarch deviates from the medieval convention to opt for an evocation at the same time more autobiographical and more philosophical.[137] If the most striking element of the *Triumphus Mortis* is the intimate, almost domestic dialogue between the poet and the shadow of his loved one, the *Triumphus Eternitatis* attempts to define the concept of eternity through the collapse of space and time, fusing the topos of the Roman triumph with the medieval motif of the *somnium*, the allegorical and prophetic dream occurring by preference in the early hours of the morning, as Petrarch specifies at the beginning of the poem. While translators conscientiously strove to imitate Petrarch's daring innovations, the appropriations of the *Triumphi* in paintings, tapestry, emblems, court entertainments and public pageantry chose a safer option:

> A fixed scheme was early arrived at for the representation of the poem which does not entirely correspond to the text. Petrarch describes the first triumph as Cupid entering on a chariot drawn by horses; but he varies this in the other episodes. It became, however, a convention for artists to represent all the divisions of the poem according to the same plan as Petrarch had laid down for the first one; that is to say, they presented the triumphs as a series of triumphal chariots, drawn by various animals, with the 'examples' of the various themes walking beside the chariots.[138]

---

[135] Amilcare A. Iannucci, 'Petrarch's Intertextual Strategies in the *Triumphs*', in *Petrarch's 'Triumphs'*, ed. by Eisenbleicher and Iannucci, pp. 3–10 (p. 5).
[136] Vittore Branca, 'Per la genesi dei "Trionfi"', *La Rinascita*, 4 (1941), 681–708 (p. 688). See also Battaglia Ricci, pp. 256–57. The form of the procession is, however, also evoked in the *Triumphus Fame*.
[137] Ernest Wilkins sees in this passage a decisive change of direction in Petrarch's structuring of his work; see 'On Petrarch's Rewriting the *Triumph of Fame*', *Speculum*, 39 (1964), 440–43.
[138] Frances A. Yates, *Astraea: The Imperial Theme in the Sixteenth Century* (London:

English poets and visual artists responded eagerly to this suggestion. The *Triumphi* were represented or alluded to in tapestries owned by Henry VIII and displayed at Westminster, Windsor and Hampton Court;[139] John Skelton's *Colin Clout*, written in the early 1520s, probably describes the ones at Hampton Court.[140] More importantly, Thomas More composed verses for pageants in tapestries ('devysed in hys fathers house in London, [for] a goodly hangying of fine paynted cloth'),[141] which may have been influenced by the *Triumphi*, since six of the nine pageants are dedicated to the same theme as Petrarch's, in the same order; the other pageants are connected to the more traditionally English motif of the ages of man.[142] Stephen Hawes's *Pastime of Pleasure* (1506/7) concludes with the four pageants that end More's poem (Death, Fame, Time and Eternity); in Wynkin de Worde's first edition (1509), these sections are accompanied by woodcuts: 'two such responses to the *Trionfi* within such a short period, together with the existence of another *Trionfi* tapestry in England by 1507, seem to suggest a predominantly visual preoccupation with Petrarch's work'.[143]

Elizabeth I was frequently the dedicatee of triumphal motifs in pageants, entertainments or paintings; an instance is the entertainment modelled on the *Triumph of Chastity* in 1578, during her progress in Norfolk and Suffolk.[144] The image of Fame also appeared in shows staged in her honour, as in the case of Bristol in 1574 and Norwich in 1578.[145] In painting, one striking example is the Sieve Portrait of the queen, completed by George Gower in 1579: the sieve itself connects the portrait to chastity thanks to the legend of the Roman virgin Tuccia, mentioned in *Triumphus Pudicitie* (I. 148-51). In the Pinacoteca di Siena version of the same portrait, attributed to Cornelius Ketel, on the bottom left

---

Routledge and Kegan Paul, 1975), p. 112.
[139] In the latter case when the palace belonged to Cardinal Wolsey. See Coogan, 'Petrarch's "Trionfi"', p. 313.
[140] Wyatt, *Italian Encounter*, p. 206.
[141] Quoted in J. B. Trapp, 'Petrarch's *Triumph of Death* in Tapestry', in *Studies of Petrarch and his Influence* (London: The Pindar Press, 2003), pp. 171-200 (p. 171).
[142] Robert Coogan, 'Petrarch and Thomas More', *Moreana*, 6 (1969), 19-30 (p. 27). Although there are French precedents, in English the only precedent of verses composed to accompany a tapestry seems to be two poems by John Lydgate (A. S. G. Edwards, 'English Poems', in *The Complete Works of St. Thomas More: Volume 1*, ed. by A. S. G. Edwards, Katherine Gardiner Rodgers and Clarence H. Miller (New Haven: Yale University Press, 1997), pp. xvii-xxxv (p. xix)). Edwards, however, considers a direct Petrarchan filiation unlikely.
[143] Edwards, 'English Poems', p. xx. For a detailed comparison of More, Hawes and Skelton's poems with Petrarch's, see *TFP*, pp. 47-54.
[144] John N. King, 'Queen Elizabeth I, Representations of the Virgin Queen', *Renaissance Quarterly*, 43 (1990), 30-74. See also Alexandra F. Johnston, 'English Civic Ceremony', in *Petrarch's 'Triumphs'*, ed. by Eisenbichler and Iannucci, pp. 395-402.
[145] David Bergeron, *English Civic Pageantry, 1558-1642* (London: Edward Arnold, 1971), p. 27; *Records of Early English Drama: Norwich 1540-1642*, ed. by David Galloway (Toronto: University of Toronto Press, 1984), p. 254.

of the picture, the column against which the queen leans, painted with scenes from books one and four of the *Aeneid*, is inscribed with the Petrarchan verse 'Stancho riposo, riposato affanno', from *Triumphus Cupidinis*, IV. 145, a line that 'comments on the futility of sexual love';[146] as has been observed, 'what the sieve portraits primarily celebrate is the rational self-control of a monarch who places marriage to her kingdom above private gratification'.[147] The Ermine Portrait at Hatfield House might also be associated with the *Triumphi*, as the same animal, a symbol of chastity, appears in the *Triumphus Mortis* (I. 19–21). Triumphal motifs were also used in courtly entertainments in Scotland. In a letter written to Sir William Cecil in 1564, Thomas Randolph describes a great feast, the Shrovetide Masque based on the *Triumphi* performed at Holyrood for Mary Queen of Scots, and sends Cecil some of the verses of the show, including a passage from *Triumphus Cupidinis* (I. 76–87).[148]

These examples show that in the passage of Petrarch's fame from his Latin works to the *Triumphi* to the *Canzoniere* we might also see an evolution of poetic taste. The sonnets would trigger a daring experiment for English poets and readers, while the longer, semi-narrative form of the *Triumphi* might be more in keeping with the medieval inheritance. The two works were adapted in two widely different media: if the *Triumphi* are often translated into visual art, in the case of the *Canzoniere* individual sonnets are translated into musical experiments, beginning with the early modern madrigals by Luca Marenzio, Sigismondo d'India or Alfonso Ferrabosco, an Italian working at the English court. These two different paths reflect the different nature of the two works, the first contemplative, the second lyrical. As far as English culture is concerned, the conceptual form of the sonnet represented an absolute novelty in England, while the *Triumphi* recalled the dream visions that had enjoyed such a successful development in English poetry in the fourteenth and fifteenth centuries. Other parts of the *Canzoniere* were imitated for their visionary or symbolic quality — this is the case of *canzone* 323 ('Standomi un giorno'), which presents six visions, and before becoming a possible source for Edmund Spenser's *Visions of the Worlds Vanitie* was also imitated by Clément Marot, by Joachim du Bellay and in Jan van der Noot's woodcuts. The exploration of the inner life of the 'I' of the poem is not expressed through meditation but through emblematic,

---

[146] Constance Jordan, 'Representing Political Androgyny: More on the Siena Portrait of Queen Elizabeth I', in *The Renaissance Englishwoman in Print: Counterbalancing the Canon*, ed. by Anne M. Haselkorn and Betty S. Travitsky (Amherst: The University of Massachusetts Press, 1990), pp. 157–76 (p. 168).

[147] Dominic Baker-Smith, 'Spenser's "Triumph of Marriage"', *Verbal/Visual Enquiry*, 4 (1988), 310–16 (p. 312).

[148] The letter is summarized and partly transcribed in Robert Keith, ed., *History of the Affairs of Church and State in Scotland, from the Beginning of the Reformation to the Year 1568: Volume II* (Edinburgh: Spottiswoode, 1845), p. 220.

symbolic images.¹⁴⁹ The genre finds an appropriate echo, perhaps beyond the Petrarchan influence, in works such as Spenser's *Faerie Queene*, or in Jacobean masques, although in this case we may suppose that equally important for the development of the triumphal form in England were the medieval legacy of the mumming, Lydgate's triumphal processions and medieval theatre, as well as the classical legacy of Ovid's *Amores*. Petrarch's work might have given distinction to a form already developing in English literature.

1.6 The English translations

Against this background, the poetic translations of the *Triumphi* seem to be attestations of a minority taste, associated with a cultural and social elite. In part, this has to do with the source language: unlike translation from Latin or French, which had a long and established tradition in the British Isles, translation from the Italian stressed rupture and had little or no historical antecedent: 'outside Italy in the fourteenth century, vernacular Italian literature offered neither fashion nor the venerable authority conveyed by vertical translations from Latin. Linguistically, it was comparatively inaccessible to English writers, although the Italian merchants and bankers living in London made some contact possible'.¹⁵⁰ By the beginning of the sixteenth century, 'vertical translation' had become a highly controversial term, as antiquity could no longer be measured on the basis of the Latin/vernacular dichotomy; at the same time, translation, rather than strictly requiring a previous knowledge of the vernacular, often became a means to acquire such a knowledge. Petrarch's subtle and complex use of language and the actual obscurity of the text created an extra layer of difficulty (even if an intermediary French translation was used). The structure of the *Triumphi*, besides, played a major role in the modes of its reception. The influence of the *Canzoniere* is due at least in part to its fragmentary nature, so that 'every lyric [...] can be considered as a unit in its own right, which allows for fruition and direct imitation without imposing a connection to a general and comprehensive order'.¹⁵¹ In the case of the *Triumphi* the epic rhythm imposed by the use of *terza rima* and the way in which each successive triumph defeats and annihilates the previous one are elements which make themselves heavily felt even when only one triumph, or indeed a fragment

---

¹⁴⁹ Bondanella, p. 19; see also Syrithe Pugh, 'Sidney, Spenser, and Political Petrarchism', in *Petrarch in Britain: Interpreters, Imitators, and Translators over 700 Years: Proceedings of the British Academy*, ed. by Peter Hainsworth, Martin MacLaughlin and Letizia Panizza (London: The British Academy, 2007), pp. 243-57 (pp. 249-52).
¹⁵⁰ Karla Taylor, 'Writers of the Italian Renaissance', in *The Oxford History of Literary Translation in English: Volume I: To 1550*, ed. by Roger Ellis (Oxford: Oxford University Press, 2008), pp. 390-406 (p. 390).
¹⁵¹ Guardiani, p. 259.

of one, is taken into consideration. Wyatt may translate simply one sonnet from the *Canzoniere* and still present it as a complete, self-sufficient literary artefact; the translator of the *Triumphi* cultivates the art of allusion, becoming part of a transmission of cultural heritage of which Petrarch himself was one of the main exponents.

Unlike the *Canzoniere*, the *Triumphi* saw two complete and a number of partial translations in the sixteenth and early seventeenth centuries:

> Complete translations:
>   Henry Parker, Lord Morley (undated, probably composed during the reign of Henry VIII);
>   William Fowler (1587).
> Partial translations:
>   Henry Howard, Earl of Surrey: *Triumphus Cupidinis*, III. 151–87 (1540s);
>   E. D.: *Triumphus Mortis*, I. 79–100 (1585);
>   Mary Sidney, Countess of Pembroke: *Triumphus Mortis* (1590s);
>   John Florio: *Triumphus Pudicitie*, 76–90, 174 (1591);
>   Elizabeth I (?): *Triumphus Eternitatis*, 1–80 (date uncertain);
>   Anna Hume: *Triumphus Amoris, Pudicitie, Mortis* (1644).

A study of early modern English versions of the *Triumphi* offers a cross-section of the contemporary intellectual world: women as well as men, aristocratic and courtier poets as well as professional writers, an English intellectual of Italian descent such as John Florio and a Scottish Calvinist such as Anna Hume. Such a range aptly instantiates Brenda Hosington's observation that 'Renaissance translations must be examined against the backdrop of contemporary social, historical, and cultural circumstances'.[152] The present book includes a complete edition of William Fowler's translation, which was last edited more than a century ago, while, in the case of Lord Morley's translation (available in an excellent 1971 edition by D. D. Carnicelli) and of Anna Hume, only the *Triumphus Mortis* is printed, together with the other, partial translations listed above. The other texts are offered in their entirety.

1.6.1 Henry Howard, Earl of Surrey

The dating of the earliest versions is extremely uncertain, but Henry Howard, Earl of Surrey (1517–1547), may be the first poet who translated a substantial section of the *Triumphi* into English.[153] In his fifty-line poem 'Suche waiwarde

---

[152] Brenda Hosington, 'Tudor Englishwomen's Translations of Continental Protestant Texts: The Interplay of Ideology and Historical Context', in *Tudor Translation*, ed. by Fred Schurink (Basingstoke: Palgrave Macmillan, 2011), pp. 121–42 (p. 121).

[153] Surrey's corpus is very difficult to establish: 'in general, Surrey is a very frustrating subject for the student with some belief in the potential of manuscript study for the assessment of an author's texts. Few of his manuscripts can be dated within his lifetime; scribal copies thus tell us little about the circulation of Surrey's verse and the milieux in

waies hath love', lines 15 to 50 are a translation of *Triumphus Cupidinis*, III. 151–87. This is a long anaphoric meditation on the paradoxical symptoms of love, and on its severity, part of a longer section which a modern editor has aptly called a breviary of love.[154] Surrey's poem fuses different love motifs from Italian and classical poets: lines 1 to 14 are indebted to Ariosto's *Orlando Furioso* (II. 1), and lines 5 to 6 contain an echo of Ovid's *Metamorphoses* (I. 468–71). The section translating Petrarch seamlessly merges with the previous one; the whole is presented in a free and original version, often deviating from the Italian and Latin models to present some of Surrey's recurring characteristics — his love for alliteration, his penchant for similes taken from the natural world — and provides a firmer closure than the Italian original.[155] At the same time, Surrey elegantly imitates Petrarch's striking anaphoric rhythm.[156] His use of poulter's measure (a form alternating lines of twelve and fourteen syllables, in rhyming couplets) has been much criticized,[157] but suits the meditative mood, and is part of that search for metrical solutions that is so important in early modern English translations of both *Canzoniere* and *Triumphi*.

1.6.2 Henry Parker, Lord Morley

Another version, roughly contemporary with Surrey's, was undertaken by Henry Parker, Lord Morley (1476–1556). One of the two full versions of the work, it was printed in 1555 by John Cawood, Queen Mary's official printer;[158] but it was probably composed much earlier, originally presented and dedicated to Henry VIII; the printed version is dedicated to young Lord Maltravers, son and heir to the Earl of Arundel.[159] A diplomat and scholar, Morley lived all his life

which it was read' (A. S. G. Edwards, 'Manuscripts of the Verse of Henry Howard, Earl of Surrey', *Huntington Library Quarterly*, 67 (2004), 283–93 (p. 292)).
[154] Ariani, p. 134.
[155] Sessions, p. 184.
[156] Arturo Cattaneo analyzes the poem in *L'ideale umanistico: Henry Howard, Earl of Surrey* (Bari: Adriatica, 1991), pp. 112–17.
[157] C. S. Lewis called it 'the very draff and scum of contemporary English poetry, the lumbering Poulter's measure' (*English Literature in the Sixteenth Century Excluding Drama* (Oxford: Clarendon Press, 1954), p. 109); Emrys Jones maintains that 'it is, though crude, a musical metre. And although it encourages a jigging or prancing movement, it does not entirely resist modification' (Henry Howard, Earl of Surrey, *Poems*, ed. by Emrys Jones (Oxford: Clarendon Press, 1964), p. xxiii).
[158] Francesco Petrarca, *The tryumphes of Fraunces Petrarcke, translated out of Italian into English by Henrye Parker knyght, Lorde Morley. The tryumphe of loue. Of chastitie. Of death. Of fame. Of tyme. Of diuinitie* (London: Iohn Cawood, 1555).
[159] For a fascinating hypothesis on the relation between Morley's translation and Elizabeth see Kenneth Bartlett, 'The Occasion of Lord Morley's Translation of the *Trionfi*: The Triumph of Chastity over Politics', in *Petrarch's 'Triumphs'*, ed. by Eisenbichler and Iannucci, pp. 325–34. Discussions on the dating appear in Axton, pp. 175–76, and in Mike Hodder, 'Petrarch in English: Political, Cultural and Religious Filters in the Translation

at court, as one of the 'courtly makers'[160] flourishing under the reign of Henry VIII. He translated from Latin and Italian, focusing on writers such as Cicero, Plutarch, Boccaccio, Erasmus, Paolo Giovio and Masuccio Salernitano.[161] He was also familiar with Petrarch as a Latin writer: in his preface to the translation of Giovanni Boccaccio's *De Claris mulieribus*, after praising Dante, he continues:

> The next unto thys Dante was Frauncis Petrak, that not onely in the Latyne tunge, but also in swete ryme, is so estemyde that unto thys present tyme unnethe [i.e. hardly] is ther any noble prynce in Italy, nor gentle man, withoute havynge in hys handes hys sonnetes and hys 'Tryhumphes' or hys other rymes. And he wrote also in the Latyne tunge certeyn eglogges in versys and another booke named 'Affrica' and 'Of the Remedyes of bothe Fortunes', with dyvers epistles and other wourkes which I over passe.[162]

While only his *Triumphi* translation was published in his lifetime, he used translation or commentary as a political tool, as in the case of *The Exposition and Declaration of the Psalme Deus Ultionum Dominus* (his other printed work, published in 1539).[163] His residence at court, where the Vellutello edition of the *Triumphi* was available, together with a number of textual characteristics, make it very probable that he was using this edition, even if he might not have availed himself of Vellutello's commentary.[164]

Morley's translation, as was the case with subsequent versions, is strongly conditioned by the choice of meter. He used the variable couplet known as 'riding rhyme', which forced him to slight expansions and occasional padding, as he translated one *terzina* as two couplets.[165] Apart from rhyming tags and

---

of the *Rerum vulgarium fragmenta* and *Triumphi* from Geoffrey Chaucer to J. M. Synge' (unpublished doctoral thesis, University of Oxford, 2013), pp. 138–47.

[160] *TFP*, p. 9.

[161] On Morley's life and literary production, see *TFP*, pp. 3–19, and the introduction in Henry Parker, Lord Morley, *Forty-six Lives Translated from Boccaccio's De claris mulieribus*, ed. by Herbert G. Wright (London: Oxford University Press, 1943), pp. ix–cv. See also Coogan, 'Petrarch's "Trionfi"', p. 315.

[162] Parker, p. 2.

[163] Bartlett, pp. 325–36. Bartlett also supposes a closeness between this version and the translation of the *Triumphus Eternitatis* attributed to Queen Elizabeth. Morley's publishing activity might make him 'the first English peer to print an essentially literary work, and the first nobleman to publish verses of his own composition' (Steven W. May, 'Tudor Aristocrats and the Mythical "Stigma of Print"', in *Renaissance Papers 1980*, ed. by A. Leigh Deneef and M. Thomas Hester (Durham, NC: The Southeastern Renaissance Conference, 1981), pp. 11–18 (p. 15)). See also Taylor, pp. 397–98.

[164] Hodder, pp. 141–44. Coogan ('Petrarch's "Trionfi"', pp. 316–17) shows that Vellutello would have been the most easily available text for Morley.

[165] Coogan, 'Petrarch's "Trionfi"', p. 320. Ilona Bell, however, notes that many additions reflect Morley's anxiety to vindicate Laura's chastity (*Elizabethan Women and the Poetry of Courtship* (Cambridge: Cambridge University Press, 1998), p. 105). On Morley's choice of metre, and his awareness of his shortcomings, see Susanne Woods, 'Lord Morley's "Ryding

repetitions, his version is generally faithful and accurate, presenting the text according to the critical tradition that saw in the *Triumphi* a long, articulated allegory. The translation includes a prefatory epistle, which begins by referring to Aesop's fable of the cock and the jewel — how the cock, 'scrapynge on a doungehill', found a precious stone which he did not prize, as it could be of no use to him.[166] The same fable had been proposed by John Lydgate and Robert Henryson, a century earlier: while Lydgate admired the cock's restraint and Christian humility,[167] Henryson led the reader along a more complicated path, demonstrating that the jasper (the precious stone in his version) 'is an actual stone that occurs in nature, which can be read as a book of instruction. But that book has already been written by the divine hand, so the narrator leads his "maisteris" from the literal to the figurative, the natural to the fabular'.[168] Whether or not Morley was acquainted with Henryson's *moralitas*, he follows his example in setting the jewel as a *figura* of the book, comparing inattentive readers to the careless cock:

> Even so there be a number of that sorte, that percase when they shall eyther heare redde, or them selfe reade this excellent tryumphes, of this famous clercke Petrarcha, shall lytle set by them, and peradventure caste it from them, desyrynge rather to have a tale prynted of Robyn Hoode, or some other dongehyll matter then of this, which I dare affirme, yea, and the Italians do the same, that the devine works set aparte, there was never in any vulgar speche or language, so notable a worke, so clerckely done as this his worke. And albeit that he setteth forth these syxte wonderfull made triumphes all to the laude of hys Ladye Laura, by whome he made so many a swete sonnet, that never yet no poete nor gentleman could amend, nor make the lyke, yet who that doth understande them, shall se in them comprehended al morall vertue, all Phylosophye, all storyall matters, and briefely manye devyne sentences theologicall secretes declared.[169]

Petrarch's erudition and *gravitas* remind us of Chaucer's *Clerk's Prologue*, introducing Petrarch as the source of his Griselda tale, or of the use made of Petrarch's *Secretum* in a late fifteenth-century English translation, in which he presents himself with these words:

> Sumtyme I was a subtyle and a notable clerke

Ryme" and the Origins of Modern English Versification', in *'Triumphs of English': Henry Parker, Lord Morley. Translator to the Tudor Court: New Essays in Interpretation*, ed. by Marie Axton and James P. Carley (London: The British Library, 2000), pp. 201–11.

[166] *TFP*, p. 77.

[167] John Lydgate, 'Isopes Fabules', in *The Minor Poems of John Lydgate: Part II*, ed. by Henry Noble MacCracken (London: Oxford University Press, 1934), pp. 566–99, lines 213–21.

[168] Edward Wheatley, *Mastering Aesop: Medieval Education, Chaucer, and his Followers* (Gainesville: University Press of Florida, 2000), p. 157. For Henryson's text, see *The Poems*, ed. by Denton Fox (Oxford: Clarendon Press, 1981), pp. 5–9.

[169] *TFP*, p. 77.

> And er I farther passe y wyll reherse myn name
> I am ye laureate poete called petrarc
> That in ytalye and Florence was of so grete Fame.[170]

This translation of the *Secretum* was meant to serve the students of Winchester school;[171] the presentation offered by Lord Morley had the same didactic purpose. At the same time it highlights the role of translation in the development of English as a literary language, noting how in France and Italy 'there is no excellente worke in the latyn, but that strayght wayes they set it forth in the vulgar'.[172] Morley decided to translate the *Triumphi* after seeing a French translation (probably Bourgouyn's), though acknowledging ruefully that, while he had 'not erred moche from the letter',[173] the *rhyme* had eluded him. English translators of the *Triumphi* appear constrained by their determination to solve a double challenge, keeping faith to a daringly innovative work and presenting a paradoxical union of the narrative and the lyrical, while attempting to create 'a poetic form for a language which had undergone such revolutionary changes in the preceding two centuries as to make it impossible for them to take Chaucer as a model',[174] not having any other established model in their own language. This preoccupation informs the prefatory material of translations.

1.6.3 William Fowler

Roughly half a century after Lord Morley, another writer took up the challenge of translating the whole of the *Triumphi*: William Fowler (1560–1612), who in 1587 completed this work and dedicated it to Jean Fleming, Lady Thirlestane. Fowler was a Scotsman who, after attending the universities of St Andrews and Paris, began a career at the court of James VI of Scotland, while also acting as a spy for Sir Francis Walsingham. He later travelled to Italy (where he spent some time at the University of Padua) and France, and came back to Edinburgh as secretary to Queen Anne, a post he maintained after 1603, when the royal household moved to London. His biography offers a portrait of a cosmopolitan writer, used to intermingling cultural and political activities and putting one at the service of the other. The survival of a great mass of his occasional papers, now at the National Library of Scotland, offers us precious clues to his

---

[170] Lines 9–12. The translation is extant in London, British Library, Additional MS 60544, fols 8r–22v. The text has been recently edited in *A Middle English Translation from Petrarch's Secretum*, ed. by Edward Wilson and Daniel Wakelin (Oxford: Oxford University Press, 2018).
[171] Alessandra Petrina, 'The Humanist Petrarch in Medieval and Early Modern England', *Journal of Anglo-Italian Studies*, 12 (2013), 45–62.
[172] *TFP*, p. 78.
[173] *TFP*, p. 78.
[174] D. G. Rees, 'Petrarch's "Trionfo della Morte" in English', *Italian Studies*, 7 (1952), 82–96 (p. 88).

personality and allows us to gauge his contribution to the public life of the time.[175] The translation of Petrarch is among his few completed works (he also translated Machiavelli's *Prince* and composed a Petrarchist sonnet sequence, *The Tarantula of Love*, as well as a number of shorter, occasional works); the survival of the presentation copy allows us to assess not only the translation but also the context in which it was composed.

Fowler's dedication has prompted queries, since the dedicatee was the wife of John Maitland, who had become Lord Chancellor in May 1586, and would become first Lord Maitland of Thirlestane in 1590. His rise coincided with the fall from favour of Francis Stewart, Earl of Bothwell, Fowler's long-time patron: through his dedication Fowler might have been seeking a more secure foothold at court.[176] It has also been argued that, given this political context, this translation 'undertakes an evangelisation of Petrarch's language which accords with the goal of harmonisation of style with subject matter as advocated by James VI's *Reulis and Cautelis*',[177] the short literary treatise James had written in 1584, marking the creation of a coterie of poets and musicians at the Scottish court (like Alexander Montgomerie and the Hudson brothers).[178] In spite of the king's strictures against translation, many of the poets of his circle (including the king himself) worked on translations from French and Italian: Fowler's version of Petrarch can be read as part of this collective effort. The work was not printed in his time, but the presentation manuscript (now Edinburgh University Library, MS Drummond De.1.10) includes a clear dating; besides, a probably earlier sonnet, signed M. B. or M. L. B. — probably Mary Beaton or Mary Lady Boyne, one of the ladies in Queen Mary's retinue — anticipated the translation of Petrarch, mentioning 'the gifts wherwith the heavens have thee instorde | If thou the learned Thuskan wolde assaye | And in thy tyme his Triumphes doe record': one more proof that this translation was meant as a form of scribal publication. Sebastiaan Verweij adds that Mary Beaton

---

[175] For a biography of Fowler, see Meikle, III. ix-xlii, and Petrina, *Machiavelli*, pp. 69-86. The papers have been collected in five volumes (Edinburgh, National Library of Scotland, Hawthornden MSS 2063-67).

[176] On this point see Hodder, pp. 147-50. The paratextual material is analysed in Alessandra Petrina, 'Approaching Petrarch's *Trionfi*: Paratexts in the Early Modern Scottish Translations', in *Thresholds of Translation: Paratexts, Print, and Cultural Exchange in Early Modern Britain (1473-1660)*, ed. by Marie-Alice Belle and Brenda M. Hosington (Cham: Palgrave Macmillan, 2018), pp. 161-82.

[177] Hodder, p. 150.

[178] On James's literary coterie, see Helena Mennie Shire, *Song, Dance and Poetry of the Court of Scotland under King James VI* (Cambridge: Cambridge University Press, 1969); Priscilla Bawcutt, 'James VI's Castalian Band: A Modern Myth', *The Scottish Historical Review*, 80 (2001), 251-59; and Theo van Heijnsbergen, 'Coteries, Commendatory Verse and Jacobean Poetics: William Fowler's *Trivmphs of Petrarke* and its Castalian Circles', in *James VI and I, Literature and Scotland: Tides of Change, 1567-1625*, ed. by David J. Parkinson (Leuven: Peeters, 2013), pp. 45-64.

'according to queen Mary's testament of 1566 was to inherit part of the royal library (all Greek and Latin books were bequeathed to St Andrews University; the remainder to Beaton), among which could be found *The Morall Triumphis of Petrark in Italiane*'.[179]

Fowler was then in his late twenties, and his youth may have accounted for the belligerent tone of his dedication, which opens the presentation manuscript. He echoes Lord Morley in praising Petrarch's work for its abundance of moral sentences, godly sayings and brave discourses;[180] but two other notes are struck. One is the theme of fame, conferred by Petrarch upon Laura and himself (obviously implying that Fowler will do the same with Lady Thirlestane and himself); the other is a savage attack on previous translations, including Morley's. In his translation of Machiavelli's *Prince*, extant only in a rough draft, Fowler appears much more cautious: the dedication to the Laird of Buccleuch describes almost solely linguistic preoccupations.[181] The difference here resides not in Fowler's greater or lesser knowledge of Italian, but in the context in which the two dedications were composed. While the dedication to Buccleuch is still a draft, composed by a writer for a nobleman who was also a close friend, in what appears to be a very private context, the dedication to Lady Thirlestane is part of a public display of linguistic prowess; the fact that the presentation manuscript includes a number of congratulatory sonnets composed, among others, by King James and Thomas and Robert Hudson, shows that the translation circulated at court. His disparaging assessment of other translators can therefore be read within a vindication of national literature, and of the national language, echoing James's own words in *Reulis and Cautelis*, which drew a sharp distinction between works in Scottish and works in English: 'albeit sindrie hes written of it in English, quhilk [i.e. which] is lykest to our language, yit we differ from thame in sindrie reulis [i.e. many rules] of poesie'.[182] The new wave of Scottish poetry presented a nationalistic agenda that overruled any qualms as to the adequacy of the language. The choice of Petrarch's text had more to do with its fame than with its moral virtues, and this is highlighted in the concluding lines of the dedication, in which the praise of the lady reaches absurd heights, as the writer wonders whether 'more fitlye can be offred these Triumphs then to a triumphing ladye, Triumphing over all vice, and who has

---

[179] Sebastiaan Verweij, 'The Manuscripts of William Fowler: A Revaluation of *The Tarantula of Love, A Sonnet Sequence*, and *Of Death*', Scottish Studies Review, 8 (2007), 9–23 (p. 11).

[180] It may be noted that in his *Defence of Poesy* Sir Philip Sidney also mentions Petrarch as a moral instructor.

[181] Edited in Petrina, *Machiavelli*, pp. 138–39.

[182] James VI, *Ane Schort Treatise Conteining Some Reulis and Cautelis to be Observit and Eschewit in Scottis Poesie*, in *The Mercat Anthology of Early Scottish Literature 1375–1707*, ed. by R. D. S. Jack and P. A. T. Rozendaal (Edinburgh: Mercat Press, 1997), pp. 460–73 (p. 461).

ellis passed her ovations and fixed Trophees in all vertew?'[183] Petrarch's text becomes an occasion for public display and celebration, of the lady, the poet and the national language.

The accompanying poems are also of interest. The sequence is opened by a sonnet signed by James VI (and appearing also in British Library, Additional MS 24195, fol. 35r), in which Fowler (though unnamed) is inserted as the last of a sequence that includes Homer, Virgil and Petrarch. In this, the king follows the example of Thomas Watson's *Amyntas*, in which the *Triumphi* had also been seen as an epic poem on the trail of the two classical ones. There follow two sonnets by E. D., identified by Theo van Heijnsbergen and Sebastiaan Verweij as Elizabeth Douglas, wife of one Samuel Coburn, and celebrated by Fowler in a funeral sonnet which is among his very few printed works;[184] as has been observed, 'Fowler's address to Jean Fleming and the "E. D." sonnets position the *Triumphs* within a textual community that evidently valued female members as readers, as patrons, and as co-creators'.[185] At the same time, the impression is that the various poets who penned commendatory poems did not actually read the translation, or did not complete their reading, with the exception of Thomas Hudson, the author of the sixth sonnet (sonnets four and five are signed respectively by Robert Hudson, Thomas's brother, and Richard Cockburn, while the sequence is concluded by a sestina signed by Alexander Colville). Even in the case of Thomas Hudson, however, the allusion to eternity, the subject of the last triumph, becomes simply a means to confer the same (transmuted into literary glory) upon the translator — an idea reiterated by the quotation from Propertius on the contents page. James speaks of triumphs of 'love, chaistnes, death, and fame', forgetting the last two; most of the others insist on the triumphant nature of the enterprise, and on the triumph implicitly bestowed on the dedicatee, reverting to a traditional, pre-Petrarchan conception that has little to do with the actual text. This supports Verweij's contention that Fowler, 'before commissioning his scribe to complete the presentation manuscript solicited from his contributors their various poems of praise, which were then delivered to the poet on single leaves'.[186] This also suggests that the translation of Petrarch's *Triumphi* was valued more for its role in celebrating a Scottish noblewoman (and implicitly the court) and in raising the tone of Scottish letters, than for any intrinsic merit.

After such premises, the reading of the actual translation may come as a disappointment: Fowler's work strikes the modern reader as prolix and

---

[183] Meikle, I. 17.
[184] van Heijnsbergen, pp. 47–63; Sebastiaan Verweij, *The Literary Culture of Early Modern Scotland: Manuscript Production and Transmission, 1560–1625* (Oxford: Oxford University Press, 2016), pp. 84–87. The funeral sonnet is edited in Meikle, I. 9.
[185] Verweij, *Literary Culture*, p. 85.
[186] Verweij, *Literary Culture*, p. 85.

convoluted, and in recent years has received little consideration, if not outright rejection.[187] Once again the choice of metre may be partly responsible: this version is in couplets, and the lines are fourteeners, following a tradition in English language translations of epic poems (from Phaer's translation of the *Aeneid* to Golding's translation of Ovid, to James VI's translation of du Bartas). Besides, Fowler normally translates Petrarch's tercets as two couplets, so that the last line of each group may sometimes seem a simple filler. Given the fact that English contains far more monosyllabic words than Italian, the choice forces Fowler to expand, often recurring to alliteration or even paronomasia. The result may be slightly embarrassing, as in the very first line ('That time that did my sobbing sobs and sorry sighs renew'), but even in this instance the reader is conscious of Fowler's search for an aural equivalent of the effect created by Petrarch. At the same time, the rhythm that is being created, in spite of some forcing and some metrical awkwardness, can have surprising effects: the fourteeners are clearly divided into two half-lines, a choice highlighted both by the fact that a fragment of the first chapter of *Triumphus Cupidinis*, extant in Fowler's private papers,[188] has each fourteener actually presented as two lines of seven syllables each, and by the layout in the presentation copy, which often inserts a space, a slash or a capital letter between the first and the second half of the line. The choice of regularly assigning four beats to the first half-line and three to the second (against the conventions regulating the fourteener) creates a lilting rhythm that evokes the ballad, highlighting the narrative structure of the *Triumphi*.[189]

When faced with this type of translation, we tend to comment that such texts 'are of little literary value in themselves. Their value as cultural indicators of their respective time periods, however, is highly significant'.[190] Yet it might be possible to go a step further. Rather than simply attesting to the vogue for Petrarchism in the British Isles, these works show the development of poetry in English in their search for a form that might adequately mirror Petrarch's original. The metrical forms chosen by Morley and Fowler, inappropriate as they may seem, reveal the effort on the part of translators to explore the possibilities of the English language for a linguistic and poetic equivalent, the attempt to establish (as was done with the sonnet) a cultural specificity

---

[187] In a review of Carnicelli's edition of Morley's translation, Katherine Duncan-Jones writes: 'It seems stranger still to give more space to the poor Scottish translation of the *Trionfi* by William Fowler (1586) than to the Countess of Pembroke's exquisite translation of the *Trionfo della Morte*' (*The Review of English Studies*, 23 (1972), 528–29, (p. 528)).

[188] Edinburgh, National Library of Scotland, MS Hawthornden 2063, fol. 39. The manuscript is described in more detail in the introduction to the text, below.

[189] I am incredibly grateful to Allison L. Steenson for her invaluable suggestions on this point.

[190] Hodder, p. 159.

that finds a model in Petrarch but develops along autonomous lines. Some of the later translators of the *Triumphi*, such as Mary Sidney and Elizabeth I, attempted closer adherence to Petrarch's metre, both as concerns the length of the line (both poets used iambic pentameter, which allowed for the same line-length as the Italian hendecasyllable) and, in the case of Sidney, the rhyme scheme, which reproduced Petrarch's *terza rima*. The result is, for the modern reader at least, more successful than the instances analysed so far; but unlike what happened with the sonnet, this did not give birth to an independent development in English poetry. At the same time, it is clear that Fowler had closely studied the original, and unravelled all of Petrarch's allusions, even the most obscure. Fowler's clumsiness and repetition are often the result of his earnest attempt to explore the Italian original and develop its semantic possibilities, as shown by the numerous semantic calques. This effort is much more evident in his translation of Machiavelli's *Prince*, partly because in this case the original is syntactically and semantically simpler, and partly because since we have a draft in Fowler's hand we can see his changes, additions and corrections. But the Petrarch version is also a fascinating instance, especially as it comes comparatively late, if we think of the European circulation of the *Triumphi* as an essentially early sixteenth-century phenomenon. It could be read as part of a wider project: in the same years Fowler was working on a sonnet sequence, *The Tarantula of Love* (the intriguing title is probably not his; the word *Tarantula* might refer both to the frenzy allegedly generated by the tarantula's bite and to the popular dance associated with it), closely following the model of the *Canzoniere*. This makes him the only poet in Britain that engaged thoroughly and consistently with the whole of Petrarch's poetic output in Italian, and the only one in King James's circle that translated directly from the Italian.[191]

Fowler's linguistic consciousness explains his translation choices much more satisfactorily than the attempt on the part of a number of scholars to read his translation as Protestant propaganda. Though it has been argued that his translation reads like a sermon,[192] this is due more to his difficulties with the Italian original than to any attempt to force the text towards a religious reading, although the public, celebratory nature of his translation (as expressed by the

---

[191] Another poet at the Scottish court, John Stewart of Baldynneis, translated an Italian text (Ariosto's *Orlando Furioso*), but using a French intermediary translation. On the *Tarantula*, see R. D. S. Jack, 'Petrarch and the Scottish Renaissance Sonnet', in *Petrarch in Britain*, ed. by Hainsworth, MacLaughlin and Panizza, pp. 259–73 (pp. 264–66); Verweij, 'The Manuscripts of William Fowler'. On the role of translation at the court of James VI, see also McClure.

[192] R. D. S. Jack, 'William Fowler and Italian Literature', *Modern Language Review*, 65 (1970), 481–92; Jack, 'Petrarch in English and Scottish Renaissance Literature', *Modern Language Review*, 71 (1976), 801–11; Hodder, pp. 165–73.

dedicatory epistle) affects his writing, often transcending Petrarch's solipsism to acquire a more public, almost exhortative tone; at other times, he opts for a rather pedantic didacticism, amplifying Petrarch's more obscure references, adding long lists of adjectives that might better define the choice in the Italian original and inserting moralizing comments so as to underline Petrarch's point (in this latter case, the comment is highlighted by the layout); the process is supported and complicated by his use of alliteration and anaphora. Petrarch's first triumph is a very clear instance of this, given the fact that the Italian poet peoples his *Triumphus Cupidinis* with immensely long lists of figures from the classical past, sometimes named and described, sometimes simply alluded to. It is unclear whether in this case the translator was prompted by his love for erudite display, or by a genuine concern for his readership, but often he adds to Petrarch's mentions additional lines of explanation or even short biographies of the characters in question. Fowler's penchant for explanation and reduplication can be plainly noted even when he is dealing with a relatively uncomplicated prose text such as Machiavelli's *Prince*; in the latter case the evidence offered by the manuscript draft often shows the writer listing a number of synonyms to translate the same word — a practice that may result in a well-considered choice or incline the translator towards hendiadys as the only way to render the semantic density of the original. In the case of the *Triumphi* we see what was probably his final choice, the result of a never-ending compromise between translating and glossing Petrarch's text. Rather than a religious reading, we might call this translation an attempt to explore the religious as well as linguistic nuances of the text. One might locate the translation within the French tradition of the reception of the *Triumphi*, in which the poem was read 'not as the culmination of the Laura lyrics in the *Canzoniere* but primarily as an extension of Petrarch's *De Remediis utriusque fortunae*'.[193]

As concerns the source of Fowler's version, there is no unanimity among scholars. Carnicelli saw in the prefatory material clear traces of Bernardo Ilicino's commentary,[194] while Hodder makes a case for Fowler having used the 1573 version of Guillaume Rouillié's edition, printed by Domenico Nicolini in Venice.[195] Hodder's hypothesis, though well-argued, is based on rather episodic evidence, and does not take into account the fact that Fowler might have used more than one version, as he probably did in the case of his translation of Machiavelli. This seems to be the case with Fowler's translation of the word *drappelletto* (Petrarch's hapax, meaning 'a small company'), appearing in *Triumphus Mortis*, I. 15. Fowler translates it as 'cloth of state', misreading the word as a diminutive of *drappo*, cloth; the mistake, Hodder argues, derives

---

[193] van Heijnsbergen, pp. 45–46.
[194] *TFP*, p. 63.
[195] Hodder, pp. 151–54.

from Nicolini's edition not presenting any gloss for this particular word. However, Morley's translation makes a similar mistake, translating *drappelletto* as 'canopy' (Mary Sidney correctly translates it as 'squadronet'; Anna Hume uses the phrase 'a little troupe'). Fowler's attack on previous translations of the *Triumphi*, in fact, makes it possible, if not probable, that he had access to them, and used them.

1.6.4 'E. D.'

William Fowler's was the last complete translation in early modern Britain. In 1585 in London the printer H. Jackson published *Prayse of Nothing*, a short and convoluted prose work attributed in the frontispiece to 'E. D.', subsequently (and controversially) identified with Edward Dyer (1543–1606), courtier and poet, and friend of Sir Philip Sidney. Ralph M. Sargent, the author of the only full-length monograph on Dyer, argues against this attribution, which indeed has no support apart from the initials.[196] Another (though quite slight) possibility is the identification of E. D. with Edward Daunce, the author of a book dedicated to Queen Elizabeth, *A Briefe Discourse of the Spanish State* (1590), though in this case the only support for this hypothesis is a vague ideological analogy.[197] *Prayse of Nothing* has little artistic merit, and develops the theme of 'nothingness' in a series of puns and classical allusions. The tract contains, on sig. G1r, a short extract in unrhymed alexandrines: these twenty lines are a translation of *Triumphus Mortis*, 1. 79–100. It is of course impossible to say whether E. D. is the translator, since the Petrarchan passage is presented as 'newly speaking in our tongue, by an unlearned translator'. The short passage, closely adhering to the original, is surprisingly elegant, insisting on strings of rhetorical questions to underline the futility of any human effort against death.

1.6.5 Mary Sidney, Countess of Pembroke

The choice on the part of the unknown translator to use the *Triumphus Mortis* is indicative of a precise preference on the part of English writers approaching the *Triumphi*. A few years later, another, much better poet, Mary Sidney, would translate the *Triumphus Mortis*, in a version that is extant in an early seventeenth-century manuscript (now London, Inner Temple Library, Petyt MS 538.43). In spite of its fragmentary nature and obscure origin, it is by far the

---

[196] Ralph M. Sargent, *At the Court of Queen Elizabeth: The Life and Lyrics of Sir Edward Dyer* (London: Oxford University Press, 1935). Sargent argues against the attribution in 'The Authorship of *The Praise of Nothing*', *The Library*, 12 (1931), 322–31.
[197] Emanuel Stelzer, 'Paradoxes on Women and Nothing' <http://textsandstudies.skeneproject.it> [forthcoming]. I wish to thank Emanuel for discussing this point with me, and allowing me access to his as yet unpublished material.

most studied among *Triumphi* translations in recent years. Known as a literary patron, Mary Sidney worked on a translation of the Psalms together with her brother Philip (or she might have completed the translation he left unfinished upon his death), and on her own translated two French contemporary works, Robert Garnier's *Marc Antoine* and Philippe Du Plessis Mornay's *Excellent discours de la vie et de la mort*.[198] Her interest in the *Triumphi* is attested by some lines from Thomas Moffett's *The Silkewormes and their Flies* (1599): in his dedication, he begs her to take some rest, in lines that might suggest an enterprise as demanding and long as the translation of the Psalms, and also gives a tentative dating for the Petrarch translation: 'Vouchsafe a while to lay thy taske aside, | Let *Petrarcke* sleep, give rest to *Sacred Writte*'.[199] The Petrarch translation was never published in Sidney's lifetime, unlike her other works: the manuscript, together with three of her translations of the Psalms, comes from a letter written in December 1600 by John Harington of Kelston (a friend of Pembroke and Robert Sidney) to his cousin, Lucy, Countess of Bedford (the extant manuscript is a copy). The text of the letter is in the same hand as the translation. Jason Scott-Warren discusses the problematic textual situation of the manuscript, which has been at various times dismembered and inserted into another composite volume, and calls the Petrarch translation 'an unexpected presence', adding that 'nothing in the dedicatory epistle forewarns Lucy about this text. Perhaps the transcriber simply inserted the poem at this point in his manuscript from another source. Or Harington's silence may have been deliberate'.[200] This means that we have no certainty either as concerns the translation's provenance or its language, both matters that have elicited much debate. The dating is also controversial; although, since most of her translations were completed between 1586 and 1601, scholarly opinion inclines to the inclusion of the Petrarch translation in this period, perhaps slightly favouring an earlier stage.[201]

Unlike what seems to have happened in the cases of Morley and Fowler, Sidney would not have sought a political or financial reward for her translation, and it may have been this that has prompted scholars to read her translation

---

[198] On Mary Sidney and her literary activity see Margaret Patterson Hannay, *Philip's Phoenix: Mary Sidney, Countess of Pembroke* (Oxford: Oxford University Press, 1990).
[199] Thomas Moffett, *The silkewormes, and their flies: liuely described in verse, by T. M. a countrie farmar, and an apprentice in physicke. For the great benefit and enriching of England* (London: Nicholas Ling, 1599). On the possibility of the extant translation being a fragment of a longer work, see Hannay, pp. 107–08.
[200] Jason Scott-Warren, *Sir John Harington and the Book as Gift* (Oxford: Oxford University Press, 2001), p. 151.
[201] Gillian Wright, 'Mary Sidney Pembroke', in *The Oxford History of Literary Translation in English: Volume 2: 1550–1660*, ed. by Gordon Braden, Robert Cummings and Stuart Gillespie (Oxford: Oxford University Press, 2010), pp. 78–82 (p. 79). See also Danielle Clarke, *The Politics of Early Modern Women's Writing* (Edinburgh: Pearson, 2001), p. 208.

as a form of autobiography. It has been linked to her mourning for her brother Philip, or more in general to a reflection on death;[202] other critics have focused on the idea of a female translator appropriating a male voice, possibly forgetting that the singularity of the *Triumphus Mortis* resides precisely in its giving voice to the female beloved. Mary Ellen Lamb, taking into account Sidney's other translations, notices how they 'reveal a preoccupation with death and with dying well'.[203] Margaret Hannay proposes an interesting range of possibilities, some of them mutually contradictory:

> It seems that Pembroke's decision to translate the *Trionfo* may have been influenced by a variety of factors: its value as a work of Christian/Senecan moral philosophy, its function as Protestant allegory, its use to praise Queen Elizabeth, and its place in the literature of consolation. She may also have been drawn to the portrayal of Laura as an eloquent figure, unlike the silent presence of the beloved in English Petrarchan sonnets.[204]

Danielle Clarke, on the other hand, offers a double reading. In her 2001 book she links the Petrarch translation to Sidney's translation of the Psalms (her versions of Psalms 51, 104 and 137 are present in the same manuscript that contains the *Triumphus*), suggesting that she 'Calvinised Petrarch, thus potentially suggesting the text as a kind of *memento mori*, which, given its connections with the representation of Elizabeth and the monarch's age, would have amounted to a pointed political comment'.[205] In a later article, she stresses the political reading, starting from a critique of a male-oriented critical stance that sees women and politics as mutually incompatible in early modern writing. Sidney's translation, from this perspective, is read as 'a veiled and ambiguous critique of the literary discourses surrounding the aging Elizabeth, by means of an extensive intertextuality'.[206] If this is to be connected with the importance of the triumphal form in royal iconography, however, it is difficult to see why Sidney should have chosen the *Triumphus Mortis*, in which the triumphal form is actually deconstructed to make way for an experimental voyage into the inner self. Both readings, besides, conflict with the fact that, as far as is known,

---

[202] Gary F. Waller, 'The Countess of Pembroke and Gendered Reading', in *The Renaissance Englishwoman in Print: Counterbalancing the Canon*, ed. by Anne M. Haselkorn and Betty S. Travitsky (Amherst: The University of Massachusetts Press, 1990), pp. 327–45 (p. 340); Janet MacArthur, 'Ventriloquizing Comfort and Despair: Mary Sidney's Female Personae in *The Triumph of Death* and *The Tragedy of Antony*', *Sidney Newsletter & Journal*, 11 (1990), 3–13 (p. 11).
[203] Mary Ellen Lamb, 'The Myth of the Countess of Pembroke: The Dramatic Circle', *Yearbook of English Studies*, 11 (1981), 194–202 (p. 197), and 'The Countess of Pembroke and the Art of Dying', in *Women in the Middle Ages and the Renaissance: Literary and Historical Perspectives*, ed. by Mary Beth Rose (Syracuse: Syracuse University Press, 1986), pp. 207–26.
[204] *The Collected Works of Mary Sidney*, p. 265.
[205] Clarke, *Politics*, p. 210.
[206] Clarke, 'Lover's Songs', p. 138.

Sidney's translation did not circulate. Finally, a connection has been suggested with the poetry of Sidney's niece, Mary Wroth, whose sonnet sequence *Pamphilia to Amphilanthus* is seen as placing her within 'a line of women writers that extend from Queen Elizabeth through the Countess of Pembroke, for whom the *Triumphs* provide an invitation to female poetics'.[207] There is, however, no proof that Wroth knew either translation, and the continuity could simply reside in the fact that Petrarchan poetry was in fashion with the literary élite in early modern England.

The translation has none of the awkwardness we associate with Morley and Fowler. D. G. Rees, in his seminal article on English translations of the *Triumphus Mortis*, was the first to notice that, in spite of Sidney's close adherence to the original, her version achieved fluency and naturalness, showing freshness and occasionally audacity.[208] Sidney is probably at her best in capturing the domestic dimension of the *Triumphus Mortis* through a startlingly homely language, as shown by instances such as her decision to translate Petrarch's description of death, bearing a dark (*oscura*) banner and dressed in black (*negra*), with a daring repetition: 'Black, and in black, a woman did appear' (I. 31); or when she renders 'omai di noi che fia?' (literally translated, 'now, what shall become of us?') with 'And now, what shall we do?' (I. 147), which has a much more intimate tone, and reminds us that Mary was the sister of the poet who wrote 'Fool, said my Muse to me, look in thy heart, and write'.[209] The elegance of her translation might also be due to the choice of metre: Sidney's decasyllables respect Petrarch's verse length and easily flow into iambic pentameter.[210] At the same time, she maintained the rhyme scheme of the original, preserving the compactness and density of Petrarch's text with the choice of *terza rima*, quite unusual in English poetry (the only other translator who attempted this is John Florio, in a very short fragment). Undoubtedly the metrical achievement is one of the most important elements of this translation. Margaret Hannay offers an excellent summing up of critical opinions on this translation:

> The 'Triumph' emphasizes the same conflict between reason and desire that informs *Astrophil and Stella*, but whereas Sidney's sequence (like Petrarch's own sonnets) presents the male frustration at the lady's coldness, the 'Triumph' permits the woman to justify her actions [...] In delightful

---

[207] Nora Fienberg, 'Mary Wroth and the Invention of Female Poetic Subjectivity', in *Reading Mary Wroth: Representing Alternatives in Early Modern England*, ed. by Naomi J. Miller and Gary F. Waller (Knoxville: University of Tennessee Press, 1991), pp. 175-90 (p. 184).
[208] Rees, pp. 83-85.
[209] Sir Philip Sidney, *Astrophil and Stella*, Sonnet 1, line 14. See *Sir Philip Sidney*, ed. by Katherine Duncan-Jones (Oxford: Oxford University Press, 1989), p. 153.
[210] 'Lady Pembroke is a master of the art of simple transposition of words to fit the rhythm of the iambic line' (Rees, p. 83).

irony, the passive mistress proves to have been in control of her ardent lover.[211]

1.6.6 John Florio

Towards the end of the sixteenth century we find two fragmentary translations that belong to very different intellectual approaches: the first is John Florio's version of a fragment of *Triumphus Pudicitie* (lines 174 and 76-90) appearing in his *Second Frutes*, the second of his language-learning manuals, containing the *Gardine of recreation*, possibly the largest collection of proverbs published in sixteenth-century England.[212] Florio had already inserted an allusion to the *Triumphi* in his *Firste Fruites*, in a passage addressing Queen Elizabeth and extolling chastity as the supreme virtue of a ruler:

> O golden worlde, when neyther Wyne, nor banquettes were knowen, then was chastity knowen in the Temple of Vesta. Then the Emperours dyd frequent the Chappel of Jupiter, then Lust durst not come to the court of Cesar, then abstinence walked through the markette in everye Cittye, then the worlde was chaste, then the world dyd triumph, but nowe every thyng goeth contrary.[213]

While this first volume seems to have been motivated by a political agenda, *Second Frutes* appears more interested in language teaching through recreation and the exploration of everyday life. Proverbs and sententious passages abound not only in the *Gardine* but also in the main section; we might read the insertion of the Petrarchan passages in this light. Beside the fragment edited here, there is a Petrarchan allusion in the dedicatory epistle, to Nicholas Saunder of Ewell:

> The maiden-head of my industrie I yeelded to a noble Mecenas (renoumed Lecester) to the honor of England, whom thogh like Hector every miscreant Mirmidon dare strik being dead, yet sing *Homer* or *Virgil*, write friend or foe, of *Troy*, or *Troyes* issue, that *Hector* must have his desert, the General of his Prince, the Paragon of his Peeres, the watchman of our peace,
> Non so se miglior Duce o Cavalliero.
> As *Petrarke* hath in his triumph of fame; and to conclude, the supporter of his friends, the terror of his foes, and the *Britton* Patron of the Muses.[214]

---

[211] Hannay, p. 109.
[212] John Florio, *Florios second frutes* (London: Thomas Woodcock, 1591).
[213] John Florio, *Florio his firste fruites* (London: Thomas Woodcocke, 1578), pp. 66-67. The passage is discussed in Diego Pirillo, 'Republicanism and Religious Dissent: Machiavelli and the Italian Protestant Reformers', in *Machiavellian Encounters in Tudor and Stuart England: Literary and Political Influences from the Reformation to the Restoration*, ed. by Alessandro Arienzo and Alessandra Petrina (Farnham: Ashgate, 2013), pp. 121-40 (pp. 137-39).
[214] Florio, *Florios second frutes*, sigs A3r-v.

Here Florio quoted *Triumphus Fame*, I. 99, but the quotation is simply an elegant embellishment of the praise of the patron. As in the case of the translated passage, Petrarch confers authority and elegance to the text. The translation is accurate and reveals a good understanding of the original, preserving also Petrarch's choice of *terza rima*.

1.6.7 The translation attributed to Elizabeth I

The second fragment we encounter, from around the same time, is of a very different nature. It is a translation of *Triumphus Eternitatis*, lines 1 to 90, generally attributed to Elizabeth I; critical opinion is divided on both authorship and date, with some scholars considering it 'a schoolgirl's exercise in versifying as well as in translating'.[215] The text is extant in the Harington manuscript, in Arundel Castle: a sixteenth-century anthology of verse which in its present state contains 324 poems, including poems by Wyatt, Surrey, John Harington and Philip Sidney, and compositions that also appear in *Tottel's Miscellany*.[216] A note added on the first flyleaf indicates that the manuscript contains writings by the queen, including a copy of 'The Doubt of Future Foes' with a prefatory letter, possibly written by Sir John Harington, in which he explains how this poem was acquired 'covertly' by Lady Willoughby.[217] The Petrarch translation, in a secretary hand, appears on fols 219v to 220v, with the subscription 'E. R.' in a different hand.

Such a subscription is of course very insufficient evidence, and the attribution of this translation to the queen is controversial; among modern scholars, David Norbrook, Michael Wyatt and Jason Lawrence accept her authorship without question, as does one of Elizabeth's earlier editors, Leicester Bradner.[218] More recent editors, such as Steven May and the already mentioned Janel Mueller

---

[215] Coogan, 'Petrarch's "Trionfi"', p. 321. See also Ruth Hughey, *John Harington of Stepney, Tudor Gentleman: His Life and Works* (Columbus: Ohio State University Press, 1971), pp. 47–48, and *The Collected Works of Mary Sidney*, p. 261.

[216] Ruth Hughey, 'The Harington Manuscript at Arundel Castle and Related Documents', *The Library*, 15 (1935), 388–444. In the recent edition of the queen's translations, the Petrarch version is marked as 'ascribed to Elizabeth'. See Elizabeth I, *Translations 1544–1589*, ed. by Janel Mueller and Joshua Scodel (Chicago: The University of Chicago Press, 2009), pp. 459–68. See also Alessandra Petrina, 'Translation and Language Learning: The English Version of Petrarch's *Triumph of Eternity* Attributed to Elizabeth I', in *Early Modern Exchanges: Dialogues Between Nations and Cultures, 1550–1750*, ed. by Helen Hackett (Farnham: Ashgate, 2015), pp. 55–71.

[217] The note was probably written by Canon Mark Aloysius Tierney, chaplain and librarian at Arundel Castle from 1824 to 1862, as noted by Ruth Hughey, first modern editor of the text. See *AHM*, I. 6.

[218] David Norbrook, 'The Rhetor', *New Republic*, 223 (2000), 41; Wyatt, *Italian Encounter*, pp. 210–12; Lawrence, pp. 32–34; Elizabeth I, *The Poems*, ed. by Leicester Bradner (Providence: Brown University Press, 1964), p. xiv.

and Joshua Scodel, appear sceptical. May does not even mention the Petrarch translation, though he dedicates a few pages to 'Wrongly Attributed Works'.[219] Although Elizabeth is known as a translator from a number of languages, there is no other extant translation of Petrarch in her name. The only other connection to the Petrarchan corpus is her slight misquotation from the *Triumphus Mortis* ('Miser é chi Speme in cosa mortal pone') inscribed in her French psalter, yet one more proof of the fascination of English and Scottish writers with this particular triumph.[220] The earliest modern editor examined the manuscript for evidence as to authorship and date, but her conclusions are very tentative:

> [The subscription is] written in a different ink, in large capital letters of printed character [...] The contraction beneath the initials is in small secretary [...] and appears to be 'scr', [with a straight horizontal line over cr] i.e. 'scripsit'. Conceivably, however, it should be read 'sec', [with a straight horizontal line over ec] i.e. 'secundus', which would refer to the second year of Elizabeth's reign, thereby indicating exactly the time of composition.[221]

Since the queen was also the object of Petrarchan imagery based on both *Triumphi* and *Canzoniere*,[222] it is conceivable that the attribution indicated in the manuscript was more the result of wishful thinking than actual fact. As for internal evidence, the corpus of translations attributed to Elizabeth I is so diverse, and spread over so many years, that it is difficult indeed to retrace common linguistic or stylistic features. My study of this translation, both in the context of the English translations of the *Triumphi* and against the background of Elizabeth's translation activity, draws me to opt either for a translation directly undertaken by the queen or realized within her circle: the attribution, I believe, would have met her implicit approval, and accompanied her construction of her political role.[223]

Whether it was actually undertaken by the queen or simply (and very discreetly) associated with her name, this translation is striking, both in the choice of text and in the result. The fragment stops before the poet turns his attention to Laura, thus eliminating any reference to the conventional Petrarchism of love poetry and leaving the reader with a severe meditation on time and immortality: 'this extract does not seem inappropriate from a theological and moral perspective for the scholarly attentions of the princess'.[224]

---

[219] Elizabeth I, *Selected Works*, ed. by Steven May (New York: Washington Square, 2004), pp. 329-31.
[220] The quotation, with the addition of the verb *é*, is from *Triumphus Mortis*, I. 85. See Elizabeth I, *Translations*, p. 400.
[221] AHM, II. 456.
[222] See for instance King, 'Queen Elizabeth', p. 47.
[223] On this point see Petrina, 'Translation and Language Learning', pp. 67-69.
[224] Lawrence, p. 32.

This highlights the extent to which Petrarchism masquerades or misrepresents the actual Petrarchan tradition, being simply translated into courtly politics, courtly mores and their representation, or into a convenient mask of courtliness used to hide political intent or quite simply the desire for advancement. This courtly trope has very little to do with the *Triumphi*. As modern editors observe, the choice of the first section of *Triumphus Eternitatis*, if it was deliberate, 'suggests that the translator was drawn more to the general Christian vision of the vanity of mortal things and of eternal beatitude than to Petrarch's personal eroticism'.[225] It might be argued that this translation resonates with Elizabeth's reflections on time and eternity, as highlighted for instance by her translation of Boethius, undertaken towards the end of her life. This closeness is underlined by some analogous lexical choices, such as the use of the word 'steady' to translate Petrarch's *stabile* and Boethius's *stabilis*, but such instances are simply too few to offer anything but scanty, unsatisfactory evidence.

As for the choice of text, Elizabeth would almost certainly have had access both to the original Italian and to Morley's translation in the royal household; a connection between Morley's version and this fragment has in fact been suggested, though it is unsupported by internal evidence.[226] This version appears superior to Morley's as concerns the rendering of Petrarch's semantic compression, the elegant turn of phrase and the economy of the sentences; as noted by Wyatt, here the translator shows 'a confident poetic voice'.[227] As in the case of Mary Sidney's version, this is almost a line-by-line translation, although in this case there is no attempt to adopt the *terza rima* scheme: the rhyme scheme is, more simply, *abab cdcd efef*, although the translator does not try to transform Petrarch's tercets into quatrains.

In a recent article, Susan Bassnett lists all the difficulties scholars face when working on an edition of Elizabeth's works, focussing on the issues of authorship and manuscript attribution, and of image manipulation, given the gap that can be noted between public and private rhetoric in her writings. As Bassnett writes, 'the private writings, particularly the translations and poems, reveal an alternative voice to the strong public rhetoric of the speeches credited to Elizabeth, a voice that speaks often out of doubt and uncertainty rather than out of assurance'.[228] The translation of Petrarch, with all the uncertainty surrounding it, is a perfect instance of the problem of identifying Elizabeth's 'real' voice, especially since the queen seems to have found a space for her

---

[225] Elizabeth I, *Translations*, p. 462.
[226] Bartlett, pp. 325-34. See also Petrina, 'Translation and Language Learning', pp. 64-65.
[227] Wyatt, *Italian Encounter*, p. 210.
[228] Susan Bassnett, 'Daring to Show Discontent: Queen Elizabeth I as Poet and Translator', in *Under Construction: Links for the Site of Literary Theory: Essay in Honour of Hendrik Van Gorp*, ed. by Dirk de Geest, Ortwin de Graef, Dirk Delabastita et al. (Leuven: Leuven University Press, 2010), pp. 211-23 (p. 212). See also Clarke, *Politics*, p. 205.

most private utterances through the medium of translation. Whether this translation can be attributed to her or not, it speaks of her to a modern reader, and especially of her effort to understand and meditate upon a text through the act of translation (particularly evident in her translation of Boethius, famously undertaken in a very short time at a moment in her life in which her duties as a monarch must have made huge demands on her attention and drastically curtailed her leisure), which she seems to have preferred to the selective excerpting or note-taking often adopted by aristocratic early modern readers.[229]

1.6.8 Anna Hume

Among the early translators of the *Triumphi*, Anna Hume is probably nowadays the least remembered, as she has left no other trace of her literary activity but a translation of the first three *Triumphi*, printed in 1644; in the same year, Ewan Tyler, the Edinburgh publisher who printed her work, also printed the *History of the Houses of Douglas and Angus*, the posthumous work of her father, David Hume of Godscroft (1558–1629?).[230] The 'Advertisement to the Reader' inserted at the end of the volume announces the future translation of the remaining three *Triumphi*:

> The first title page should have told thee that all the three Triumphes were translated out of the *Italian*, a circumstance I considered not then, since it is thought necessary to say so much, I will now say more: I never saw them, nor any part of them, in any other language but *Italian*, except the poore words in which I have cloathed them. If they afford thee either profit or delight, I shall the more willingly bestow some of my few leasure hours on turning the other three Triumphs, of *Fame*, *Time*, and *Divinitie* or *Heaven*. Farewell.[231]

However, this second volume never appeared.

It has been suggested that Anna Hume was associated with William Drummond of Hawthornden and his circle on the basis of a letter written to Hume by the latter (now Edinburgh, National Library of Scotland, MS 2061);[232] but the letter, rather affected, acknowledging in Hume 'so pregnant and rare a Wit', and 'so sound a Judgment', contains no real allusion to anything other than, perhaps, laudatory verses for Drummond himself.[233] The translation is

---

[229] I would like to thank Oscar Meana for discussing this point with me. On the early modern habit of excerpting, see Andrew Hadfield, *Shakespeare and Renaissance Politics* (London: Thomson, 2004), p. 18.
[230] For this information see Sarah M. Dunnigan, 'Hume, Anna (fl. 1644)', *ODNB*.
[231] *Anna Hume*, ed. by Roche, p. 99.
[232] Dunnigan, 'Hume, Anna', *ODNB*.
[233] The letter is reprinted in William Drummond of Hawthornden, *The Works* (Edinburgh: James Watson, 1711), p. 139.

dedicated to Princess Elizabeth of Bohemia (1618–1680), daughter of Elizabeth and Frederick V of Bohemia, and James I's granddaughter; however, we have no proof of any contact between the two women. The dedication is articulated into two short poems, of which the first insists on the conventional praise of the patron and the distance between the latter and the humble translator:

> That my rude lines durst meet the dazeling rayes
> Of Majesty, which from your Princely eyes
> Would beat the owner back, blame them not, they
> Want sense, nor had they wit to bid me say
> Thus much in their behalf: else having heard
> Y'are mercifull, they could not be affeard:
> Or doubting some arrest of sudden death
> Made haste to be reprived by your breath!
> True glory of your sex, whose single name
> Protecteth vertue, and commandeth fame.
> Now you have sav'd them with a looke, the rest
> Assume like boldnesse, and desire to taste
> Like honour, since they justly think their claim
> Better, by vertue of great Petrarch's name:
> Whom if they lamely follow tis more grace,
> Then t'have outgone a meaner Poets pace.
> Your milder judgement must the sentence give,
> For which they humbly wait to make them live.[234]

In the second poem, Hume reiterates the humility topos, underlining the fact that she writes

> to approve my selfe a reall friend
> To chaste Lauretta, whom since I have tane
> From the dark Cloyster, where she did remain
> Unmarkt, because unknown.[235]

The image of the 'dark Cloyster' has been taken to indicate Hume's anti-Catholic attitude, but as Sarah Dunnigan notes, it may simply mark 'Laura's emergence and emancipation from "unmarkt" anonymity to symbolic recognition'.[236] A short poem to the reader completes the introductory section, in the nature of a warning against expectations of facile entertainment.

A series of arguments and annotations, added by the translator, accompanies

---

[234] *Anna Hume*, ed. by Roche, sig. A2.
[235] *Anna Hume*, ed. by Roche, sig. A3.
[236] Sarah M. Dunnigan, 'Daughterly Desires: Representing and Reimagining the Feminine in Anna Hume's *Triumphs*', in *Woman and the Feminine in Medieval and Early Modern Scottish Writing*, ed. by Sarah M. Dunnigan, C. Marie Harker and Evelyn S. Newlyn (Basingstoke: Palgrave Macmillan, 2004), pp. 120–35 (p. 125). See also Germaine Greer, et al., eds, *Kissing the Rod: An Anthology of Seventeenth-Century Women's Verse* (London: Virago Press, 1988), p. 101.

each triumph, offering useful guides, especially as concerns Petrarch's learned allusions. Often the annotations refer to an 'Italian Commentar' that might be either Bernardino Daniello da Lucca's 1549 edition or the Vellutello commentary (or both). Fascinatingly, in a passage of the *Triumphus Mortis* (II. 146-49), Hume finds her own reading at variance with that proposed by the Italian commentary;[237] though she preserves her interpretation in the main body of her translation, she not only offers the alternative explanation in the notes, but also proposes a variant translation. Her notes have prompted critical speculation: the commentary has been called

> a compound of 'daughterly' loyalty to, and rebellion from, the early Renaissance Italian tradition of Petrarchan commentary [...] her commentaries are frequently rebarbative, audacious, and arguably 'proto-feminist' in the tradition of the seventeenth-century European female *philosophe* or *précieuse*, and claim the sanction or patronage of the Princess Palatine.[238]

Notably, 1644 was also the year in which René Descartes dedicated to Elizabeth of Bohemia his *Principes de la philosophie*, and in his dedication the princess is saluted as a remarkable thinker; however, Elizabeth's intellectual circle comprised far more men than women, and was too isolated an experiment to allow us to suppose that by the 1640s the tradition of the *femme philosophe* was established; it is even more controversial to presuppose that such a tradition, if it existed, had spread as far as Scotland. Hume's notes and comments to the translation strike the reader as being examples of intelligent and attentive reading, and, as in the instance noted above, she is prompted by what today we would call philological curiosity; the idea of a literary coterie behind them is rather forced.

As a poetic effort, the translation may be disappointing — Rees talks of 'joyless competence',[239] observing how Hume 'scatters little moral *sententiae* throughout her verse, sometimes with some basis in the original, but often on her own initiative'.[240] Unfortunately the choice of rhyming couplets (in iambic pentameter) accentuates the pedestrian quality of her writing, though I find Rees's condemnation far too sweeping. Hume appears to have worked directly from the Italian original, and the hypothesis that she might have availed herself of William Fowler's version is probably unfounded; although Sarah Dunnigan writes that 'her later text seems to constitute an almost conscious stylistic refutation of the earlier translation',[241] the two versions are too distant.

---

[237] *Anna Hume*, ed. by Roche, sigs G3 and G5.
[238] Dunnigan, 'Daughterly Desires', p. 121.
[239] Rees, p. 90.
[240] Rees, p. 91.
[241] Sarah M. Dunnigan, 'Scottish Women Writers, c.1560–c.1650', in *A History of Scottish Women's Writing*, ed. by Douglas Gifford and Dorothy McMillan (Edinburgh: Edinburgh

Her translation, especially in chapter one, is generally faithful to the original and attempts to translate line by line; occasionally, however, she inverts the lines in order to highlight sententious passages or moralizing moments. She also occasionally simplifies the original, eliminating some of Petrarch's more obscure references, substituting classical allusions with Christian ones, and making Petrarch's rich system of images somewhat plainer, but also clearer. In the dialogue between Petrarch and Laura in chapter two, Hume is much freer with her material and eliminates a number of Petrarch's lines; her simplifications and her opting for direct questions and shorter sentences create an interesting similarity with Sidney's translation, as opposed to Morley and Fowler's more tortuous and slow versions.

1.7 Conclusion

This overview of early modern translations of Petrarch's *Triumphi* allows us to highlight two fundamental points in the English and Scottish reception of this text: the importance of the *Triumphus Mortis*, and the role played by the paratexts that accompany a number of these translations.

Theodor Adorno famously wrote that 'death is imposed only on created beings, not on works of art, and thus it has appeared in art only in a refracted mode, as allegory'.[242] In the *Triumphus Mortis*, the meditation on death prompts a reappraisal of love, transcending courtly and even religious conventions. It marks a decisive move from the traditional iconography of triumphal forms: the conventional pageant of death is considerably underplayed, in favour of an intimate reflection on the distance death creates between us and our loved ones. Even the long lists of names and learned allusions to the Bible, classical lore, and past and recent history that so delighted Petrarch in the previous triumphs are here renounced in favour of a bleak landscape, in which the only proper nouns refer to the far-away places (India, Cathay, Morocco) that fill the vision with dead bodies. In this annihilation of the historical, the personal finds a new dimension. The triumph of death astonishingly offers the occasion for Laura to acquire her own voice — a surprising development in Petrarchan poetry. Here, as has been noted, Laura

> never lectures or fulminates or rhapsodises. For all her dignity, she is sweetly companionable — even familiar, in the sense of communicative, to a degree hardly imaginable in Beatrice [...] This kind of spiritual intimacy between a man and a woman is something new in Italian literature.[243]

University Press, 1997), pp. 15–43 (p. 36). For a different view, see *Anna Hume*, ed. by Roche, p. xii.

[242] Theodor W. Adorno, *Essays on Music*, ed. by Richard Leppert (Berkeley: University of California Press, 2002), p. 566.

[243] Kenelm Foster, *Petrarch: Poet and Humanist* (Edinburgh: Edinburgh University Press, 1984), p. 45.

The very parade of figures of the past in *Triumphus Cupidinis* or *Triumphus Fame* gives the poet an opportunity to allude to another medieval form, the *ubi sunt* poem,[244] an elegy on the transience of all living beings, which enjoyed great popularity in late medieval English and Scottish literature. The irony suggested by the depiction of a procession of figures whose glory is irrevocably consigned to the past, in a sort of *danse macabre*, becomes an object of reflection in the *Triumphus Mortis*: all the historical and literary figures evoked in the other triumphs could appear here. So the victims of Death have no name, with the exception of Laura, and appear as a multitude of figures designated by their status rather than their individuality. The line concluding this passage from the triumph to the dance of death ('e 'l vostro nome a pena si ritrova', I. 90) is the most frequently translated Petrarchan line in early modern English: apart from the versions presented here (by Morley, Fowler, the anonymous E. D., Sidney and Hume), there is yet another version by William Fowler. Hawthornden MS 2063 (now in the National Library of Scotland, Edinburgh), is a collection of writings, notes and occasional papers mostly penned by Fowler.[245] Fol. 4 is headed 'The Triumphe of Death — 1 chap', and presents the argument of a poem (not extant) lamenting the 'Untimly death' of Sir Francis Walsingham, who died in 1590, composed 'be Mr Wm. Fowler of Hawick'. On the verso there is a dedication 'To the right Honorble Lady, My Ladye Eleanor Baes, wyffe to the right hon.bl Mr robart Bowes of Ask, Embassadour for his ma.tie the King of Scotland' for yet another funerary poem that has not survived. Here Fowler writes of those whose name has been obscured by death, adding:

> as the florentene poete has song in his 'triumphs,'
> E'l nome loro a pena si retrova — -
> Scarse can thair name bot even with pane [i.e. pain] be found?

It is a very different version from the one in his translation.[246] Evidently the line resonated with the *ubi sunt* motif that plays such an important role in English poetry.

A comparative reading of the prefatory material to the English and Scottish translations of the *Triumphi* shows both an articulate knowledge of and a complex approach to this poet and his literary output; at the same time, however, it shows that, the more Petrarch's fame grew in northern Europe, the easier it was to *use* his name, and the text that was being translated, as a vehicle for an ideology that was far removed from that of the Italian poet — a process that we can also detect as we look at the various translations from a diachronic perspective. The difficult and experimental nature of the *Triumphi* made them an ideal terrain on which translators could work, and what we

---

[244] Coogan, 'Petrarch's "Trionfi"', p. 308. Carnicelli talks of 'conflating the Triumph of Death and the Dance of Death' (*TFP*, p. 46).
[245] A description of the manuscript is available in Petrina, *Machiavelli*, pp. 101-03.
[246] See Petrina, 'Approaching Petrarch's Trionfi', pp. 161-82.

find in both translations and paratextual material tells us that even that most popular of Renaissance readings of Petrarch, Vellutello's transformation of the Italian poetic corpus into an autobiographical narrative, was simply one among a variety of possible approaches. The organic nature of Renaissance translation makes it possible for the original work to be subsumed within a number of different agendas, thus becoming, in turn, a linguistic or stylistic challenge, a book of moral instruction, a step in the path towards fame, or even a pretext for anti-Catholic propaganda. At the same time, the translation was a means to measure one's poetic abilities against a master whose stylistic, linguistic and ideological innovation posed a constant challenge to translators, across languages and centuries, in a never-ending dance *dal centro al cerchio, e sì dal cerchio al centro* ('twixt centre and circumference to or fro').[247]

---

[247] Dante Alighieri, *La Divina Commedia: Paradiso*, ed. by Umberto Bosco and Giovanni Reggio (Florence: Le Monnier, 1979), XIV. 1. Translation taken from Dante Alighieri, *The Divine Comedy*, trans. by Geoffrey L. Bickersteth (Oxford: Blackwell, 1981), p. 615.

AC.d.13

THE TRIVMPHS OF THE
MOST FAMOVS POET M^R.
FRANCES PETRARKE
TRANSLATED OVT OF
italian into inglish by M^r
W^m. Fouler P. of
Hauicke.

Giuen to the colledge of Edmb.
by
William Drummond
1627.

Frontispiece of William Fowler's translation (Edinburgh, Edinburgh University Library Special Collections, MS Drummond De.1.10, fol. 1r)

WILLIAM FOWLER'S TRANSLATION OF PETRARCH'S *TRIUMPHI*

Fowler's translation is extant in two manuscript sources: Edinburgh University Library, MS De.I.10, and National Library of Scotland, MS Hawthornden 2063. The first is part of the collection known as the Drummond manuscripts, bequeathed to the library by William Drummond of Hawthornden in 1626.[1] Together with MS De.3.68, in the same collection, it contains William Fowler's Petrarchan works; the second manuscript includes *The Tarantula of Love*, Fowler's sonnet sequence. Ms De.1.10 is a paper manuscript, with modern binding and tooling supervised by the antiquarian David Laing around 1827.[2] A typewritten note inserted between fols 2 and 3 reads:

> Scottish. 16th cent. A manuscript of the Triumphs of Petrarch translated by the Scottish poet, William Fowler, who was secretary to Queen Anne, wife of James VI. The page on the left is in the typical Elizabethan 'secretary' hand; the poem on the right is in italic, a cursive version of the revived Caroline script which gradually established itself as the standard English form for everyday use. Presented to Library by William Drummond of Hawthornden in 1627.

It is a very clear manuscript, with borders ruled in pencil (the text occasionally overflows the border) and a small catchword on every page. On fols 1r to 5v we find an articulated paratext, including a list of the Triumphs (1v), the dedication to Jean Fleming (2r–v), and a list of sonnets in praise of Fowler, beginning with the one by James VI (3r–4v); the last poem, by A. Colville, is in a different ink and markedly different hand, and rather than a sonnet is a six-line poem. Fol. 5r presents the Argument, 5v is blank. Then follows the translation proper (6r–43v), with each chapter clearly demarcated and given a new page. The very few corrections are in paler ink and in a slightly different handwriting (possibly the same hand that inserted the Colville poem); towards the end of the translation there appear a few scribal mistakes. Bound with this are three other documents (the whole manuscript is marked Drummond De.1.10/1–4): Fowler's printed epitaphs of Robert Bowes and John Seton, and his funeral sonnet on Elizabeth Douglas. The *Triumphi* translation is not in Fowler's hand: it is a clear secretary hand, rather different from Fowler's. Verweij makes a very strong case for John Geddie, a pre-eminent calligrapher as well as a courtier, as the scribe responsible for the decorated title page, the titles of the dedication

---

[1] On Drummond's donation, see Verweij, *Literary Culture*, pp. 1–2.
[2] A full description of the manuscript can be found in Meikle, III. xlix.

and of the first chapter — something that underlines both the importance of this presentation manuscript and the fact that it was the result of a strongly knit scribal community.[3]

The second manuscript, NLS Hawthornden 2063, includes only a short opening section from the *Triumphus Cupidinis*, corresponding to lines 1 to 32 in the University Library version. This manuscript belongs to the Hawthornden collection, comprising fifteen volumes, five of which contain most of Fowler's papers (Hawthornden 2063-67).[4] The volume under examination here is composed by ix+275 folia; it includes a mass of scribblings and notes, proverbs, impresas, anagrams and other ephemeral writing, with sections in Latin, Italian, French and Greek. The various sheets were put together by David Laing in the nineteenth century, and there is little certainty that their present order reflects an original arrangement. The Petrarch translation appears on fol. 39, and two lines at the top of 40r refer back to it (fols 40 and 41, in prose, also seem related to the Petrarchan material, but are extremely difficult to decipher). There are some differences between the texts of the two manuscripts (noted in the commentary below), but the main difference is the layout: while the Drummond manuscript clearly sets out the translations in rhyming couplets of fourteeners, Hawthornden opts for shorter lines, that divide each line in Drummond in two, and suggests through the layout a division in octaves, rhyming *xa xa xb xb*. Elsewhere in the same volume (fols 4r-5v) we find a composition titled *The Triumphe of Death*, which announces a 'deploration of the Untymly death' of Sir Francis Walsingham; the text of this 'deploration', however, does not appear anywhere in the collection.[5] As in the case of the Petrarch translation, it is reasonable to suppose that other folia have been lost. In the same volume, we also find a page in Fowler's hand headed 'my works' which includes, among other sometimes more puzzling items, 'petrach translated'. On the reverse of the sheet we read 'is tomis sit notus WF' ('by these works WF shall be known', fol. 107v).

External evidence does not help us to establish which of the two versions was composed before the other. It is arguable that the fragment in Hawthornden 2063 presents a metrical structure, based on the ballad, which indicates a conservative attitude, and thus a first, tentative approach on the part of the translator, who then developed, in the second version, a more sophisticated metre, more suitable for a version that was meant for scribal publication in a courtly circle. It should be added, however, that the Hawthornden version is not in the nature of a draft, and that the chaotic and incomplete nature of the

---

[3] Verweij, *Literary Culture*, pp. 93-101.
[4] The collection is described in Meikle, III. xliii-xlix, and in Petrina, *Machiavelli*, pp. 87-111.
[5] Printed in Meikle, I. 307.

Hawthornden collection makes it impossible to establish whether the fragment we have is what is left of a longer version, whether it indicates a first attempt, subsequently abandoned, or whether it is a re-elaboration of the material in the Drummond manuscript, prepared for a different readership. This second hypothesis is supported by the fact that there is a distinct anglicization in the spelling of the Hawthornden version, and more elegant semantic choices.[6]

Among the paratextual material, the opening sonnet, by James VI, appears also in London, British Library, Additional MS 24195, fol. 35r;[7] the 'E. D.' sonnets appear also in NLS Hawthornden 2065, fol. 4v, while the other commendatory poems appear only in MS De.I.10. Henry Meikle, in his edition of Fowler's works, inserted the translation of Petrarch in the first volume, dedicated to poetry (published in 1914), and transcribed the Hawthornden version separately. The present edition is based on both manuscript and printed sources, and uses as its main references MS De.I.10. In this manuscript Fowler (or perhaps the scribe) also divides the text into stanzas of varying lengths, a division I have followed in this edition. Significant variants in the Hawthornden manuscript (which sometimes amount to whole lines) are inserted in the footnotes, marked 'Hawthornden'.

---

[6] I would like to thank Allison Steenson for discussing this point with me. The suggestions in this paragraph are mostly hers.
[7] James Craigie, in his edition of James's poems, prints both versions. *The Poems of James VI. of Scotland: Vol. II*, ed. by James Craigie, Scottish Text Society (Edinburgh: Blackwood, 1958), p. 104 (the Drummond MS version is printed on p. 105).

THE TRIVMPHS
OF M^R. FRANCES PE-
TTRARCHE.

The first triumphe of Loue.

CAP. I.

THAT tyme quhen my soddayn sobbe and sorye sighs teares
Throughe painfull remembrance of that day on whilk my cares first roote
Vhich was the first begynnar of my paines and futur smart
And of my Lonesome martyrdome that martirised had my hart
The Sunn alreddye warmed had the Bull his Doubled horne
And Tithan with Aurora cleir vpryseing redde at morne
The yce and miste frostye hie had from his feet Dueste
onto his woonted antient place for auld frequented roote.
Loeue greif disdaine and plaining plaints and seasons of the zeir
had caused me to a secreit place my self for to retere
Whair all the causes and passions that did oppresse my sowl
mycht hamly act afflicted be and all my doole auent.

I saw on the graß and plesant greine my boyet his plaints mad weith
my wateringe eyes retired grones sleip at lenth him rest did tak
Anear then I saw a illustrious light and in the same mure we
with litill Joy and silence still out as me semed so
Amidst quhairof I saw a Duik victorious light of myght
Lyk on who to see rapitule triumphs in charyot bryght
Than I rose was not myche acquent with such buquented sight
him throwgh this noysum wilked worle so full of wast and flight
In whilk to sone I sibe alace and it of valent voyce
bot full of pryde of vrache hair whilk brutes hie Dispytes
The sable proude before busks all neus and by argument
I seme bleßd with tarssyde eyes hir feable forhead faint
Throwgh Imperyus force and success sleir this first I did Disterne
he that I had no eyes my eyen such a sycht to lerne.

Their teares I saw for comsled feirs more whyte than anie swan
a goddess boy and yonny lyer laid in hyus hair to span
```

Opening page of William Fowler's translation of the *Triumphus Amoris* (Edinburgh, Edinburgh University Library Special Collections, MS Drummond De.1.10, fol. 6r)
```

The triumphe of loue.
Cap. 1.

In that time that I did my sobbs
  and heauie sighs renewe
through sueet remembrance of the day
  on which my loue first grewe
which was the first beginner off
  my pains and loving smart
and off this longsome martirdome
  which galled hathe my hart
The sunn Alcidio scortched had
  the bulls doubled hornes
And Titans chyld aurora cleere
  bpuysing roade at morne
Al Icye and most frosen lyke
  had then her selfe adrest
Unto her wonted ancient place
  her mansion and her rest.
Loue rage disdaines and blubbring plaints
  with seasone of the yeere
did leede me to a solitude place
  to which I did retere
where euery weried hart ouer charged
  with boundles of there greif
doth lay thame vp and set asyde
  for there more fresh releif
there then amongst the heaths and plants
  my twee beflaits milde house
and woryed vexs exclaming with caire
  sleepe did to rest entres.

Opening page of William Fowler's translation of the *Triumphus Amoris* (Edinburgh, National Library of Scotland, MS Hawthornden 2063, fol. 39r)

2.1 Text

The triumphs of the most famous poet m^r. Frances Petrarch, translated out of Italian into English by M^r. W^m. Fowler P. of Hawick.[8]

The contents of this book.
1.
The Triumph of Love.
2.
The Triumph of Chastity.
3.
The Triumph of Death.
4.
The Triumph of Fame.
5.
The Triumph of Time.
6.
The Triumph of Eternity.

Ingenio stat sine morte decus.[9]

---

[8] This title takes up fol. 1r; at the bottom of the page we read, in a different hand: 'Given to the college of Edinb. by Willian Drummond. 1627'. 'P.' stands for Parson, and refers to the fact that Fowler had been rewarded by the Earl of Bothwell, his first patron, with the parsonage of Hawick, in the presbytery of Jedburgh, on the Scottish border.

[9] Propertius, *Elegiarum*, III. 2: 'the honour paid to genius is eternal'. This quotation does not appear in the Petrarchan original. The inference is that the Scottish translation, as is also made clear in the dedicatory epistle, emphasizes the theme of immortality achieved through literary merit.

To the right honourable and most virtuous Lady Jean Fleming, Lady Thirlestane, spouse to the right honourable Sir John Maitland Knight, principal Secretary to the King his Majesty, and great Chancellor of Scotland

Madam, there be two causes, speaking morally, which both in war and in peace encourage men in the enterprise and execution of great things. The first is honour and renown; the second is profit and commodity. Noble hearts and generous, high aspiring minds, do chiefly choose the first; the baser and less noble search for the other, which are the wages only of avarice. So that these things being so well considered by that ornate orator, Marcus Cicero, he is moved in his oration for Archia Poeta to set down for a settled sentence: that by nature we are all driven to a desire of praise and commendation, and that he that is of most account and most greatest is most covetous of renown and seeketh for no other guerdon[10] of his virtue than glory.[11] And in his pithy and eloquent defence of his accused Milo, subjoineth that the valiant men and most endowed with wisdom do not endeavour themselves so much to practice and exercise their virtues for reward of gain, than for the praise and honour that arises of their actions.[12] Which things being so well engraved in the marble breasts and more deeply imprinted in the plots of the Roman hearts than of any other nation, they have sought both above and beyond all others besides the recompense of profit: by the price of eternal fame and ever-living glory to illustrate and make more commendable the names of their virtuous, wisest and valiant victors by thrice hundred and twenty victorious and un-decaying Triumphs, unto the declining time of their decaying empire after Probrus.[13] In imitation whereof, our Laureate Poet Francis Petrarch, a noble Florentine, has devised and erected these Triumphs in the honour of her whom he loved, thereby to make her more glorious and himself no less famous. Which, when I had fully perused, and finding them both full and fraughted in stately verse, with moral sentences, godly sayings, brave discourses, proper and pithy arguments, and with a store of sundry sort of histories embellished and embroidered with the curious pasmentis[14] of poesy and golden freinyeis[15] of eloquence, I was spurred thereby and pricked forward incontinent by translation to make them somewhat more popular than they are in their Italian original. And especially when as I perceived both in French and English

---

[10] guerdon] reward.
[11] The reference is to Cicero, *Pro Archia*, § 26. See Marco Tullio Cicerone, *Le Orazioni: Volume II. Dal 69 al 59 a.C.*, ed. by Giovanni Bellardi (Turin: UTET, 1981), p. 1014.
[12] The reference is to Cicero's *Pro Milone*, § 96. See Cicero, *The Speeches*, ed. by N. H. Watts (Cambridge, Mass.: Harvard University Press, 1953), p. 114.
[13] Probably a misspelling for Marcus Aurelius Probus, Roman Emperor from 276 to 282.
[14] pasmentis] ornamental trimmings.
[15] freinyeis] friezes, ornaments.

traductions[16] this work not only traduced, but even as it were magled[17] and in every member miserably maimed and dismembered, besides the barbar[18] grossness of both their translations, which I could set down by proof (were not for prolixity) in two hundred passages and more. But Madam, as I purpose not by debasing of their doings to enhance my own, nor by extenuating their travails and derogating from their deserts to arrogate more praise to myself, so do I now expose the same to the sight and view of all the world, whose judgement and censure I must underlie; and consecrate them to your ladyship, whose courtesy, gravity, godliness, goodness, wisdom, honesty and honour is such that it driveth not only the devotion of them who are acquainted with the same in a farther continuance and liking of your ladyship, but enforced also the unacquainted beholders and hearers thereof with wonder to reverence, and almost amazed to marvel at the same. Which thing, as they bring forth in you the desserts and proofs of perfect praise, so I rather choose to be a true reporter thereof, when I am asked then with my unexercised style to debase such graces so worthy a highest commendation. Neither am I ashamed in this point to make confession of my weakness, who now, standing at the brink and riverside of my Lord Chancellor your husband's and your ladyship's own proper praises to make a willing entry and passage therein, am let in my enterprise and stayed in the promptitude of my intention through the largeness and deepness of the same, who more increasing and enlarging by his famous virtues the great glory his worthy father has left him and his peerless prince procured him, does deserve the first place among these whose names and renown surviveth to this day. But, Madam, seeing I have too much matter ministered onto me, and both your honour and your praises be more than my page, I am forced to shorten this preface surceasing.[19] Will better time and opportunity afford the occasion to pen, some day, your praises in a more larger discourse which now abruptly I drive to a short connection. But in this I rest satisfied, that although I am not a sufficient praiser of both your virtues,[20] yet your honour's deserts shall be an open testimony of my opinion. And the world shall see that, albeit I want cunning to commend you, I lack not goodwill to speak what I think of you truly. These things then considered, to whom either in respect of former favour, present credit, or future fortune and better hap (if poets may be prophets), more fitly can be offered these Triumphs than to a triumphing lady, triumphing over all vice, and who has else passed her ovations and fixed trophies in all virtue. So, having assured hope of your ladyship's accustomed courtesy, that your honour will favourably receive this voluntary obligation as pledge of my greater

[16] traductions] translations. The choice of this word allows the pun on 'traduced', below.
[17] magled] disfigured (attested in *DOST*).
[18] barbar] barbarous.
[19] surceasing] by concluding.
[20] i.e. I cannot sufficiently praise the virtues of both.

service and affection, I humbly take my leave. Submitting myself to the censure of the learned, and committing your ladyship to the protection of the almighty, from Edinburgh, the 12 of December 1587,

> Your honour's humbly to command
>
> M. W. F.[21]

---

[21] As noted by Meikle, the initials (for Master William Fowler) are added in a different hand, possibly Drummond's. The same hand has also inserted corrections.

Sonnet to the author[22]

We find by proof that into every age
In Phoebus' art some glistering star did shine,
Who, worthy scholars to the Muses sage,
Fulfilled their countries with their works divine:
5   So Homer was a sounding trumpet fine
Amongst the Greeks into his learnèd days;
So Virgil was amongst the Romans since,
A sprite sublimed, a pillar of their praise;
So lofty Petrarch his renown did blaze
10 In tongue Italique in a sugared style,[23]
And to the circled skies his name did raise;
For he by poems that he did compile
    Led in Triumph[24] Love, Chasteness, Death and Fame;
    But thou triumphs o'er Petrarch's proper name.
                        J. Rex[25]

E. D. in praise of Mr William Fowler, her friend[26]

The glorious Greeks do praise their Homer's quill,
And cities seven do strive where he was born;
The Latins do of Virgil vaunt at will,
And Sulmo thinks her Ovid does adorn;[27]
5   The Spaniard laughs (save Lucan) all to scorn,
And France for Ronsard stands and sets him out;
The better sort for Bartas blows the horn,
And England thinks their Surrey first but doubt.[28]
To praise their own these countries go about:
10 Italians like Petrarca's noble grace,
Who well deserves first place among that rout.

---

[22] What follows is a series of sonnets and other poems, written by various authors, praising the translator's work (and occasionally the dedicatee). The first sonnet, written by King James, appears also in London, British Library, Additional 24195, where it is headed 'A Sonnet on Mr W. Fullers translation of Petrarchs triumphe of love'. This, together with line 13 of the sonnet, makes it possible to suppose that, when he wrote the sonnet, James had seen only a partial translation.
[23] Italique] Italian.
[24] In Additional 24195, 'In triumphe ledde'.
[25] J. Rex] Jacobus Rex.
[26] This poem appears also in Edinburgh, National Library of Scotland, Hawthornden MS 2065, fol. 4v. Verweij (*Literary Culture*, p. 85) supposes this to be Elizabeth Douglas's hand.
[27] Sulmo] Sulmona, Ovid's birthplace.
[28] but doubt] doubtless.

But Fowler, thou do now them all deface,[29]
>No vaunting Greece nor Roman now will strive;
>They all do yield since Fowler doeth arrive.

E. D. in commendation of the author and of his choice

When Alexander entered Phrygian land,
Achilles' tomb he weeping did behold:
O happy wight who such a trumpet fand![30]
And happy thou who has his virtues told!
Then happy Laura, thou by Fame enrolled! 5
And hap to thee, O Petrarch, does befall:
Thy glory she, her praise thou do unfold.
How may thy Fame, O Fowler, then be small,
Who sings dame Laura's praise, but feignèd all?
This virtuous dame, to whom thy work thou gives, 10
To her of right these triumphs sing thou shall:
No Laura here, but Lady Jean it is.
>O lady live! thy Fowler thee extolls,
>Whose golden pen thy name in Fame enrols.[31]

Sonnet in Mr William Fowler's commendation

I saw once all the Muses in my thought,
With poets also bedecked in scarlet gowns;
before with sacred troop Mercurius brought
A youth upon whose face was yet but downs;
There saw I them present him laurel crowns; 5
And with the rest the Tuscan Petrarch came,
Who said: 'My son, receive these right renowns,
As he who duly does deserve the same;
But more triumphant has thou made thy name
Upon the throne of memory to stand 10
To choose for patron such a worthy dame,
Who only is the Laura of this land.'
>Than Fowler's laud so loud I heard them sound,
>That through the world his praise shall ay rebound.
>>Ro. Hudson[32]

---

[29] deface] make them lose face, make obsolete.
[30] fand] found.
[31] enrols] inscribes.
[32] Robert Hudson, one of the members of King James's intellectual circle.

In commendation of the translator and the Lady to whom these Triumphs are directed

If pithy Petrarch who these poems penned
Has purchased praise promulgated else by Fame,
Reviving her whose life by Death took end,[33]
And after Death triumphant made her name,
5 Then poets praise his Triumph to proclaim,
Whose compassed course conducted has with care
From Florence here, and fraughted Petrarch home,
Decked with his dames ascending in the air,
Into Triumph; and to augment it more,
10 To you, madam, these dames be all direct,[34]
Who on including all their virtues rare,
Is with Triumph above them all erect:
    As Petrarch's place triumphing here we see,
    So Fowler self, and you, Madam, all three.

                                      M. R. Cockburn[35]

A summary and a sonnet upon the Triumphs and the translator[36]

If conquering Cupid, captain of renown,
Who chains his captives to his chariot bright,
By Chastity is chased and beaten down,
And by her virtue spoilèd is of might;
5 If Death, the daunter of the human wight,[37]
Triumph upon that dame and doeth her thrall,
Surviving Fame claims but her proper right
To live through land or lake as doth befall:
But thou, O Time, that long and short we call,
10 The Triumph of the rest thou wouldst retain,
Were not Eternity confounds them all,
As nothing more triumphant may remain.
    Then what abide to Fowler them has penned? —
    Eternity, to which he does pretend.

                                       Th. Hudson[38]

---

[33] A truism that is in line with the whole poem.
[34] direct] directed.
[35] Probably Sir Richard Cockburn of Clerkington (the 'M.' would indicate that he had a Master's degree), son of Helen Maitland, John Maitland's sister (van Heijnsbergen, 'Coteries', p. 55).
[36] In the margin, the evocation of each Triumph is marked by a sequential number.
[37] Death who terrifies everyone.
[38] Poet and musician, he was Robert Hudson's brother, and also a member of the King's coterie.

When matchless Homer his Achilles sings,
Achilles only meaning to decore,[39]
Himself to greater praise by praising brings,
And so begets by giving all his glore;[40]
     So Fowler eternisèd has his name
     With noble Petrarch and his Laura's Fame.[41]
                            A. Colville[42]

---

[39] decore] adorn.
[40] glore] glory.
[41] These six lines are in a different hand from the rest of MS De.I.10. Verweij (*Literary Culture*, p. 84) conjectures the scribe to have been Colville himself.
[42] This has been variously identified with Alexander Colville of Blair, or, more convincingly, with his father Alexander Colville, commendator of Culross. See van Heijnsbergen, 'Coteries', p. 53.

The Argument[43]

Our famous and moral poet in these, his moral Triumphs, purposeth to describe the diverse states and conditions of man, who being formed mortal is endowed with two principal powers and faculties: the one is a sensual appetite, the other is a natural reason. The one of these having sovereignty in his youth, at that time when the senses has most force and vigour. The other again when youth and lustiness decayeth. Who, being dead, yet has his memory surviving by his famous acts through a more and longer Fame, which at last even as all other things under heaven, is overcome and vanquished by Time, which entombeth Fame in an eternal oblivion. Yet, seeing that turning Time is a thing bounded, limited, and in itself finite, does remain subdued by immoveable Immortality, by whose aid and help Fame is delivered from the injury of consuming Time, does live as fermour[44] in the revenues and possessions of Eternity. For which cause the first Triumph of our sensual parts and youthly[45] affection is deciphered by Love. The second is of Reason, when we by more riper and mature age with the wings of discretion does subdue our affection. And this is figured under the name of Chastity in the person of his lady Laura. The third is of Death, who defaces all the operations of our appetite and power of our reason which were wont to be wrought during our lifetime. The fourth is of Fame, when men after their death recrease[46] and re-flourish their renown. The fifth is of Time, that suppresses and extinguishes the same. The sixth and last is of Immortality that overcometh all Time, because of things that are infinite there is no proportion. It is more to be noted that these first two Triumphs of Love and Chastity are in this life the third, when our soul is in departing from our body, and the other three after it is free of the same. Which six Triumphs our Poet does depaint[47] partly by vision, partly by imagination, particularly interlacing the discourse of his estate and his lady's, and how her Chastity overcame him, and again Death her;[48] yet how by Fame she reviveth again, when although that Time does prease[49] to dark the glory of her famous name, yet shall it be through Immortality eternal.

---

[43] The passage that follows is a translation of the first half of the *soggetto* prefacing Giovanni Andrea Gesualdo's edition of the *Triumphi*, printed in 1541 (Meikle, III. 6).
[44] fermour] firmness.
[45] youthly] youthful.
[46] recrease] grow once more, are reborn.
[47] depaint] paint, represent.
[48] How Laura's chastity overcame the poet, and how Death overcame Laura.
[49] prease] strive.

The Triumphs of Mr Francis Petrarch

The first Triumph of Love

That time that did my sobbing sobs and sorry sighs renew,[50]
    Through sweet remembrance of that day on which my love first grew[51]
Which was the first beginner of my pain and future smart[52]
    And of my longsome martyrdom that martyred had my heart,[53]
The sun already warmed[54] had the Bull his doubled horn   5
    And Tython's wife, Aurora, clear uprising ready at morn[55]
All icy and most frost-like[56] had then herself addressed
    Unto her wonted ancient place, her old frequented rest.[57]
Love, grief, disdain and plaining plaints, and season of the year,[58]
    Had caused me to a secret place myself for to retire,[59]   10
Where all the causes and fashereis that did oppress my heart[60]
    Might thereby all affected be and all my dole avert.[61]

There, on the grass and pleasant green, my voice by plaints made weak,[62]
    My watching eyes o'ercome through sleep at length some rest did take,[63]

---

[50] Hawthornden: 'In that time that did my sobbs | and heavie sighs renew'. Petrarch refers to spring, which was the season of his first meeting with Laura. The Drummond version highlights Fowler's love for alliteration.

[51] The couplets are highlighted not only by the rhyming scheme, but also by the layout and by the use of a capital letter only at the beginning of the first line of each couplet (although in the manuscript this is not always regular).

[52] Hawthornden: 'longing smart'.

[53] my longsome] Hawthornden: 'this longsome'. that martyred] Hawthornden: 'which galled'.

[54] Hawthornden: 'scortched'.

[55] The word 'Tython' is the result of a double correction. Originally, the manuscript read 'chylde', then this was corrected to 'Titans', and finally to 'Tython'. The Hawthornden manuscript has 'Titans chyld'. The reference is to Tython, lover of the dawn, though it may also be to Titan, with an allusion to the fact that Aurora was believed to be the daughter of the Titan Hyperion. See also the reference to Aurora in *Triumphus Mortis*, II. 5.

[56] Hawthornden: 'frosen lyk'.

[57] Hawthornden: 'her mansion and her rest'.

[58] grief] Hawthornden: 'rage'. plaining] Hawthornden: 'blubbring'.

[59] Hawthornden: 'did leede me to a schut-up place | to which I did reteere'. Here Fowler misses Petrarch's allusion to Vaucluse, *chiuso loco* (line 8 in the original). On this point see Meikle, III. 6, and Svjetlana Atić, 'An Analysis of William Fowler's Translation of Petrarch's "Trionfi"' (unpublished MA thesis, University of Padua, 2009), p. 94.

[60] fashereis] trouble, bother. The choice of words creates an assonance with Petrarch's *fascio* (burden). See Atić, pp. 94–95. Hawthornden: 'where every weried hart, o'rcharged | with bondles of there greif'.

[61] Hawthornden: 'doth lay thame up and set asyde | for there more fresh releeif'.

[62] Hawthornden: 'There then amongst the hearbs and grass | my voice and plaint made hoarss'.

[63] Hawthornden: 'and weryed eeys o'rcummd with caire | sleepe did to rest enforce'.

15   Where then I saw a marvellous light and in the same much wo[64]
         With little joy and sadness full.[65] And as me seemèd, lo,
Amidst thereof I saw[66] a duke victorious, high of might,
         Like one who to the Capitol triumphed in chariot bright;[67]
Then I, who was not much acquainted with such unacquainted sight,[68]
20   E'en through this noisome wicked world, so full of craft and slight,
In which too long I live, alas, and it of valour void,[69]
         But full of pride, of graces bare, which virtue has destroyed,[70]
The habit proud, unseen, unused, all new and unacquainted,[71]
         I there beheld with careful eyes, both heavy, tired, and faint,[72]
25 Through lingering love and drowsy sleep, this sight I did discern[73]
         For that I had no other joy than such a sight to learn.[74]

There then I saw four coursers fair, more white than any snow,
         A childish boy and youngling raw in fiery chair to draw,[75]
Who in his hand his bow did bear, his arrows by his side,
30   As neither helmet nor yet target their piercing shots can bide.[76]
Above his shoulders there were placed two flying feathered wings,
         Embroidered with ten thousand hues,[77] all bare in other things;
And round about him there did stand and round about his chair
         A number of such mortal men that none can them declare
35 Whereof then some were prisoners by him in battle tane,[78]
         Some piercèd by his piercing darts and some by him lay slain.

---

[64] Where] Hawthornden: 'Whils'. a marvellous light] Hawthornden: 'a lightning greate'.
[65] Hawthornden: 'With solace schort and breef delyte'.
[66] Hawthornden: 'spyed'.
[67] The image of Love as a victorious captain appears in Ovid (*Metamorphoses*, v. 365-70; see Ovid, *Metamorphoses: Books I-VIII*, ed. by Frank Justus Miller and G. P. Goold (Cambridge, Mass.: Harvard University Press, 1977), pp. 262-64) and Virgil (*Eclogues*, x. 69; see Virgilio, *Bucoliche*, ed. by Luca Canali (Milan: Rizzoli, 1978), p. 162). Fowler's 'duke' is a calque of Petrarch's *duce*.
[68] Hawthornden: 'I not much wont for to enjoy | Such aspect grace and sight'.
[69] Hawthornden: 'In which I live alas to long | and it of verteu void'.
[70] Hawthornden: 'and emptie of al worthines | yet filled is with pryde'.
[71] Hawthornden: 'The proud attyre and fashion strange | unused and al new'.
[72] Hawthornden: 'be rearing up my fainting eyeis | and heavie I did veue'.
[73] Hawthornden: 'and in this moode and drousines | this sight I did discern'. This line is not in Petrarch.
[74] such a sight] Hawthornden: 'things unsene'.
[75] Hawthornden: 'Upon a fyrie chariot | a youngling boy to draw' ('a youngling boy' is also inserted at the end of the first line, and then crossed out).
[76] Hawthornden: 'might bide'.
[77] Hawthornden: 'a thousand hues'.
[78] tane] taken.

I wondering then to know some news of him and of his train[79]
    And so far forward marchéd on, all wearied, all with pain,[80]
Did then perceive myself e'en one of such a flock to be,
    When love from life long time before had far divided me.[81]   40
Then stayéd I a while to see if any one I knew
    Within the thickest of that troop that Love so with him drew,
Who is a king, that fasting is, and hungry ay for tears,
    Who makes men die, and daily does them feed with lingering fears;[82]
But none there was I could discern, and yet, if there was one   45
    With whom I once acquainted was, and now to Death is gone,
His face was changed and countenance, by prison or by death,
    Whom cruel weird or fatal Parcae bereavéd of his breath.[83]
Thus as I was astonishéd and looking there and here,
    Behold there did rencounter me and to me did appear   50
A sight and shadow somewhat less than that I saw before,
    Sad, pensive, dark, obscure, and pale, unknown to me the more[84]
Which by my name me called and said, 'Let nothing this thee move
    For all this pomp and this Triumph is purchaséd by Love'.
Whereat I marvelled very much and said in speeches plain,   55
    'How kenst thou me when surely I do know thee not again?'[85]
He answered then, 'This comes to pass and this does so appear
    E'en through the burden of my bonds and chains that I do bear,
And by this thick congested air and by this foggy mist,
    Which duskish is that so thy eyes with darkness do resist.   60
But I am he, e'en he, thy friend to thee was traist and true,[86]
    In Tuscany bred and therein born, where first our friendship grew.'

His speeches then and friendly words and reason, which of old
    He wont to use did quickly then this much to me unfold,

---

[79] wondering] Meikle has 'wandring' (closer to the manuscript reading), which he explains as eager, desirous.
[80] all wearied, all with pain] This half line has no counterpart in Petrarch.
[81] Fowler here misreads Petrarch: the Italian poet affirms that Love has deprived each lover of life, while Fowler is speaking of the poet only (Atić, p. 96).
[82] This line has no counterpart in Petrarch.
[83] 'Weird' is the Old English word for fate, used by early modern Scottish poets such as Alexander Montgomerie; the Parcae were the figures of destiny in classical mythology. Fowler often uses synonymic couples to underline cultural syncretism.
[84] This line is the result of a misreading on Fowler's part. Petrarch writes that this shadow is *men che l'altre trista*, less sad than the others, possible with an allusion to his corporeality (critics are still uncertain as to the identification of this character).
[85] kenst] know.
[86] traist] trusted.

	Discovering at that instant time that which his face did hide
65	
	As afterwards we sat us down each one at other's side.

Discovering at that instant time that which his face did hide
    As afterwards we sat us down each one at other's side.
Where he began to speak to me: 'Long time is since, I thought,
    To see thee here with us among, and in this band be brought.
Because that we e'en from thy age and tender years did see
    The very things within thy face that Love should captive thee.'
Then answered I, 'That is most true; at first I was so bent,
    And truly I had yielded to love my heart and whole consent;
But oh, alas, these troubled cries that lovers do sustain[87]
    Afraid me and made me from that course for to refrain,[88]
So that I left my enterprise to which I first did tend;
    But in my breast the reviving rage of love may yet be kend.'[89]
So said I then; but as yet, as he did hear in what a sort
    I answer made, he smiling then to me did this report:
'O my dear child, what flames for thee be kindled and prepared!'
But oh, alas, at that time I did not his words regard,
Which now so deeply be imprinted within my head each one,
    That none more fast nor solidly be graved in marble stone.

Since I, who by my nearest age which so does rage and burn
    Already learned both tongue and mind the use, to speak and mourn,
Demanded of this shadow dark, 'I pray thee, tell of grace
    And courtesy, what folk be these that marches in this place'.
Then he replied, 'Within short time thou by thyself shall know,
    For of this company thou shall be e'en one of them, I show,
And by this lord thou shall be led, so fettered fast and bound;
    This thou shall prove and yet not know how thou may cure thy wound.
Thy fortune is, thy fates are so, thy destinies and thy lot,
    That this shall chance or thou dissolve, or yet unloose that knot.[90]
Thou first thy pleasant face shall change, thy hair shall first be grey,
    Ere from thy neck and rebel feet these bands be tane away.

But yet, that I may satisfy thee in thy young desires,
    What thou now cravest I will thee tell, and show what thou requires;
And first of him I will declare that greatest is of state,
    Who does at once the life of man and liberty abate.
The same is he who by this world is namèd bitter Love,

---

[87] troubled] The final d is a later correction; originally the manuscript had 'troubles'.
[88] afraid] frightened.
[89] kend] kindled.
[90] or thou dissolve] before you loosen the knot (Fowler then offers a synonym).

But better shall thou know the same, and better shall it prove,[91] 100
When that his force shall thee subdue, and so shall captive thee,
    That over thee he shall be lord and thou his vassal be.
In youth a meek and modest child, but in his years and age
    A cancard throward tyrant, strong, of fierceness full and rage.[92]
Woe, woe to him that kenst so well! and thou the same shall know 105
    Before a thousand years be past. Awake, for I it show.
He also gendered is and bred of idleness and sloth,
    With wantonness of mankind's mind; his nourishing and his growth
Is of such thoughts within themselves do seem both douce and sweet,[93]
    And deified and made a god of people indiscrete. 110

To whom he is there only Death and whom with hardest laws
    Do under thousand chains and nails keep fast within his claws,[94]
They leading on and drawing forth their days and lingering life,
    Sharp, hard, severe, and bitter also, all full of sturt and strife.[95]
This is the principal of this pomp and high triumphant Lord 115
    Whose Triumph is by many men so gloriously decord.[96]
But whom thou seest so lord-like go and stately first does come,
    It is the monarch Caesar great, the emperor first of Rome,
Whom that Egyptian Cleopatra in Egypt land did bind
    Among the flowers with beauty brave, and bounty of the mind. 120
Now she over him triumpheth, so with reason, love, and right,
    That he who did the world o'ercome so with his manly might
Should be subdued by her again, and he such change might see,
    And that the victor's honour might the vanquished glory be.[97]

The next to him it is his son Augustus, great by name, 125
    Whose fervent love more loyal was and juster more his flame;
Who though he might his Livia by force her get and gain,
    Yet would he with most humble suit unto her love attain.[98]

---

[91] In playing on the consonance between 'bitter' and 'better', Fowler attempts to echo Petrarch's paronomasia between *amore* (love) and *amaro* (bitter). See Atić, p. 98.
[92] A cancard throward tyrant] a bad-tempered, perverse tyrant.
[93] douce] gentle, pleasant.
[94] nails] This word translates the Italian *chiavi* (keys).
[95] sturt] discord. The locution 'sturt and stryfe' is found frequently throughout the poem.
[96] decord] celebrated. Lines 113–16 are Fowler's addition.
[97] Fowler seems to have misunderstood Petrarch's corresponding line. Petrarch writes, 'del suo vincitor sia gloria il vitto', that is, the vanquished should be the victor's glory. By having both 'honour' and 'glory', Fowler makes the line obscure.
[98] Livia was already married to Tiberius, and had children, when Augustus persuaded her husband to divorce her, and married her.

And by her husband's own consent obtained her at his hand
130   Suppose she was with child that time to join in marriage band.[99]
The third that marchèd with these two was Nero the unjust,
    Despiteful, bloody, cruel, fierce and faithless, void of trust,[100]
Who passèd on with visage full of ire and proud disdain,
    And yet for all his force and strength Sabina has him tane.[101]
135 And Mark Aurelius likewise there went with this valiant king,
    Full of all praise and honour, also in glory most condign,
Whose golden tongue and sacred breast full of philosophy
    Was for the love of Faustina made a sign and mark to be.

These other two that standeth by, so fearful by mistrust,
140   Is Alexander Phereus and Dionysus the unjust,[102]
Ta'en both in love and in their love afraid night and day,
    Whose jealous minds through jealousy did purchase their decay;
And this effect thereof did rise. Now he who next comes on
    Is that Aeneas that laments upon Antandrum stone[103]
145 Dame Creusa's death, king Priam's child, who reft from him his wife,[104]
    Who from Evander took his son and reft him of his life.
Has e'er thou heard one reason of, or yet of him to talk,
    That to his stepdame's furious lust and bed would no ways walk,
Whom Phaedra so with prayers prayed, with lovely looks and sighs;
150   Yet he thereto did take no heed, but shunned that dame by flight.
But woe, alas, his chaste intent, his goodly thoughts and mind,
    Did bring his death, and also her hate, both terrible and unkind.
And yet therethrough she wrought her death: by love she thereto ran,
    A vengeance just for Hippolyte whom she exilèd then.
155 For Theseus' consent thereto, and also Ariadne,
    From whom her sister reft her spouse and had from her withheld,
But yet not justly may she plain, nor think her much misused;

---

[99] These two lines are Fowler's addition — the detail about Livia being pregnant when she married Augustus appears in Suetonius, *Augustus*, § 62. See Caio Svetonio Tranquillo, *Le vite di dodici Cesari. Volume I: Cesare — Augusto — Tiberio — Caligola*, ed. by Guido Vitali (Bologna: Zanichelli, 1973), p. 152.
[100] As is typical of Fowler, Petrarch's two adjectives (*dispietato e ingiusto*) become here a long string of seven.
[101] Sabina] Fowler gives a name to Petrarch's generic *femina*.
[102] Alexander Phereus' translates Petrarch's *Alessandro*, a tyrant of Pherae in Thessaly. Dionysus was tyrant of Syracuse.
[103] Aeneas] Here, too, Fowler gives a name to Petrarch's *colui*. As in the Italian original, Aeneas is not associated with Dido, but with his wife Creusa.
[104] This explanation is Fowler's addition. reft] tore away.

She wrought her brother's dreadful death, and father had abused.[105]
Some people be who others blame when they themselves should blame,
  And spieth faults in other men, and seeing not their shame;   160
Yet he who maketh sports and play and doth in fraud delight
  He should not much grieved be if he get quite for quite'.[106]

There saw I then his father next, with all his pomp and praise,
  Led prisoner in that Triumph on whom my eyes did gaze
To see him there twixt sisters two, brought there in that convoy   165
  And Ariadne of his death and he of Phaedra's joy.[107]
He that is next is Hercules, that martial man so bold,
  By Dejanira and Iole and Omphale made thralled,[108]
The other who doth favour him is that Achilles stout
  Who in his life had all his love e'en full of dole and doubt.[109]   170
Here standeth likewise Demophon, with him doth Phyllis move,
  Who for his stay and long abode did hang herself for love.[110]
This Jason is, with him his dame Medea, Aetas' child,
  That followed him and Love also, through towns and deserts wild;
And look how much she guilty was against her father dear,   175
  Or cruel in her brothers' death, so void of shame and fear.
So was she more crueller and moved in furious ire,
  In great despite against Jason's love, to set his house in fire,
And not content with this revenge she further off did go,
  To cut in blades before his eyes the children of them two.   180
She thought this rigour nothing great, nor yet to hurt her heart,
  Not yet believed that by her fact revenge did pass desert.[111]

Then after came Hypsipyle who seemèd to complain
  That by the barbar love of one she was brought in disdain.[112]
Then saw I her who by her face of beauty bears the name,   185

---

[105] Here Fowler expands the original, adding Ariadne's story.
[106] After 'much', the scribe has inserted 'be'. This word seems to me to be a scribe's mistake, and should be eliminated. These last four lines are written out much more clearly than the rest, in the same style the scribe occasionally uses for proper nouns. What is being underlined here is the sentious quality of the passage.
[107] This seems to be a misreading of the original (Atić, p. 101).
[108] made thralled] enslaved. The list of women who caused Hercules' downfall is Fowler's addition.
[109] love] I am here emending the manuscript, which has 'lwkt' (luck?). Petrarch has *amore*.
[110] This line is Fowler's addition.
[111] Lines 178–82 are Fowler's addition.
[112] barbar] barbarous.

Fair Helena, Menelaus' wife, the fairest Grecian dame,[113]
Who had with her that shepherd there, that to his great disgrace
    Did fix his eyes and gazed upon her fair and heav'nly face;
Wherethrough great tempests of great wars, great murders wild and strange
190   Did rise thereby and all the world did up and downside change.
I after heard Oenone amongst these troops full sad,
    Weep for the death of Paris too, and for his love die mad.
There likewise Menelaus was, who did for Helena moan,
    To see her thoughts not fixed on him, but on him that was gone;[114]
195 And after was Hermione who for Orestes cried[115]
    To succour her from Pyrrhus' hands, who had her beauty spied.[116]

There also I did there behold Acastus' daughter fair,
    Laodamia, much making for her Protesilaus' care.[117]
With her I saw true Argia, most faithful to her spouse,
200   That made his funerals for his corpse e'en with her tears and vows;
More just, more true and faithful more, more loving in effect
    Than Eriphyle that for a chain Amphiaraus did detect.

O, Petrarch,[118] hear the sad complaints, the sighs and grievous sounds,
    That from these lovers miserable so miserably rebounds,
205 Who are about to render up to him their sprites and life
    That in such sort them governeth and guideth in such strife.
I cannot all their names rehearse that were about that chair,
    Not only men was them amongst, but e'en the gods were there.
Their press and number was so great whom Cupid led in chains
210   That all the shadowing myrtle woods were fillèd with their trains.

For there I saw the Cyprian dame, dame Venus bright and fair,
    With mighty Mars, both neck, feet, arms bound by Vulcan's snare;
And Pluto that Proserpina did ravish to the hell
    Who half the year did with her dam, the other with him did dwell;[119]

---

[113] As is his custom, Fowler adds this explanatory line.
[114] This line is Fowler's addition.
[115] Hermione] The manuscript originally read 'Herminione'; the word has been corrected by a later hand.
[116] This line is Fowler's addition.
[117] The character of Acastus is added by the translator.
[118] This exclamation (Fowler's addition), the first of a few we shall find scattered throughout the translation, seems part of the translator's strategy to call attention to the importance of the source.
[119] This line is also Fowler's addition — here and throughout, he adds details that help the reader recognize the mythological and historical figures.

There Juno jealous did I see, and brave Apollo bright 215
    That did despise Cupid's age, his youth, his bow and might,
Yet for all that this youngling boy his puissance made him prove,
    When in Thessalia he him shook and made him for to love.

What shall I say then, to be brief and in this passage short;
    Behold these gods and goddesses that Varro does report, 220
All prisoners and captive now, and charged with thousand chains,
    And with the same e'en Jove himself his chargèd legs forth strains,
And goes enfettered hard afore this high triumphant chair,
    Subdued by Love and led by Love, to make his pomp more fair.[120]

The second chapter of the first Triumph of Love

Already these my wearied eyes, all wearied so to view
    That brave Triumph and princely pomp that bravely did ensue,
And yet therewith not satisfied, desirous more to see,
    Now here and there to this and that I did convert mine ee;[121]
Which things for to repeat and show as I did see them frame 5
    So short an hour will not permit nor thole I show the same.[122]
Then did my heart from thoughts to thoughts by intercourse so pass,
    When as I spied two folks apart together them amass,[123]
And hand in hand so jointly joined, promening softly went,[124]
    And reasoning in sweetest words they thus their progress spent. 10
Their uncouth habit, light and strange, did make me much to muse,
    And speech unknown, to me obscure, which none but they did use;
Yet all their talk and conference which was betwixt these twain
    My marrow and interpreter and truiche man made it plain.[125]
And after that I knew them both, I nearer did approach, 15
    And boldly did myself enquire, and on them both encroached,[126]
Where I perceived the one to be a friend unto our name,
    The other an adversary severe and enemy to the same.
Unto the first I me addressed and thus began to say:

---

[120] This conclusion (lines 223–24) is Fowler's addition.
[121] ee] eyes.
[122] thole] suffer. These six opening lines correspond to Petrarch's first tercet.
[123] amass] unite.
[124] promening] walking.
[125] marrow] companion. This word is often used in the poem. truiche man] interpreter.
[126] As in line 13, here Fowler adds a line that essentially repeats and strengthens what had been said before. This strategy goes beyond the requirements of metre, and points at the translator's desire to clarify his meaning.

20   'Masinissa, princely prince, forgive me, I thee pray,
E'en for thy Scipio's sake, and hers by whom I now begin,[127]
       That thou would pardon what I speak and not be grieved herein'.
Thereafter then he me beheld and speaking thus began,
       'I willingly then first would know what art thou for a man,
25 Since thou well[128] in me had spied and dost so well discern
       My double love unto these two so stable and eterne'.[129]
I humbly answered him again, 'O peerless prince of praise,
       My poor estate will not permit that thou me know these days.
Base is my port, obscure I am, my means are mean and might,[130]
30   And from my small flames that far are placed there cannot come great light.[131]
But thy renown and royal fame through all the world arrives,
       Whose force is such that is conjoins the hearts, the sprites, and lives
Of those that never have thee seen nor shall hereafter see,
       With knots and bands of lasting love that shall ay lasting be.
35 Now tell me if this gracious Duke in whose Triumph you go
       If that in peace and quietness he does conduct you two,
Which couple makes me think such things to be so strange and rare
       And of the faithful rarest faith that any can declare.'

Then answered he, 'Thy tongue does prove, in naming me so prest,[132]
40   That thou dost know e'en by thyself my state and all the rest.
Yet for to chase far from my heart the dole which does it grow[133]
       And so results e'en by her death who now no more does live,
To thy request I yield consent.[134] I having then my heart
       Upon that high victorious Duke whose love has wrought my smart,
45 So steadfastly emplaced on him which no thing might supplant
       That Lelius in this respect with no small pain could vaunt,[135]
Wherever might his standard then or ensign be found

---

[127] A slight misreading on Fowler's part. Petrarch has *cominciai* ('I began to say') as a verb unconnected to the lady.
[128] Meikle inserts 'so' before 'well'.
[129] eterne] eternal.
[130] This line is Fowler's addition.
[131] there] I accept here Meikle's emendation to 'thair'; the original has 'they'.
[132] prest] ready. Fowler is proposing a calque for Petrarch's *si presta* ('so ready').
[133] dole] grief, sorrow.
[134] Although there is no interruption in the translation, at this point the scribe leaves a blank line. It is worth noting that, by amplifying the original, here Fowler introduces an allusion to Laura's death which is absent in Petrarch, who never refers to it in the first two Triumphs (Atić, p. 107).
[135] vaunt] boast, brag.

There was I likewise pressed in arms to combat on the ground.
To him was fortune favourable; from him she did not swerve,
    Yet not so far as did his acts and doughty deeds deserve.   50
Such valour was emplaced in him, such manhood in his mind,
    His like was never seen before nor yet shall come behind.
Now after that the Roman arms with honour was besprent[136]
    And sparpled to the utmost parts of east and occident.[137]
With him I me adjoinèd then, and Love with her me joined   55
    In such a sort that Death herself yet not has us disjoined.[138]
Was never such a sweetly flame two lovers' breasts did burn,
    Nor never shall, as I believe, for which I moan and mourn,
And weepeth that such few short nights, which makes me care and cry,
    Should all my pleasures overcross and my deserts all dry.[139]   60
For, being in vain conducted both unto our marriage bed,
    And all our just and lawful links to broken be and shed,
And therewith all my truce despised and no excuse prevail,
    In this my fury and my love that did me so assail
By him whose valour in itself than all the world was more,   65
    By him whose words were holy all and full of fame and glore,[140]
By him who had no pity on of both our sighs and woe,
    By him and by his holy speech we parted were in two.

From thence, alas, did rise our dole, and yet I must confess
    In doing so he has done well, suppose my joys are less   70
I saw such perfect proofs of grace in him, such virtue flame
    Within the mind of Scipio that ay shall live in Fame.
And as the man is stony blind that cannot see the sun
    E'en so is he[141] that not remarks the splendour he has won.
Great justice is to lovers true a sore and great offence,[142]   75
    So that his counsel grave and wise, that stayed our good pretence,
Was e'en a rock and craggy stone to break that enterprise
    Which we by force of fervent love amongst us did devise.[143]

---

[136] besprent] sprinkled.
[137] sparpled] scattered.
[138] This line is Fowler's addition.
[139] overcross] lie across. This word is to be found only in Fowler. This line shows Fowler's misreading, having the speaker, Masinissa, attribute to himself the *pleasures* that in Petrarch are attributed to Scipio.
[140] glore] glory.
[141] I accept Meikle's insertion of 'he'.
[142] The scribe highlights this line, underlining its sententious import (it is also proverbial in Petrarch).
[143] This line is Fowler's addition.

By age to me he brother was, by love my son, I say,
80   By honour e'en my father dear, whom I must needs obey,
Suppose I was with heavy heart, with sadness full and woe,
     And with a lowering countenance constrainèd to do so.
From whose command and counsel came my Sophonisba's death,[144]
     Who seeing herself so prosecuted by Romans' spiteful wrath
85 And almost brought within their bands, she chusèd first to die[145]
     Than to be brought in servitude, and through them shamèd be.
And I myself e'en of her death the minister even was:
     She prayed me to do that which her prayers brought to pass.
So doing that which she desired and bringing it to end,
90   Have wrought offence against myself that would not her offend.
So that I then her sent a cup within a poisoned drink
     With such a woeful sort of thoughts and sorrow you may think,
As I do know and she believes, and thou thyself may trow,[146]
     If that such coals of kindled flames had kindled been in you.

95 And now the heirship which I have and partage by my wife[147]
     Are only plaints, grief,[148] and woe and long and lasting strife;
In her did rest my only hope, in her was all my bliss;
     There have I lost for to conserve my faith but stain or miss.
But search if that thou now may see in all this troop and dance
100   A thing so wonderful and strange, and of so rare a chance;
Consider this in time, because the Time is light and swift[149]
     And there is matter more than day that bides a longer drift.'

As I was pausing, full of ruth and pity for them two,[150]
     And of the short time of their love, so wrappèd full of woe,
105 Together with their fervent fire which fiercely had begun,
     Me thought my heart was made of snow and set against the sun;
And thusways[151] musing in my mind I heard her as she went
     Say to her love, 'This man me grieves, and makes me malcontent.

---

[144] Fowler specifies the name of the heroine, while Petrarch only has *mia cara*.
[145] chused] chose.
[146] trow] trust, believe.
[147] heirship] inheritance. partage] portion.
[148] Meikle adds 'doole', a synonym of 'grief', presumably to preserve the rhythm of the line.
[149] This is 'a good example of Fowler's trying to be exhaustive in his process of translation. The Italian word *leve* (71) is used to indicate something light or transient' (Atić, p. 110). This linguistic effort explains many of the reduplications in this translation.
[150] pausing] Meikle reads 'pansing', which does not seem to make sense in the context. ruth] compassion.
[151] thusways] thus.

I firmly keep within my mind and earnestly in thought
    To hate him for his nation's sake, who our destruction wrought'.[152]   110
Then this to her I spoke again, 'Do this for my request,
    O Sophonisba, be at peace and put your mind to rest.
Your Carthage has by these our hands been wracked and ruinèd thrice,
    And at the third time all upraised and on the ground now lies.'
But quickly she this spoke again: 'Show me this other thing: 115
    When Africa wept, did Italy then either laugh or sing?
For proof hereof cast o'er your books and these your stories write,
    And they will show if you enquire, for they of both indite.'
And thus our friend, her love, also did smiling then depart
    And to the thickest of the troop their steps they did convert,   120
So that these eyes, these lights of mine, that on them gazed afore,
    Through multitude e'en of the press could not behold them more.

Then, as a man by doubtful ways does at adventure ride,
    Now stands, now rests at every place, and cannot tell what side,
Or yet what way to turn him to, but looketh here and there,   125
    So that his doubtful wandering thoughts his passage do impair;
E'en so the number of these men who captive went with Love
    Did make my going doubtful slow, wherever I did move.
And yet I had a more desire and seemèd more content
    To know how much and through what fire these lovers all were brent.[153]   130
Where on my left hand I had espied without the common way[154]
    E'en one who does resemble him who earnestly does pray,
And covets things with great desire, and in his suit has sped,
    Both blithe and blushingly departs, his former steps to tread.
E'en in such sort I saw that king who gave his loving wife   135
    And chosen spouse unto his son, to lengthen his lingering life.[155]
O Love, O Love in high degree, O courtesy most strange,
    O wonder great, more far again to see her in that change
And that excambion so content that she but blushed for joy;[156]
    This marching on they to their troop did then themselves conwoy,[157]   140
Conferring on their sweet desires, but sighing that she cost

---

[152] A misreading. In the original Sophonisba maintains her hatred for all the nation, but makes an exception for *costui*, this man.
[153] brent] burnt.
[154] without] outside, away from.
[155] Seleucus renounced his wife, Stratonica, and gave her to Antiochus, his son, who was sick for love for her.
[156] excambion] exchange (a Scottish legal term).
[157] conwoy] convey.

The Syrian sceptre and her crown and kingdom thereby lost.

I drew me near unto these sprites that were about to stay,
    Consulting how that they might go and take another way,
145 And saying to the foremost man that nearest was my side,
    'I pray thee now most instantly that thou would me abide'.
And he, e'en at the first resound of that my Latin tongue,
    With troubled face depaint with ire, unto a musing doung,[158]
Restrained his steps to know who called and quickly did divine
150   What was my will and my desire; and so me answered syne:[159]
'I am Seleucus; here with me Antiochus goes my son,
    Who had great wars against you all, and both by them undone.
But right nor reason contrary force has neither room nor place,
    And this is she, first was my wife, whom now my son does brace,[160]
155 Whom I did quit and did resign to be his lawful wife
    To free from Death and chase away the danger of his life,
To which his lovely hid desires and closet secret flame[161]
    Conducted him. And so that gift was lawful then but blame.
Stratonica she namèd is, and so our chance and lot
160   Is as thou seest indivisible, and by this sign the knot
Of this our long and lasting love is yet so tough and strong
    That no thing that can separate which first was us among.
She was content to quit to me the kingdom,[162] I my wife,
    Then my belovèd dearly spouse, and he again his life;
165 So warily went he in his love so far by reason forth[163]
    That he more made him so esteemed of one and other worth.
And if it had not been by skill, by help, and aid discreet
    Of that expert physician with practice full complete,
Who well espied where lay the cause that did his health down ding,[164]
170   His youth e'en in her flower had ended and finished in her spring;
For he in silence and in love did run unto his death.
    His feet him failed, his voice was weak, his powers life and breath,[165]
Fates caused him love, his virtue made him hide it to the end,

---

[158] depaint] painted. unto a musing doung] cast into reflection, fallen into meditation.
[159] syne] since.
[160] brace] embrace.
[161] lovely] loving.
[162] Probably a misreading of the original: in Petrarch, Stratonica is content to leave her husband and the kingdom.
[163] This line is Fowler's addition.
[164] down ding] cast down.
[165] This line is Fowler's addition.

And my paternal pity the succour has extend.'
Thus as he spoke, then as a man that does make change for change, 175
    Of hailsing others mutually, does both by other range,[166]
So at the end of these his words he turned his steps and heel
    That I with great difficulty might bid him then farewell.

Then after that from these my eyes the shade away had gone,
    Which were with pity heavy made; I sighing progressed on 180
For that my heart from these words was not unbound nor loosed,
    But ruefully remembered that which he to me disclosed.[167]
At last to me that time was said, 'Thou standeth too, too much
    Upon one thought in diverse so and of variety such,
Which shortness of the sliding time as thou too well dost know 185
    Will not permit in large discourse that I them to thee show'.
Not Xerxes to the seas of Greece convoyéd such a band
    Of arméd men by naval host as there with them did stand;
E'en such a troop of lovers, all both naked, bound and tane[168]
    As that my eyes unable were to such a sight sustain. 190
They were in tongues so different and of such diverse lands
    As scarcely I e'en one can name of thousands led in bands.
So that the story which I write and poem I compile
    Shall be of these and them a few, whom I there knew that while.

And Perseus first shall prease in place, whose love made me desire[169] 195
    To know how that Andromeda did set his heart on fire.
And how in Ethiopia land that virgin, black of hue,
    Did with her eyes and crispéd hair him to his love subdue.
Next him was there that lover vain, whose beauty was his wrack,
    Who through too much desire was quite destroyed and all sacked, 200
And only poor made by his wealth and by abundance scant,
    And now transforméd in a flower that seed and fruit does want.
Beside him was that Echo, nymph who for Narcissus cried,[170]
    Whose corpse was changéd in a stone, and voice in rocks was dried;
With her was Iphis in that rank, so bent unto her death, 205
    That hated herself for others' love and reft herself of breath;[171]

---

[166] hailsing] saluting. This line is Fowler's addition.
[167] This line is Fowler's addition.
[168] tane] taken prisoners.
[169] prease] strive.
[170] Fowler adds Echo's name, to make the reference clearer.
[171] reft herself of breath] took away her own breath. Here Fowler enlarges the original, adding a reference to Iphis, but mistaking him for the nymph of the same name.

And many other damnèd souls condemnèd to like pain,
    And in their march did all like cross and fortune hard sustain:
A people who through too much love did loath in life, lo, live
210   Through rigour of their careless dames, whose pride them most did grieve;[172]
Where also I did there perceive of this our age a host
    Whose names for to recount or tell were work and labour lost.

With them were those whom Love has made eternal marrows two,[173]
    True, just, and faithful Ceice and constant Alcio,[174]
215 Who at the border of the seas and at the showers his side
    Did big their nests e'en at the best and calm of winter tide.
Along from them was Aesacus, who pensive there did stand,
    And searching for Hesperia, now sitting on the land,
Then on the watery floods again, and now to mount more high;
220   And Scylla, Nisos' cruel child, far from her father fly.
There then I Atalanta saw by apples three of gold,
    And with the beauty of a face overcome and controlled;
With her, her lower Hippomenes, who far above the rest
    Of all that troop of lovers were and wretched runners best,
225 Who only by his valour did her vows and oaths supplant,
And joyful of the victory so marching on did vaunt.

Among the fabulous lovers vain which poets do rehearse
    Was Galatea, Acis eke, and Polyphemus so fierce,
Who Acis slew while as he did within her bosom lie;
230   And so with noise and rumour great these three then passèd by.
There Glaucus, fleeting on the waves to enter in that band,
    But Scylla whom he did desire and with such zeal demand,
And blaming Circe namèd her a lover fell and fierce;
    With them was then these other two which Ovid does rehearse,
235 Canence with her Picus chaste, sometime one of our kings,
    But now by Circe made a fowl that chatters and not sings,[175]
Whose sorcery did change him from his name and embroidered robes,
    For which her well-belovèd low ay sighing wails and sobs.[176]

---

[172] This line is Fowler's addition.
[173] Those whom Love had made eternal companions.
[174] Alcio] Alcyone, a Thessalian princess, who married Ceyx, king of Trachis.
[175] Circe transformed Picus into a woodpecker. Both Scylla and Circe are alluded to by Petrarch, but not explicitly named — as often happen in this text, Fowler makes implicit allusions explicit.
[176] This line is Fowler's addition.

I saw likewise Egeria's tears, and Scylla have for bones
  In place thereof a hard sharp rock that sounds, that roars and groans, 240
And from her name the crag so called, so that unto that sea
  Where it is placed does ever grow great shame and infamy.
I also Canace beheld who having in one hand
  A fatal naked sword, as did her father her command,[177]
And in his right a pen to write in dole and deep despair, 245
  And to her lover then her love her dolent death declare.[178]
With her was there Pygmalion, with him his dame did bide,
  And thousands more, who singing then were at the fountain's side,
Of Aganippe and Castalia, where then I saw in end
  Cydippe with that apples scorned Acontius did her send. 250

The third chapter of the first Triumph of Love

So much my heart was then amazed, so much of marvel full,
  That I there stood, e'en as a man that stupid stands and dull,
And cannot speak, but holds his tongue and looks if any man
  Be near, of yet him round about, to give him counsel then.
When that my shadow and my friend began thus for to say:[179] 5
  'What dost thou now, what looks thou on, whereon thy thoughts do stay,
Knowest thou not well that I am one e'en of this troop and band
  Whom Love does lead, with whom I go that cannot him withstand?'
Then answered I, 'My brother dear, thou best my state dost know,
  And also the love that in my breast does to such kindling grow, 10
Whose force is such that e'en what things of thee I should require,
  Together with such like affairs, are stayed by great desire'.

Then he thus spoke again, and said, 'Already I have known,
  Though thou through silence speak nothing what thou wouldst have
                thee shown;
Since thou would know what folk be these and people thou hast spied, 15
  I will thee tell, if to my tongue the use be not denied.

Behold that great and glorious man, so honourèd of all,
  He Pompey is that leads, with him Cornelia withal,

---

[177] Canace's name is Fowler's addition, as is the reference to Canace's father.
[178] dolent] painful.
[179] my friend] Fowler translates Petrarch's simple *l'amico mio*, adding 'my shadow'. Thus he establishes the function of this ambiguous Petrarchan figure, reinforcing the analogy with Dante's Virgil in the *Divine Comedy*. The word 'shadow' is used a number of times to refer to Petrarch's mysterious companion (see, for instance, line 113 in this chapter).

Who with her salt and watery tears condoles his dolent death[180]
20   Which Ptolemaeus that wild did cause, through terror more than wrath.[181]
He whom thou seest more farther off is that great valiant Greek,
    Conductor of the valiant host. And here Aegisthus eke,
That murderer, adulterer, that poltroon paliard priest,[182]
    This cruel Clytemnestra is that cruel godless beast
25 By whom it may now well be known and by them we may find
    If Love inconstant be and vain, insensate, furious, blind.[183]
But yet behold yon other dame, of greater faith and love,
    That faithful Hypermnestra fair, and so did Linus prove;[184]
See Pyramus and Thisbe both, to stand the shadow by,
30   With Hero at the window and in seas Leander lie.
This shadow that thou pensive seest is that Ulysses, whom
    His chasteful wife does long expect and prayeth to come home;[185]
But Circes, that enchantress, through Love does him detain
    And does impeach his forward steps and makes him stay again.
35 This other whom thou dost behold it is Amilcar's son,
    Bold Hannibal, who stoutly did with the Romans conjoin,[186]
Whom Rome thought not in many years nor Italy might abase,
    Yet has an abject woman him of Puglia led in lace.

She that with hair both cut and short does follow so her lord
40   Was queen of Pontus that for love does now to this accord,
With servile clothes and such attire Mithridates to serve,
    That in his journeys and conflicts from him did never swerve.
This other dame is Portia, bold Brutus' faithful wife,
    That sharps her sword hard by the coals and ends by them her life.[187]
45 There also Julia thou may see that wept for her spouse,
    For that unto his second flame he more inclines and bows.

Now turn thine eyes and them convert unto that other side
    Where our great father Jacob scorned does with these folk abide,[188]

---

[180] dolent] painful.
[181] The second half of the line is Fowler's addition.
[182] paliard] dissolute.
[183] An instance of misreading on Fowler's part. Petrarch states that Agamemnon is so blinded by love that he cannot see Aegisthus, so is unable to defend himself; in Fowler's version, the blindness of love is attributed to Aegisthus and Clytemnestra.
[184] Fowler probably means Lyncaeus, Hypermnestra's husband (unnamed in Petrarch).
[185] chasteful] chaste, full of chastity.
[186] Once again Fowler enlarges and clarifies Petrarch's mention of the son of Amilcar.
[187] sharps] sharpens.
[188] As with Mithridates, above, the name of Jacob is added by the translator, who, on the

And yet for all that does not forethink or meant from her to swerve,
> For whom with constant loyal love he twice seven years did serve. 50
O lively Love! O force most strange that does not only last,
> But grows by griefs and always is by troubles more increased!
Behold the father of this man, with him his goodsir too,[189]
> Departing from his dwelling place, and Sara like to do;
Then after look how cruel love and wicked, David won, 55
> Enforcing him to do that work from whence he, after then,
Within a dark and secret cave, withdrawing him apart,
> Wept for his faults and for his sins in anguish of his heart.

Behold also how such a mist and such like darkened cloud
> Does so obscure his son his face, and darkness overshroud, 60
And covet the praise of all his wit and make the same be smored,[190]
> Which published was through all the world by our supernal Lord.
Then Amnon spy who at one time did Thamar love and hate,
> And how she then to Absalom her brother did repeat,
Disdainful and most dolorous, the cause of all her woe, 65
> His raging lust and hate again his kindness to o'erthrow.
Before a little thou may see one stronger more than wise:
> I Samson mean, who with his wife did foolishly devise
And through her clattering trifling tries then she did then delair,[191]
> Did put his head within her lap that cut away his hair. 70

Behold also how that among so many spears and swords
> Love sleep; and also a widow fair with many pleasant words
And with her comely, cleanly cheeks, accompanied with her maid,
> Has killed Holofernes the proud, and vengeance him repaid;
And they, returning to their town, and in their hands his head, 75
> At midnight given God the thanks to which they haste with speed.
See Sichem and with him his blood, how that the same is mixed
> With circumcision and with death and with the slaughter next
Of both his father and all these that pissed against the wall;[192]
> O force of Love, both strong and great, that made such sudden fall! 80
Behold Ahasuerus, in what sort he begging seeks his love,

---

other hand, deletes a reference to Rachel. It may be deduced that he expected his audience to be more familiar with biblical than with classical lore.

[189] goodsir] grandfather.

[190] be] I accept Meikle's emendation — the original reads 'the'. smored] smothered.

[191] delair] the word is unattested elsewhere, and finds no explanation in *DOST* or in *OED*.

[192] A rather surprising addition on the part of Fowler, who does not translate, or perhaps misreads, Petrarch's *ad un veschio* ('in a snare').

That he in peace may her possess, and how he does remove
And so unloose his former knots, and free him of these bands
That bound him fast, I mean his wife that kept not his commands;
85 And how that by another knot again he has him bound,
Which only is the salve that may in contrary love be found.
And all such malice to efface, there is no better thing
E'en as a wedge another doth, and nail and nail forth bring.[193]

Now would thou see within one heart the bitter with the sweet,
90 And loathsomeness with love again e'en in one mind to float?
Behold Herodes cruel, fierce, of kindness full and rage,[194]
Whom Love with cruelty and hate so long time does assuage;
Regard how that the first does burn and lie in fervent flame,
And after how he gnaws his[195] heart in memory of the same,
95 And calling for his Marion which then does not him hear
Too late he now repented him of such his rage severe.

Behold again these other three, both good of life and love,
Deidamia with Arthemise and Procris so did prove;
Now see likewise these three, so curst and touched with raging flame,
100 Semiramis with Biblis eke and Myrrha void of shame.
How every one of them appears for shame to blush and stay,
That they can have no licence for to walk with them that way.
But for to take the thrown street and e'en of that denied,[196]
Behold that troop that fills with dreams the papers on all side,
105 Whose works do make the vulgar sort to read them and require,
And vainly through their erring dreams so for them have desire.
These are the wandering loving knights of Arthur's table round,
Where Guinevere with her Lancelot with others may be found,
As Tristan with Isotta fair, the king of Cornwall's wife;
110 And also that count of Rimini who lost for love their life,[197]
Lord Paul of Malatesta's house and Franceschina fair,
In making moan and sad laments and wailing marchèd their.'[198]

---

[193] This line, proposing a moralizing simile as a conclusion to the section, is highlighted by the scribe.
[194] Herodes] Herod.
[195] Here I accept Meikle's addition of 'his'.
[196] the thrown street] the crooked path.
[197] count] Possibly a scribal mistake for 'couple' (in Petrarch, *coppia*).
[198] This short section dedicated to medieval romance lovers is translated with some amplification and great care: 'it seems as if he spent a good amount of time working on these lines. He mentions explicitly the Round Table and he arranges the names in pairs' (Atić, p. 122).

Thus as my friend and shadow spoke, I at that time did stand
    E'en as a man that is afraid for ill that is at hand,
And trembleth fast before he hears the trumpet show his doom, 115
    And feels his dolent death before the same by sentence come.
So was my state e'en at that time, my face such colour kept,
    As one drawn forth e'en of his grave wherein he long did sleep;
When then with paleish face and wan before me I espied[199]
    A lively Nymph, more fairer than a dove, stand by my side, 120
Who there me took and captive led; and I who would have sworn
    To have defended well myself and men of arms o'erborn,
Was with the smirking of her eyes and smiling of her face
    And with her pleasant gracious words then snarèd in her lace.

As I was thinking on this thing and for the truth to show 125
    My friend more nearer did approach and towards me did draw,
And laughing rounded in my ear (whose laughter caused my woe
    That at my losses he should smile) and thus began he so:
'Now has thou licence for to speak e'en what thou and please,[200]
    To show how Love e'en in his mood does both thee pain and ease 130
Since now we both sail in one bark and both one liquor like,[201]
    And both together markèd like, and touchèd with one pike'.[202]
I then became as one of those who more is discontent
    Of others' hap and better luck and prosperous event,
Than of my loss and hapless chance, and so more grieved was I, 135
    When as I did the dame me led in peace and freedom spy.
And after, as too late my loss and damage I did know,
    So from the beauty of my dame I made my death to grow
For burnt with love and with his flame and with envy enrage,[203]
    And jealous was then my heart which nothing could assuage, 140
Nor would I turn my staring eyes away from her fair face,
    But as a man by fevers weakt so seemed I in that case,[204]
Who, though he sick and feverish be, yet has a greedy will[205]
    For that which to his taste is sweet but to his health is ill.[206]

---

[199] In this line, 'my ee' has been corrected by a later hand to 'me'. Fowler adds the detail of the young woman being pale and wan; in Petrarch she is simply purer than the white dove.
[200] The line is defective, missing a verb after 'thou' (Meikle, III. 52).
[201] bark] boat.
[202] These three lines translate Petrarch's simple image 'ché tutti siam macchiati d'una pece' ('since we are all defiled with the same pitch').
[203] enrage] enraged.
[204] weakt] weakened.
[205] This line is Fowler's addition.
[206] This line is highlighted in the manuscript.

145　So that to any other joy which more might glaid my mind[207]
　　　　My ears were deaf and stoppèd both, my eyes were shut and blind,
　　In following her whose steps me led by many doubtful pace
　　　　So that in thinking on the same I tremble yet, allace.[208]

　　For ay since syne[209] my eyes through tears were on the ground fixed weak,
150　　　　My heart was sad and pensive ay the ins that I did take;
　　And solitary resting place was then the wells and woods,
　　　　The fountains, rivers, mountains, hills, the craggy rocks and floods,
　　Sensyne the papers and the scrolls which I have spersed always[210]
　　　　With thoughts, with tears, with ink to pen my pains and paint her praise,
155　Sometimes through love, sometimes through wrath, I forcèd was in spite[211]
　　　　To tear them all in pieces small and o'er again to write.

　　Sensyne I know how Love retains within his cloister now
　　　　Doubt, dread, despair and deep distrust,[212] and hope with constant vow,
　　So that the man that well would know the feats and fruits of love,
160　　　　The pains, the plagues, the lingering times that lovers hourly prove,
　　If he can read then lift his eyes unto my forehead now,
　　　　When he shall see all these effects fair written on my brow.
　　And her I see so careless walk, that fair and gallant dame,
　　　　Not touched with ruth for all my pains, but careless of the same,[213]
165　And reckless both of them and me she taketh no account
　　　　Now whether I sink or yet I fleet, I fall or yet I mount.[214]
　　Such graces now do grow in her, such beauty she does shroud,
　　　　That of her virtue now she goes and of my spuilyei proud.[215]

　　And on the other part I spy and see on other side
170　　　　E'en Love himself to stand in fear, and from her him to hide;
　　Although he winneth all the world, he cannot her subdue,
　　　　So that past hope of help am I, nor Love can make rescue.
　　In my defence there none that stands, no succour comes to me,
　　　　And in my aid no boldness can, nor force can make supply;

---

[207] glaid] gladden.
[208] allace] alas.
[209] syne] This word repeats and reinforces the preceding 'since'.
[210] Sensyne] since. spersed] dispersed.
[211] I thus emend the manuscript, which has 'and spyte'.
[212] This series is highlighted by the scribe's choice of calligraphy, as well as by alliteration.
[213] ruth] compassion.
[214] This line is Fowler's addition.
[215] spuilyei] spoil.

For Love himself in whom I hope and confidence do bide, 175
    Whose custom is most cruelly to flite if lovers hide,
And flesh with mine their skin from them[216] dally with his dame,
    And flatteringly caresses her, yet cares she not the same,
Nor any be that more or less may force yet or constrain
    This rammage and rebelling maid with Love for to remain.[217] 180
But going by herself alone, and free from Love his lace
    Withdraws her from his ensign a long and distant space.

And truly in his beauty she, and in her port and pace,
    And in her smiles and high disdains and in her words and grace,
She in this sort surpasses so, compared with other dames, 185
    E'en as the sun the little sparks exceedeth by his flames.
So fair appears her hair to be, that they do seem of gold,
    All shaking softly by the wind which does their tress unfold;
Her eyes like heav'nly lamps and lights that so inflame my heart
    That through their grace I am content that they increase my smart. 190
Who can with her behaviour and angel-like address,
    With manners meek and customs high compare, or yet express?
For he who would in poem praise condignly to report
    Her virtues, deeds and glorious acts, I think he should come short.
It far my learning does surpass, my wavering pen does shake, 195
    My style, my verse, my voice, my phrase are over-base and weak;
No pen can more depaint her praise or yet advance her glore[218]
    Than little strands the largest seas do by their course make more.

O things most new and never seen before unto this day,
    Nor more but once, nor after shall their glory more bewray! 200
It is a thing shall never be, her like shall never come,
    And on her virtue and her grace all voices shall be dume.[219]

So do I find myself now bound, and she in freedom free,
    And I exclaiming in this sort, O star, how guides thou me?
O cursèd star, O fates unjust, what things do ye portend. 205
    How chanceth it that for my pains I ripe no fruit in end?
I day and night bewail my woe, and ay do call and pray
    To her who cares not for my moan, nor yet to here will stay,

---

[216] Here Meikle adds 'dois', i.e. 'does': although unnecessary from the point of view of meaning, this added word would restore the metre.
[217] rammage] untamed.
[218] glore] glory.
[219] dume] dumb.

So that with great difficulty, with travail, toil, and pain,
  I scarcely for ten thousand words can one obtain again.
O law severe of Cupid's court! yet though it crookèd be,
  And indirect, yet must we all to follow it agree,
Because it is so ancient, so universal old,
  That it conjoins to the heaven earth so low and cold,
Whose potent power and strong effect not only man has proven
  But e'en the manhood of the gods by it has been o'erthrown.[220]

And now since Love has me subdued I know and have espied
  How that he does the heart of man far from his course divide,
And how he can give pain and peace, long lasting wars with truce,
  And doleful tidings to despair, and then more better news,
And how he forces outwardly men for to hide their woe,
  When inwardly their breasts burnt suppose it seem not so,
And how e'en in one instant time the blood in haste departs,
  And quickly from his vanes does run and in his cheeks converts,
If so it chance that any fear does then his mind possess
  Or shamefastness constrain him blush, or terror him oppress.
I know how that the serpent lies all hid within the flower,
  The snares, the girnis, the nets and baits the lovers do devour,[221]
And also how he jealous wakes[222] and sleeps in dread and doubt,
  Suspecting ay his rival foe by love should thrust him out.
I also know how this my life does languish by despair,
  And how I dying never die, nor Death can end my care.
I also know how for to trace the footsteps of my foe,
  And how for fear to find her since I stand in dread, then go.
I also know in what a sort and what a guise so strange
  The lingering lover in his love does him transform and change;
And how among so longsome sighs and shortened smilings I
  Can change my state, my will and hue, and colour soon thereby;
And how to live and stand but life when as my woeful heart
  Is sundered from his sprite and soul, her lively vital part.
I also know how Love has led me in this dance this while
  A thousand ways, and vain deceits myself for to beguile.
I also know how for to burn in following so my fire,
  Where it does fly, and how at hand so freezes my desire;

---

[220] As sometimes happens at the end of a stanza, the last couplet has been added by Fowler. This whole passage has undergone radical amplification in the process of translation.
[221] girnis] A synonym of 'snares'.
[222] My emendation. The manuscript has 'walkis', which might be a scribal mistake for 'wakis', more closely corresponding to Petrarch's *vegghia*.

And farther off does rage again, and burn in greater flame, 245
    And nearer then how I congeal and freeze in the same.
I also know how Love does bray and rout above the mind,
    And how it does all reason smore and chase unto the mind.[223]
I also know the diverse arts that Love through craft does use
    For to subvert the lovers' heart and how him to abuse. 250
I know how that a gentle mind is suddenly disgraced,
    And how that by a little cord it strongly is unlaced,[224]
When it is left unto herself disarmed of reason then,
    And when none is to make defence against the lusts of man.
I also know how Love does shoot, and then does fly away, 255
    How that he boasts and striketh both, and puts all in a fray.
I also know how that he rubs and plays the thief perforce,
    How that he revis and spuilyeis all his pillage but remorse.[225]

And how unstable is his wheel, how doubtful is his hope,
    How certain is his wrack and woe, and how his course and scope 260
Is for to make such promises that are of faith devoid,
    By which the true and faithful heart is scornèd and destroyed.
I also know how in his bones the raging flame does lurk,
    How in his veins the hidden hurt does his consumption work,
From whence does come his open death and fire through smokes expressed 265
    That secretly in secret did harbour in his breast.

In end, for one conclusion, I know the lovers' life
    To be inconstant, wandering, vain, and full of sturt and strife,
Both fearful and both hardy too, and how does Love repay
    The little sweet with bitterness so long to last for ay. 270
        I know their customs, manners, use, their sighs, their groans and song,
Their broken words, their sudden peace, their silence dumb and long,
    Their shortest smiles, their long complaints, their tears, their grievous
                                                                                                       fall,
Their pleasures with displeasure crossed, their honey mixed with gall.[226]

The fourth chapter of the first Triumph of Love

When after that my fortune had and Love me forwards thrust
    Within an other's force and strength and so had brought to dust,

---

[223] smore] smother.
[224] Possibly a scribal mistake: Fowler may have meant 'is enlaced' to translate Petrarch's *s'allaccia*.
[225] revis and spuilyeis] robs and spoils.
[226] Petrarch's four-line conclusion is rendered here with eight lines.

And cut in two the veins and nerves and freedom of my will,
    And liberty, which long time I free remainèd still;
Then I, who was afore as free and wild as any hart,
    Was quickly tamed and soon subdued with little pain and art,
And brought to know the luckless lot and unexpected chance
    With these my marrows miserable whom Love led in his dance.[227]
Then did I spy their travails, pains, their cummer and lament,[228]
    The throwin ways,[229] the crookèd lanes, the path and straits they went,
And by what art and labour they conducted thereto were,
    Where all that lovely flock and troop did then so wandering err;
And while I rolled in every side my gazing restless ene,[230]
    If I could spy there any man whose fame so clear has been,
By histories of ancient times, or poems in our days,
    In which more late and recently included is his praise,

I saw e'en then fair Orpheus: of him I first will tell,[231]
    Who only loved Euridice, and following her to hell
Obtainèd her with him again, yet lost her then again,
    And being dead yet calls on her with tongue most cold in vain.
I Alcaeus saw, so pregnant prompt of love, that could indite,
    And Pindar with Anacreon that of the same did write,
Who had their muse, their rhymes and verse, all pennèd in behove
    Of Cupid's court, whose poems lay within the port of Love.
I Virgil saw, and him about his brave companions stood,
    Brave poets of a high engine and of a merry mood,[232]
Whose works this world so esteems, that they them first elect
    Extolling them in highest praise and honourable respect:
Ovidius with Corinna caught, and Tibullus Plania,
    Propertius who so hotly sang in praise of Cynthia,
Catullus also there I spied, whom Lesbia led in love,
    With her, that learnèd Sappho Greek that passions like did prove,[233]
Resounding with her noble voice with poets who view there
    Her sweetest songs, and show her style to gallant be and rare.

---

[227] marrows] companions.
[228] cummer] distress.
[229] throwin ways] narrow, tortuous paths.
[230] ene] eyes.
[231] As often happens in this translation, Fowler enlarges and explains the original, in which Orpheus is simply alluded to as *colui* ('that one').
[232] engine] This word is often used here with the meaning of mind, intelligence.
[233] Fowler adds the names of the poets' loved ones, and clarifies Petrarch's allusion to Sappho.

So, looking here and there again, to this and to that side, 35
    Upon a flowery pleasant green I quickly then espied
A people speaking on to walk, and reasoning as they went;
    And so I saw then first appear e'en Dante incontinent
With Beatrice, Selvaggia next, and Cino of Pistoia bred,
    And Guido of Arezzo was with them in that troop led, 40
That seemèd for to be displeased and angry, malcontent,
    That he was not there first with love and foremost with him went.
With them two other Guidos were, and those of Sicily,[234]
    And that good-natured Bolognese, an honest man was he,[235]
Sennuccio with Franceschin there likewise did them show,[236] 45
    The gentlest men and courteousest that ever men did know.
And after such a sort of folk in vulgar clothes I spied
    And habits of such strange attire that marchèd on that side,[237]
Amongst them first they were in preiss Arnaldo Daniell,[238]
    A master great in Cupid's court that did in love excel, 50
Who yet does by his pleasant speech and his inventions new
    Renown his native country soil by these their sight and view.
There also was, whom lightly Love with little pain o'ercame,
    One Peter, and Arnaldo was the other of less fame.[239]
There also was these sort of men subdued by greater war. 55
    Two of one name, Rombaldi called that sang in Mountferrar,
Upon their dames, fair Beatrice;[240] with him Giraldus lo,[241]
    And aged Peter of Auvergne; with him was Falchetto[242]
That gave the name to Marseilles town and did from Genoa awfer,[243]
    And changed his country clothes and state, and better had for war, 60

---

[234] The allusion is to Guido Guinizzelli and Guido Cavalcanti, foremost poets of the Dolce Stil Novo school. In the second part of the line, Petrarch alludes to the Sicilian school of courtly poetry (flourishing at the court of Frederick II).

[235] Fowler might have misunderstood Petrarch's reference to the poet Onesto from Bologna.

[236] The poets Sennuccio del Bene and Franceschino degli Albizzi.

[237] attire] Fowler might have misunderstood Petrarch's *drappello* (small group), reading it as a diminutive of *drappo* (cloth).

[238] in preiss] in the crowd. Arnaldo Daniell is the Provençal poet Arnaut Daniel.

[239] In this instance, too, there is a misunderstanding on Fowler's part. Petrarch writes 'l'un Piero e l'altro, e 'l men famoso Arnaldo' ('one and the other Piero, and the less famous Arnaldo'), referring to the French poets Peire Vidal of Toulouse, Peire Rogier of Auvergne and Arnaut de Maroilh.

[240] The allusion (possibly misunderstood by Fowler) is to Raimbaut of Aurenga and Raimbaut de Vaqueiras, both twelfth-century poets; the latter loved Beatrice, daughter of the Marquis of Monferrato.

[241] The troubadour Giraut de Bornelh.

[242] Fowler here misspells the name of Folco (or Folchetto) of Marseilles.

[243] awfer] A Latinism, meaning 'come from'.

Giaufre Rudd also was, who more through love than wrath
      Did use the speed of sails and oars to speed his fereth death.[244]
And also there that William was,[245] who with this lover's songs
      Does free his name from all decay, that much his praise prolongs.
65 Amerigus and Bernard too, and Hugo with Anselm,[246]
      And thousand more who used their tongues for lance, sword, buckler,
                                                             helm.

And now, since it is seemly that my dolour I divide,
      I have converted my dazzled eyes, all wearied, to that side,
Where I have spied my faithful friend, good Thomas, that does grace
70   Bologna town with lasting fame, and makes his praise increase.
And by his songs and sonnets so Messina makes to grow
      More fat in praise and rather more and more in braver show.[247]
O fleeing sweet! O fading joy! O wearied, painful life![248]
      Who is it that does unto me procure this sturt and strife?
75 Who is it hath then ta'en from me my friend and only joy,
      Who quickly now before his time does him to grave convoy?
But whom and but whose company? such now is my mishap
      That I can neither space nor pace not further go a step.
Well now I know which thing I might have better known afore,
80   How that the life of mortal men wherein so much we glore[249]
And like in the same to live is but a stage of noise,
      A sick man's dream, or foolish conceit, and fable full of toys.[250]

I was a little somewhat forth out of the vulgar way,
      When Socrates and Lelius did first themselves bewray;[251]
85 With them it me behovèd then to walk and farther go
      And search for learning in their works and for their science know.[252]

---

[244] The allusion is to the poet Giaufré Rudel. his fereth death] his untimely death.
[245] Guilhem de Cabestanh.
[246] Aimeric de Pegulhan, Bernart de Ventadorn, Uc de Saint Circ and Gaucelm Faidit.
[247] Petrarch simply has *Tomasso*, but Fowler evidently recognised the allusion to Tommaso Caloria of Messina, a friend and fellow student of Petrarch's.
[248] The scribe highlights this line not only with calligraphy, but also by employing exclamation marks, a very unusual practice in this manuscript.
[249] wherein] After this word, a letter m has been erased, with 'so' superimposed, and another 'so' after it. glore] glory.
[250] This ironic description of life (translating Petrarch's simpler 'sogno d'infermi e fola di romanzi') contains surprising assonances with Shakespeare's *Macbeth*, v. 5.
[251] Petrarch's friends, Louis Sanctus of Beeringen and Lello di Piero Stefano.
[252] This line is Fowler's addition.

O what abundance of my friends, with virtue so decord,[253]
    Was led at that triumphant chair whose gifts none can record,
Whose ornate talk and eloquence, nor wit can none rehearse,
    In facile prose, in lofty style, in rhyme and stately verse!   90
And with these two I walking went, and searchèd diverse ways,[254]
    To them I opened up my plaints and hurt, my heart's assays,
From them no other time nor place shall ever me divide,
    But as I wish to do I hope with them so long to bide
Unto the last gasp of my breath and never to retire[255]   95
    Until the cinders of my corpse be burnèd on the pyre.
For with these two I have obtained that glorious laurel bough
    Which does the temples of my head environ and my brow;[256]
Which has perchance before the time my forehead so bedecked
    In mind of her whom yet I love and do so much respect.   100
But yet of her whose praise I paint and fills my heart with thought
    I never could get branch nor leaf which I with service sought,
Nor any pleasure could obtain, so stable was the root,
    And so unjust to which she leaned, that I could ripe no fruit;
From whence although sometimes my grief and grievous dole did rise,   105
    As his who has received offence to stay his enterprise,
Yet she on whom my eyes did gaze so ruled and ranged my will
    That now no more I do regret that she refused me till
A matter sure of stately style and of heroical verse
    To which no dolts nor ignorants can yet attain or pierce.   110
Nor yet such poets of such stuff, of base and vulgar rhyme,
    May well conceive how I did see Cupido ta'en that time.
But first to tell I will proceed, and first I will recount
    How Love so leading us in links did so o'er us surmount;
Then after this I shall forth show what he of her sustained   115
    And how my dame did vanquish Love and all his arts disdained.[257]
This work and subject is not mine, nor only made by me,
    But long before by Orpheus penned and Homer seems to be.
Then followed we the noise and sound of Cupid's purple pens
    And of his fleeing horse that ran through thousand dykes and dams,   120
And through a thousand hills and dales at last in end we came

---

[253] decord] decorated.
[254] Fowler omits Petrarch's subsequent line.
[255] This line is Fowler's addition.
[256] environ] surround, adorn.
[257] With this line Fowler anticipates the subsequent Triumph, in which Petrarch muses on the fact that Laura might never have loved him. It is one of the instances in which the translator intervenes to underline the connections between the various chapters.

Unto his mother's country, where sojournéd then that dame,
And in which way where we through brayes,[258] through briars and bushes went,
Through mountains, meadows, hills and woods, our chains did not relent,
125 Nor yet were we unloosed of them, but hurlèd, meinyeit, ran,[259]
As none of us knew where he was nor wist how he was drawn.[260]

Beyond where that Aegean Sea does sigh and mourn so oft,
There lies an isle delectable, more pleasant, plain and soft
Than any other isle that is both wet and washed with sea,
130 Or warmèd with the sunny beams, or yet enflamèd be;
In midst thereof there is a hill of shadow full and green
With savour sweet and fragrant scent, with water sweet and clean,
Whose virtue is and whose effect to take out of the mind
All sad and pensive blots and marks that has with grief it pained.
135 This is the land wherewith so much fair Venus is content
Which consecrate was to that queen that time by men's consent,
Whiles as the truth was lying hid and verity unshown,
And Christ his incarnation was not revealed nor known,[261]
And yet albeit this day it be of virtue lean and bare,
140 Yet does it hold and it retains some customs keepèd there[262]
That seems to these, whose reason, love, and virtue do exclude
Both pleasant, sweet and very douce, and bitter to the good.[263]

There then triumphèd over us that sovereign gentle lord,
And carried at his golden chair there, coupled in a cord,
145 These whom he took in circling so the world round about,
E'en from the Indies to Thule Isle, the westmost part without.
There in that place he did expose his spoil, his prey and gain,
And from his bosom pullèd forth the lovers' thoughts most vain;[264]
He had their vanity in his arms, their sudden fleeing joy,
150 Their constant woe, their solid grief, their stable, firm annoy,
Their roses gathered in that time when winter's blast does boast,
Their ice e'en on the hottest days, at midsummer their frost,
He also had before him then distrust and doubtful hope,

---

[258] brayes] hillsides.
[259] meinyeit] mixed.
[260] wist] knew.
[261] By adding this line, Fowler clarifies Petrarch's meaning.
[262] keepèd] kept.
[263] douce] sweet.
[264] These two lines are Fowler's addition.

And backward on his shoulders then again he carried, bound with rope,
Repentance with displeasure sore, and anguish with annoy;[265]   155
    Most like the same that was in Rome and in the wasted Troy.
The valley where this Triumph was with murmur did rebound
    Of waters, brooks, of birds and fowls that gave a clamorous sound,
Whose banks were all embroiderèd with flowers of variant hue,
    Some white, some green, and some again red, yellow, and some blue;   160
And there, besides clear rivers, from so lively fountains ran
    Where then upon the cold, fresh herbs the sun to shine began,
There also was a shadow thick of trees both high and fair,
    Out of the which then did come out a sweet and breathing air;
And after, when the winter tide does make the season cold,   165
    Yet there the sun so does his flames most temperately unfold,
And so does make the place and ground and meets almost lukewarm,
    And through an idleness, all slow, the simple heart encharms.
And as that place so was the time and season then, I say,
    When as the equinoctial line does victor make the day,   170
And when that Procne laughs and chants, and does at morning spring,
    Returning to her sister then, on their lovers to sing.
O trustless stay, O stayless faith of all our chance and lot![266]
    For to resist or to withstand that lord it vailèd not[267]
Within that place, that season, time, and in that instant hour,   175
    Where Love required us from our eyes a larger due[268] to power.
He in that hour, that place and time, whom vulgar do adore,
    Would then triumph in chariot bright, as victor full of glore.
So there I saw what service he and servile Death does prove,
    And to what vengeance is he brought that is infect with Love.[269]   180
And since the time and place is shown, so will I now declare
    Which things were then placed round about his high triumphant chair:
First error, next deluding dreams, and deadly shapes and pale,[270]
    And false opinion at the port that does o'er minds prevail;
Then slippery hope and sliding trust was in the ladder steps,   185
    And damnèd gain with gaining lost, that casts men in mishaps;
The nature of the grace was such that they that highest went

---

[265] This long list of opposites related to love is a recurring topos in Petrarchan poetry.
[266] stayless] unstable.
[267] vailèd] availed.
[268] My emendation: the original has 'at larger dew', but the initial 'at' may be a scribal mistake. Petrarch has *più largo tributo*.
[269] vengeance] Here this translates the Italian *strazio* (extreme suffering, torture).
[270] The scribe highlights the opening lines of this, the most allegorical part of the vision of Love, by using small capitals for most of the virtues and vices.

The lower and the deeper down again was their descent.
Then wearied rest was on the high, and their repose in pain,
190   With open shame and glory obscure and duskish did remain.
Unfaithful faith, disloyal Love, and oaths but true in show,
    Solistful fury, madful care, and reason sweet and slow,[271]
Twix these a preiss it was to which we came by open way,
    But narrowly with straitness pain our out-gate did assay;
195 The steps thereof and entries was both downward sliding quick,
    The passage out and going forth was high and rare unthick;[272]
Within was all confusion and trouble mixed with annoy,
    A fray of certain woe and dole and of uncertain joy.
These ills did never broil so fast nor bray in burning rage,
200   Of Vulcan, Ischia, Lipari, whose flames none can assuage,
Nor Stromboli with Etna mount, Mountgibell called by name,[273]
    As did that place and prison strong combur in burning flame.[274]
So that I think he hates himself and less himself does love
    That would by practice know that yoke and by his peril prove.

205 Within that cage and dungeon dark, that prison stark and strong,
    We captivate were prisoners and there enclosèd long,
Where that my hair and wonted flight were turned by Time's eclipse,
    And unto paleness all the fresh and ruddiness of my lips,
So that my soul, so touched with care for that, her freedom past,
210   Which great desire makes prompt and light, was comforted at last
When as it spied (though but in dream) these things so hard and strange,
    Coequal with my state and place and so go in their change;
But viewing there so many sprites which in that pit did wun,[275]
    My piteous heart did melt like snow so set against the sun;
215 And like as one who in short time does view some pictures long,
    Wherein are draught and variant lines and stories them among,
With one foot forward goeth on, yet after with his ee[276]
    Does backward look, with better sight, the more to mark and see:
E'en so did I there cast my eyes and roll them round about,
220   The more perfectly for to view that band again and rout.[277]

---

[271] Solistful] anxious, solicitous. madful] mad.
[272] rare unthick] really narrow. 'Rare' is here used as an adverb.
[273] Petrarch uses *Mongibello*, the Sicilian-Arabic name for Etna.
[274] combur] burn.
[275] wun] dwell (cf. German *wohnen*).
[276] ee] eye.
[277] As is his custom, Fowler concludes with two lines of his own invention.

The second Triumph called the Triumph of Chastity

When then I saw e'en at one time and in the self-same place
    The courage daunted of the gods whom Love did so deface,
And likewise with these gods, e'en those who mortal men were called,
    And to the world did live like saints subduéd all and thralled,[278]
By their estate and guilty fall I did example take   5
    And by their losses and their harms this profit did I make.
So thereby comfort came to me, which eased me of my woe,
    When as I spied me tread that trace when gods and men did go:
For there I saw and did behold fair Phoebus full of glore,[279]
    With Cupids bow and with his dart lie stricken very sore;   10
With him also that lusty youth, Leander, Hero's love,[280]
    The one a god, the other a man, and so his death did prove.
I likewise saw within one snare with Juno Dido led,
    Who for the woe her husband dead her vital blood forth shed;
Not as the public voice does bruit, or common fame does tell,   15
    Because Aeneas went his way and would not with her dwell.
Thus seeing then wherefore should I regret, or yet lament,
    Or yet bewail my freedom lost, or yet seem malcontent,
If now I be by Love o'ercome whilst as I was but armes,[281]
    Young, reckless, and not well advised, unaware of all my harms,   20
Or wherefore should I then complain if Love and not my love,
    Or might not make my friendly foe his puissant power prove,[282]
Nor yet have I just cause of dole that there I saw again
    Love in habit naked, spoiled, so poorly there remain,
Bereavèd of his feathered wings, and spoilèd of his flight,   25
    Though sorrow made me to complain for to behold that sight.

And thus when Cupid soon espied,[283] e'en as wild lions two
    With roaring rumour other beasts in rage rencounter so,
Or as two thundering thunderbolts down dingeth here and there[284]
    All things, they find where'er they light in heaven, earth, and air,   30

---

[278] thralled] enthralled.
[279] glore] glory.
[280] Petrarch only refers to the young man of Abydos.
[281] armes] poor, defenceless. Though unattested in both OED and DOST, the word does appear in MED as the adjective 'arm'; it has twenty-three attestations with this meaning, though all of them are early (eleventh–twelfth century). Compare modern German *arm*.
[282] These two lines are Fowler's rather convoluted translation of Petrarch's *se la mia nemica Amor non strinse* (if Love did not capture my enemy, i.e. Laura).
[283] The grammatical subject is 'I'.
[284] down dingeth] cast down.

No otherwise I Cupid spied address him to my dame
    With all the arguments he might her to his yoke reclaim.
But she upon the other part against him did proceed
    With swifter course, so that she passed both wind and fire through speed.
35 No greater sound, more terrible, did Etna mountain make
    E'en at that time Enceladus the giant it does shake;
Nor Scylla with Charybdis seas so rages in their ire,
    That day nor night their sturdy storms do other waste or tire,
Than was e'en at the first conflict for to be seen and heard,
40   So full of doubt was that assault, it cannot be declared;
Then every man retired himself unto the highest place
    The better for to mark and view who, in that cruel case
And enterprise so horrible, victorious most should be,
    With heart and eyes of plaster made, such success for to see.[285]
45 This conqueror who first did prease to give the first onset[286]
    Did take in his right hand his dart, in left his bow did get,
Then for to put my dame in fray and in a greater fear
    He had already bended it and drawn it to his ear.
And this did he so hastily that not the flying heart
50   More speedily to ford and wood his course does so convert,
Pursuéd by the leopard dischargéd of his chain,[287]
    Or yet that in the wildest woods in freedom does remain;
Yea, they had both been late and slow there in respect of Love,
    Who, with his visage full of flames, did fast him forwards move.

55 There might be seen, within my breast which all was set in fire,
    A sore conflict and doubtful fight twixt pity and desire.
Desire me moved for to desire that Love should victor be
    And that my dame by him subdued I might my marrow see;
But pity then did plead remorse, and caused me say again
60   It pity were, and hard to see my Laura so lie slain.[288]
Yet virtue that does never from the virtuous folk estrange[289]
    E'en at that instant show herself that she does never change,
Nor yet them leave who trust in her, though some thereby her blame,
    From whom she has herself withdrawn, to lodge them next their shame.
65 Was never such a scrimeur then so able was and quick[290]

---

[285] plaster] Thus Fowler translates the Italian *smalto*, enamel.
[286] prease] strive.
[287] Leopards could be kept for hunting, and thus chained.
[288] Once again, unlike Petrarch, who never mentions her, Fowler uses Laura's name.
[289] This line is highlighted by the scribe.
[290] scrimeur] swordsman (from the French *escrimeur*; Petrarch has *schermidor*).

> For to award or to eschew the blow, the stogg and prick;[291]
Was never mariner so prompt, nor so ready a hand
> To turn the ship forth of the rocks, and from the sinking sand.
There was my lady Laura fair, who with a bold defence,
> With honesty and shamefastness did let his high pretence; 70
She suddenly her visage fair did from his strikes so hide,
> That she both sharp and eagerly did Love's assaults abide.
I was that time with eyes attent and bent for to behold[292]
> The success and the end of this great fight and battle bold,
And hoping that the victory should fall on Cupid's side, 75
> Where it is wont, and not from Love herself does oft divide.
And in this hope I so became then through too much desire,
> E'en as a man unmeasurably who does some thing require,
And first his suit first put in writ, or he to speak begin,
> And in his eyes and forehead has his tongue and talk within. 80
'I would,' I say, 'O thou, my lord, if thou me worthy think,
> That with this dame if thou o'ercome I chainèd were and link.[293]
Fear not I swerve from thy empire, or yet myself shall free
> Forth of these knots, wherewith thou hast so bound and coupled me.'
Whilst thus I spoke and this did say, I saw my dame again, 85
> With face depainted full of ire and full of proud disdain,
Demure within her countenance, sad, sober and so grave,
> That no man is to show the same or able to conceive,
Although his wits were singular and almost all divine;
> How then can I the same display, that is of base engine? 90
For there it might have well besene Cupido's golden darts,[294]
> That kindled were in fiery flames, and wasted so men's hearts,
Through outward blast of beauty brave, with honesty quite quenched,
> And through the coldness of my dame his ardent pleasures staunched.
So great her mind and courage was, with valour of the same, 95
> That neither was the Volscian queen, nor Amazonian dame
That did support the Trojans and the Greeks of life bereft,
> And usèd ay for to combat and shoot ay with the left;[295]

---

[291] stogg] stab.
[292] attent] attentive.
[293] link] linked.
[294] besene] Meikle reads this as a scribal error for 'been seen' (Meikle, III. 89).
[295] This time Fowler omits Petrarch's explicit reference to Camilla (the Volscian queen); he is faithful to Petrarch's description of the Amazons as female warriors, but misunderstands Petrarch's reference to *la sinistra sola intera mamma* (alluding to the story alleging that Amazonian warriors would cut and cauterize their right breast in order to shoot more easily).

In any point of worthiness with Laura to be compared,
100   Whose valour far surpassed them both that I afore declared:[296]
Not Caesar great, that worthy wight who in Pharsalia field
           Defeated Pompey with his host, and made him to him yield,
Was ne'er so sharp nor ardenter or bolder on his foes,
           Than was my dame in contrare him who does all armour lose.[297]

105 With her then armèd were at once e'en all the virtues fair;
           O, what a heav'nly company and glorious troop was there!
They progressed so in this their pomp and brave triumphant band,
           All pair and pair, and two with two, and marching hand in hand;
Upon the vanguard there was placed high honesty,[298] that dame
110   With shamefastness who trimly did conduct and guide the same,
Two noble virtues of great praise, and in themselves divine,
           Which made my lady Laura fair above the rest to shine.
Wit then with modesty ensued, and were their neighbours next,
           Delight and good behaviour, who in her were fixed;[299]
115 Then perseverance marchèd on, and glory came behind,
           Entreaty fair[300] with good advice of a foreseeing mind.
And round about that valiant dame they were in middle guard,
           Rare courtesy and cleanliness for which she much ay cared.
Then fear of shame, desire of glory, and thoughts in youthful age,[301]
120   And concord rare (within this world) all rancour to assuage;
In rear-guard true Chastity and Beauty brave did go,
           And in this sort my lady fair went to her fighting so,
Against that sovereign lord of Love with full intent to win,
           With favour of the heavens and all the blissed souls therein.
125 And as my eyes unable were their fullness to behold,
           So is my tongue the meanest part thereof for to unfold.[302]

There saw I this clear company from Love and from his bands
           A thousand thousand famous souls[303] spoil by their spoiling hands,

---

[296] These two lines are Fowler's addition.
[297] in contrare him] against him.
[298] All the virtues listed in the following lines are highlighted by the scribe.
[299] While the line makes good sense, the metre is defective, suggesting that after 'her' a word (possibly 'eyes') might be missing.
[300] Thus Fowler renders *Bella Accoglienza*, Petrarch's version of *Bel Accueil* from the *Roman de la Rose*.
[301] With the oxymoron 'youthful age' Fowler translates Petrarch's *canuti* (aged, white-haired).
[302] This line is Fowler's addition.
[303] Following Meikle's suggestion, I thus emend what in the manuscript is 'sonnes'.

And shake and stripe forth of the same with victors' voice and psalms,
    A thousand thousand branches brave of clear victorious palms.   130
That sudden fall and overthrow was never then so strange
    To Hannibal that victor long, who did the Romans range,
And sixteen years in Italy did brangill their estate,[304]
    And in the end by Scipio was vanquished and defait.[305]
Nor yet that giant Goliath with fear was more abashed   135
    When that the Hebrew child his brains and head with stones had dashed;[306]
No Cyrus more astonishéd when that widow came
    And killèd him and all his rout with lasting glory and fame;
As then that time appeared Love who stood e'en in that place,
    Resembling him who now is whole, but in a little space   140
Is suddenly in sickness brought, with wonder is amazed
    To see his welfare and his health so suddenly upraised;
Or e'en as one who touched for dole for things he not foresees,
    Does with his hands both wipe and rub shame forth out of his eyes.
Love even so did there remain, yea, in a worser state,[307]   145
    For all his forces and his folks were bravely there defeat.

There might be seen then in his face both dolour, dread, and fear,
    And at one trait both shame and ire and anger great appear.
The stormy seas not rages so when they so angry grow,
    And by their contrary wind tides their borders do o'erflow,   150
Not yet that isle Inarime which lies on Tipheus' back,[308]
    Which he with boiling foaming rage and painful pain does shake;
Nor yet Mountgibell brayeth so when that Enceladus sighs,
    And bursteth forth his raging sobs from boldened breast and lighs,[309]
As Love did then both chafe and rage, and sighingly did plain,[310]   155
    To see himself and all his folks discomfited remain.
Thus passéd this great company so glorious in their train,
    That for to tell their valiancy my tongue I must restrain;
I am unable that charge to take, lest I their praise impair.
    I therefore turn unto my dame and to the rest were there.   160

---

[304] brangill] shake.
[305] defait] defeated. Fowler adds the name of Scipio, while Petrarch simply alludes to the young Roman.
[306] Fowler makes Petrarch's allusion to Goliath explicit (in the original he is simply 'that great Philistine', *quel gran filisteo*).
[307] worser] far worse.
[308] Inarime] The ancient name for the island of Ischia.
[309] lighs] lungs.
[310] plain] complain.

She had that time upon her back a glorious gown of white,
        And in her hand that crystal targe that wrought Medusa spite,[311]
And in the same a pillar was erect of jasper stone,
        Wherein a chain of diamonds were placèd one by one
165 And topazes mixt in the midst which virtuous dames did use;
        But now no more they keep that use, since they themselves abuse.[312]
There saw I her before my ene so fast Cupido tie,
        And plaguing him so cruelly where he did vanquished lie,[313]
That surely then it seemed to me the vengeance too too much,
170   But yet I was content therewith and thereat did not grouch.
My wits are weak, my Muse too slow, and slender my engine
        To pen the number of these dames and virgins most divine;
Nor Clio with Calliope and all these of that sect[314]
        Be able what these ladies were to show or yet detect
175 Of many yet few shall suffice and of these will I tell
        Who on the top of honesty and dignity did dwell.

Amongst the number of these dames that stately there did stand
        Was fair Lucretia, first in place, and kept the right hand,
To whom Penelope was next, who by her force and might
180   Despoilèd Love of all his arms and of his wingèd flight;[315]
And reaving from that forward lord his quaver, bow, and darts,
        They crushed, they burst, they threw and broke them in a thousand parts.
Then next approached Virginia; with her, her father fierce,
        Armed with disdain and pity, and with a blade to pierce
185 And wound his chastely daughter's breast, which both to her and Rome
        Brought change of state, and by her death their freedoms both did come.

Then afterward the German dames marched forward in that band,
        Who for to save their chastity did in themselves put hand:
Juditha chaste, that Hebrew dame and widow wise and strong,
190   Was with these other dainty dames triumphing them among;
Next her that brave courageous dame that Hippo height by name,[316]

---

[311] In this brief ekphrasis all precious and symbolic materials (crystal, jasper, etc.) are highlighted by the scribe. targe] a light shield.
[312] Fowler omits Petrarch's reference to the fact that the chain of diamonds and topazes has been dipped in Lethe, meaning that the virtues symbolized by the stones are no longer practised.
[313] ene] eyes.
[314] i.e. the Muses.
[315] Despoiled] The manuscript has 'bespoyled'.
[316] Once again, Fowler adds the name of the heroine.

> To save her body undefiled and free herself from shame,
Did with a valiant worthy mind her hard mishap to save
> That to her chaste and comely corpse she made the sea her grave.
With her and other blessèd saints I saw triumph in glore 195
> My dame and love who o'er the world had first triumphed before.

Amongst the same I there perceived the Vestal virgin chaste,
> Fair Tuccia who falsely was by infamy disgraced,
Who for to purge her of the same this miracle did give:
> She brought from Tiber flood to church forth water in a sieve.[317] 200
And after her Hersilia, that brave Sabinian dame,
> Whose worthiness does every book and story forth proclaim.
With her was these, her country maids, whom Romans through defeat
> Had ravished to be their wives for to prolong their state.
And there, amongst these strangers also I her did there espy 205
> That for her faithful loving spouse did take her death thereby.
Let then the vulgar people peace, it Dido is, I say,[318]
> Who for the dole of Sicheus' death she put herself away;
Though Virgil write and public bruit by Aeneas do her shame,
> It was but care of honesty that pushed her to the same. 210
And in the end there, pressed in place, one who did her enclose
> Within a place at Arno side, but she her time did lose,
For what she would effectuate and purpose bring to pass
> Her honest thoughts and chasteful mind by force impeachèd was.[319]

This valiant and victorious band went forward in that time 215
> When that the winter waxèd hot, and spring was in his prime;
And so they all passed joyfully together in that way,
> Where that the saltish watery waves do break on Baiae's bay.
And so they walkèd on apace and towards the right hand
> They marchèd on, till they did come unto that solid land, 220
From whence betwixt these mountains two of Barbary and Averne[320]
> They progressed on, till they did come unto Sibylla's derne.[321]
And further off they passèd on, until Linterno fort,
> In which so solitary a place that great man did resort
And chieftain brave, who has his name from Africa with praise, 225

---

[317] The story of the virgin Tuccia (once again unnamed by Petrarch) is also evoked in the Sieve Portrait of Queen Elizabeth I.
[318] peace] be silent.
[319] The poet is here alluding to Piccarda Donati, celebrated by Dante in *Purgatorio*, III.
[320] Averne] Avernus.
[321] derne] Attested in *DOST*, with the meaning of a secret hiding place.

For that he was the first who there did by his sword make ways;
Who did not there in any sort diminish or abate
By his renown and purchased glory the newness of their state,
But with his eyes most pleasantly them pleased with merry cheer,
230 And she that was most chaste in life most fairest did appear.[322]
In others' pomp it would him grieved so in their bands to walk[323]
Who only was (if men's belief be not in vain and talk)
The only man born to triumph and thereto to aspire,
And only bred to countries win and conquer an empire.
235 Whereafter they and all arrived unto that sovereign town,
And first unto that holy church, so famous by renown,
Which chaste Sulpicia had erected and to that end did frame
To quench within the mind of man, all mad and raging flame.[324]
And after they their progress made unto that church whose name
240 Is Chastity, that honourable and most renownèd dame,
Who kindleth in a gentle heart chaste will and high desire,
Not of the vulgar sort, but such as unto praise aspire.

Where in that church that glorious dame did all her spoil expose
Before that goddess' goodly feet, and there likewise depose
245 Victorious leaves and sacred palms which she before had tane[325]
And reft from Love that to her glory the same might there remain.
There was with her that Tuscan youth, Spurinna height by name,
That magled had his visage fair for to eschew defame,[326]
Whose beauty was of such great force all women to subdue,
250 That they were win all to his Love at his first blink and view.
There did that youth with Laura fair display and did unhide
His bloody wounds and magled cheeks with Chastity to bide.
With her compered many more whose names my guide did know,[327]
And at the time of their Triumph he did them to me show
255 Who did despise Cupido's force and power in that band,
And whom among fair Hippolite and Joseph just did stand.[328]

---

[322] This whole line is highlighted by the scribe.
[323] Fowler here appears to misunderstand Petrarch, who writes that Scipio Africanus was not displeased in following another's (i.e. Chastity's) triumph.
[324] The temple of Venus Verticordia, which was dedicated by the paragon of Roman chastity, the matron Sulpicia.
[325] tane] taken.
[326] magled] disfigured (attested in *DOST*).
[327] compered] appeared.
[328] This time the translator does not add concluding lines, as is his habit.

The third Triumph of Death

Chap. 1

This stately, brave, and well disposed, this gallant, glorious dame,
    That is a naked sprite and piece of earth within the same,[329]
Who sometimes was the pillar high, the fortress full of store
    Of valour and of worthiness, returnèd back with glore,[330]
Most joyfully from these her wars,[331] triumphing o'er her foe,   5
    That all the world does with his craft and his deceit o'erthrow;
And not with other arms or strength this foe she has subvert[332]
    Than with a visage fair and mild, and with a chastely heart,
With thoughts most poor, with speech most wise, with language most discreet,
    That ay were friends to honesty with shamefastness replete.   10

A wonder great it was to see a thing both strange and rare:
    The arms, the bow, the shafts of Love, for to lie broken there.
And round about him to espy so many there lie slain,
    With many captived prisoners that did in life remain.
This lady with her chosen folk back making their retreat   15
    From her triumphant victory marched under cloth of state;[333]
In number few her people were, this is no strange to hear,
    Because that true and solid glory is seldom seen appear.[334]
Yet everyone who was with her deservèd worthy praise,
    In history, in lofty verse, in stately style and phrase.   20

At that time was their ensign within a field of green
    An ermine white depainted was, all lily white and clean,
Whose neck did bear a topaz chain, inset with finest gold,
    To witness well that purity which they did always hold.
No human pace nor earthly steps their walking was and trace,   25
    But heav'nly all, and all their words were full of heav'nly grace.
O blessed be these, well be these blessed, and happy thrice again,
    That to such destiny created be, and such good fate sustain!
As twinkling stars they all appeared, in midst a sun of light,

---

[329] piece] My emendation. The manuscript has 'peace'.
[330] glore] glory.
[331] My emendation; the manuscript reads 'wayes'.
[332] subvert] subverted, overcome.
[333] Fowler misunderstands Petrarch's *drappelletto* (a small group, a small company), reading it as a diminutive of *drappo* (cloth, flag).
[334] This line is highlighted by the scribe.

30	Decoring them e'en with these beams which dazzled not their sight.[335]

Their heads with garlands were bedecked, of red incarnate rose,
    With violets of bravest hues and flowers of bravest choice;
And as a noble gentle heart great glory does obtain,
    So did this joyful company with joy each footstep train.

35 When then I saw e'en suddenly a banner borne of black,
    And in the same of that same hue a furious woman shake,
Sad, pale, obscure and senseless, she appeared, alas, to me,
    With furies wrapped and furies worn at that time seemèd she,
The sight hereof so hideous was as scarcely I can tell
40   If such a sight at Phlegia was when that the giants fell.[336]
Then did this grisly, ghostly ghost address her to my dame,
    With trotting trace and hasty voice did call her by her name:
'O lady fair, that so does go decored with youth and grace,
    And does not know of this thy life the fixèd term and space,
45 I she am, she, that importune and cruel called by you,
    Who are a people deaf and blind, and makes all creatures bow,
Who fearfully does all arrest, e'en by my force and might,
    That shortens the day and hastens before or evening come the night.
I she am, she, that has convoyed the Greeks unto their end,
50   The Trojans and the Romans too I have made to descend
Within their dreadful grave and tomb by this, my fatal brand,
    That shears and slays, that pricks and cuts, and killeth out of hand,
With many other people more, both barbar, gross and strange,[337]
    Arriving first before they know their life for death to change,
55 Ransacking all their pensive thoughts, long lodgèd in their mind,
    And breaking down their vain conceits to Death they have declined;
And now to you when you must list to live in life so long,
    I do address my deadly curse with deadly dart and strong,
Before dame fortune with her wheel in some unhappy hour,
60   With luckless hap o'ercross your hope and mixed your sweet with sour.'

Then answered she, who was within this world only one:
    'Thou hast not in these companies no right, nor reason none;
Thou may in me far less pretend but if that thou wilt have
    The only spoil is that thou shalt my corpse convoy to grief.

---

[335] Decoring them] decorating, illuminating them.
[336] The Phlegrean plain is mentioned in classical poetry as the place where the giants fought against the gods of Olympus. Sidney has, more correctly, Phlegra, while Morley refers more generically to the fall of the giants, and Hume drops the reference altogether.
[337] barbar] barbarous.

But there is one who shall have more displeasure by my death, 65
    For in my welfare and my health depends his life and breath;
It shall to me most thankful be from this world to go,
    Which is the port of misery and harbour for our woe.'
Then, as a man who bends his eyes on uncouth things and new,
    And seeing them more than first he spieth far otherwise ensue, 70
With wonder is astonishèd, and then himself does blame,
    So does this fierce and cruel Death with wonder pause for shame.
And as by chance she mused awhile, these words at length she spak:[338]
    'I know the time wherein my teeth are dressed to spoil and sack',
So afterward with calm face, less ugly than before, 75
    She thus began to speak, 'O dame adornèd so with glore,
That does conduct this chastely band yet, though thou has not known
    My poisoned shafts and deadly darts which many has o'erthrown;
If to my counsel at this time thou both give trust and ear,
    What I enforce is for the best, and so it shall appear, 80
Old, hoary, loathsome, crookèd age I far from thee shall chase,
    With all the cares and fashereis that do with age recrease;[339]
I am resolved and purposed now such honour thee to do,
    Save thee, to none was ne'er before such favour shown unto.
Thou shalt exchange thy life for death, thy sprite shall part, but fear 85
    No sorrow thereby shall thou feel, nor dolour shall thee deir.'[340]
This earthly saint this spoke again: 'E'en as it pleases the lord
    That stands in heav'n to rule from thence all things in good accord,
Who governeth all this universe and rules this massive round,
    Do he to me and in such sort as other folks has found'. 90

Thus, as she spoke, then suddenly, behold! the spacious place
    Was quickly with dead bodies filled, whom Death did so deface.
The number was so huge and great as none could have them penned,
    Suppose he should in prose and verse them prease to comprehend,[341]
Of India, Cathay with Morocco, and of Spain, 95
    Of all these people was the midst replenished with the plain,
The lowest parts and hollow place the multitude upfilled,
    Whom Death with longer tract of Time had cruelly so killed.

There was these men whom men most called most happy and most blessed,
    Triumphant kings and emperors and popes, whose feet men kissed, 100

---

[338] spak] spoke.
[339] fashereis] troubles, annoyance. recrease] increase.
[340] deir] hurt.
[341] prease] strive.

Who now lies spoilèd of their pomp and scant does plague their pride,
    And poorer are than beggars be who oft for crumbs has cried.
Now tell me then, where is their wealth, where is their glory great?
    Where are their gems and precious stones, and sceptres of estate,
105 Where are they now, where are they gone, where are their princely crowns,
    Where are their forkèd mitres now, where are their purple gowns?
O wretched he, and miser more, that fixes so his trust
    On mortal things to which all men that mortal be have lust.
But who is he that does not so? yet they shall be in end
110   With reason, justly scorned and scuffed that to that course did tend.
O blinded folk to toss you so, what joy can you befall?
    Unto your mother old you must return, both one and all,[342]
And then your titles and your styles shall so obscurèd lie
    That you shall all forgotten be, none shall you have thereby.
115 Then tell me now, for what effect do you your care intend,
    Although one gain for thousand pains do to you rise in end?
Who does not see [that] all is vain, a folly flat expressed?
    Or what avails that by your force such countries be possessed,
Which are not yours, and tributary to make the stranger's soil,[343]
120   With damage of your corpse and soul, that for your sins shall thole?[344]
Or, after perilous enterprise, both bloody, vain, and wrong,
    To purchase land by loss of blood, that does you not belong,
Or yet to make and gather gold and so your hands defile?
    It better for your souls had been to live with bread this while,
125 And water more had you beseemed, rough trees and brittle glass
    Had more beset than gems and gold, in which your glory was.
But now will I draw in my sails, and to my purpose turn,
    Which is the subject of my woe that makes me so to mourn.

So when I say the hour was come, alas, that latter hour
130   Of that her short and glorious life which Death did so devour,
Wherein she must that doubtful pace and passage than assay,
    Whereof the fearful world stands in dread and in a fray,
There came a troop of valorous dames, a band so chaste and fair,
    To see if this fair lady lived, or Death her life would spare.
135 About her bed they gathered them, to mark and view the end
    To which but once but no more oft, must all incline and tend;
As all his friends and neighbours near, her beauty did behold,

---

[342] your mother old] Nature.
[343] tributary] paying a tribute.
[344] corpse] Here in the sense of 'body'. thole] suffer.

Death rooted up and did dissolve her hair as fine as gold,³⁴⁵
So that the chosen fairest flower that in this world did sprout
    Death foully to the world's disgrace did rive and pull it out.   140
Nor for to hate, nor yet envy that he to it did bear,
    But that in things most excellent his power might appear.
Sore sad laments and sparpled tears, deep sighs and ruthful cries³⁴⁶
    Was there amongst these women all that rave to ruth the skies.
O, what a heartbreak was it to see these eyes so fair and bright,   145
    For which I many a sonnet made, to lose their lucent light.
Betwixt so many scalding sighs, and heavy lays of woe,
    Betwixt so many shrilling shouts, and sobs in number more,
That heav'nly dame, that lady fair, did peacely sit but bruit³⁴⁷
    And of her virtues' deeds did reap the glorious gain and fruit.   150

'O mortal goddess, go thou hence, in peace dost thou depart!'
    So said the people who were there, with sad and mournful heart.
'What shall become or yet befall to other mortal wights,
    Since such a dame has burnt and freezed and past in such few nights?'
Their speech, forsooth, deservèd praise but it not much availed   155
    Against that Death that in her rage so roughly her assailed.
O trustless hope of human things! O hope both blind and vane!
    Uncertain are thou in thy course, and so shall ay remain.

If that for pity of her death the earth was washed with tears,
    As he best knows who saw it so, so let him think that hears.   160
It was the sixth day of April, thereof the primal hour,
    In which my fervent flame began, by Cupid's puissant power,
And look what hour she did me in her loyal love ensnare.
    The selfsame Time now by her death renewèd has my care,
At that same day that has me bound the same has set me free,   165
    As fortune in her fickle course her style does change, we see.

None ever yet did so complain, none ever so bewailed
    His freedom lost or dreadful Death that over him prevailed,
Than I of this my liberty, brought by her loss of life,
    Whose thread by greater right should been first cut by fatal knife;   170

---

³⁴⁵ Petrarch speaks of *un aureo crine*, a single golden hair, possibly alluding to an analogous passage in Virgil's *Aeneid*, in which Dido's death is described (IV. 698–99); see Virgilio, *Eneide*, ed. by Rosa Calzecchi Onesti (Turin: Einaudi, 1967), p. 158. Fowler misunderstands or simplifies the passage.
³⁴⁶ sparpled] scattered.
³⁴⁷ peacely] peacefully.

For thou should first, O Death, me killed, my debt by age was due,
    That foremost stood upon that front from which her glory grew.
Who can believe my doleful woe, my dolour and my care,
    My sadness and my loud laments, my sorrow and despair?
175 No, none there is imagine may the greatness of the same;
    How then can I in prose and verse them boldly forth proclaim?

These ladies fair that stood about that lady's chastely bed,[348]
    With woeful woe, with mourning moan, and cheeks with tears o'erspread,
Began to cry: 'Now, now, alas, dame virtue is decayed,
180   Fair beauty[349] now has lost her lamp, and courtesy is a-strayed.
Woe, woe, alas, who shall us save, what shall become of us?
    Since she is dead what shall we hope? who shall this doubt discuss?
Who ever saw in such a dame such perfect proofs of praise?
    Who ever heard so sweet a speech, so full of wit always?
185 Who ever heard or yet did see, though he should live so long,
    From such an angel angel's voice so angelic a song?'[350]

Her sprite, before it did depart from bosom of her rest,
    And from that place which too, too short it shortly had possessèd,[351]
With all his virtues and his gifts conjoinèd unto one
190   Did light the air in every part, and clear the heav'ns anon.
Nor none of all the furious sprites durst then once undertake
    For to compare before that dame with visage foul and black,
Before, alas, that dreadful Death, that dame, but blame or fault,
    Upon her chastely comely corpse had finished his assault.
195 But after they had end their plaints and left their loud lament,
    And by despair were made secure, they had their eyes all bent
Upon her visage meek and mild, and marked her angel's face
    Most beautiful, most angelic, and full of heav'nly grace.[352]

Not as a fire, or flaming flame blown out by bustling blast,
200   But as a spark that through herself consumes and dieth last,
And as we see a sweet clear light that cometh to decay,
    Whose nourishing by piece and piece does softly wear away,
And to the end his ancient use and customs keep each on,

---

[348] chastely] chaste.
[349] This word is highlighted by the scribe (a very rare occurrence in this chapter).
[350] The repetition of 'angel' is necessary for metrical purposes, so cannot be attributed to a scribal mistake. Fowler probably means 'from the angelic voice of such an angel'.
[351] This line does not appear in the original.
[352] These two lines do not appear in the original.

So to his fading dying life her dying day drew on,
And so but pain, so died my dame, her life so passed and went, 205
    Her heav'nly soul to heav'nly rest in peace did part content.
Not pale that lovely lady lay, but whiter than the snow,
    Which gathered is in flakes but wind, and does together row;
And as a man through travel long and exercise is faint,
    In such a sort my lady lay when Death did her attaint. 210
Her soul then being parted so, that which made foolish men
    Call ugly Death, a pleasant sleep did in his eyes seem then,
So that the deadly monster wild that does all folk disgrace
    Did then appear most beautiful within my lady's face.[353] 110

The second chapter of the Triumph of Death

The night that after did ensue this woeful, ugly chance,
    That Death my dame so suddenly did to her grave advance,
That night in manner made the sun his lucent light to lose,[354]
    And sped him from the earth in haste, in heaven to repose.
So being left, I knew not well whose footsteps for to train; 5
    I lost my guide and I did like a blinded man remain.[355]

When that the sweet and summer frost was sparpled by the air,[356]
    And while Aurora did begin again to earth repair,
That does despoil and take away, e'en by her wholesome streams,
    The coverture and mantle braid of false confusèd dreams; 10
E'en at that time a lady fair did to my sight appear,
    Resembling right on every point the season of the year.
She was bedecked with precious pearls and crowned with orient stones;
    Yes, crowned she was with thousand crowns of jewels brave at once,
Who, moving softly in herself, she towards me did walk, 15
    And lovingly besides my side did set her down to talk.
And stretching out her pleasant hand, that hand so long desired,
    She, sighing, speaking, yield it forth and me to speak required;
From whence has risen the pleasant joy and that eternal bliss
    That in my woeful heavy heart so long so lodgèd is. 20

---

[353] In the second half of his translation Fowler is generally more faithful to the original: amplification occurs without normally adding extra lines, and at the end of each chapter he tends not to add concluding couplets, as he does in previous chapters.
[354] in manner] in a way.
[355] Petrarch's three opening lines are amplified into six.
[356] sparpled] scattered.

'Knowest thou not her', thus spoke my dame, 'who first thy wandering pace
  Has turned aside from vulgar way and from the vulgar race?
Knowest thou not her who thee withheld from that which youth did rage,
  Whose chastely heart both caused thy love and also thy lust did assuage?'[357]
25 This pensive dame, in deeds most wise and in her acts discreet,
  Sat down where meekly she did me to sit with her entreat.
It was a pleasing bank, that place whereon we then reposed,
  With laurel green and branchly beech o'ershadowed all and closed.

Then answered I, e'en as a man who speaking sheds his tears,
30 And through the greatness of his grief his tongue from talk forbears:[358]
'O Laura, thou! O lady fair! O goddess of my mind,
  My eyes do know thee very well, O glore of womankind!
Tell me, my dame, tell, heav'nly soul, from whence my grace does grow,
  If thou be living, or yet dead, because I long to know.'
35 'I am in life, not dead,' says she, 'I live and thou is dead,
  And shall be, while the later hour that Death to earth thee lead.
And now, for that the time is short, our will is always long,
  I counsel that thou it, that so thou go not wrong.[359]
Lose not the bridle to the same, thy speech to good employ,
40 Before the day that draweth near thee to thy grave convoy.'
Then I in end repliéd thus, 'Tell me, my heav'nly dame,
  That now in life and death has proven the practice of the same,
And knowest the proof what is to live and what to die again,
  If Death a thing so fearful be, or yet so full of pain'.
45 Then answered she: 'So long as thou with vulgar folk will hold,
  Whose judgement is ay wavering and to their will enthralled,
And their opinions so embrace, that blind are, hard and old,
  Thou never happy shall be named, nor blissèd shall be called.

To noble sprites and gentle minds Death is the end of care,
50 Of prison strong, of dungeons dark, of dolour and despair;
But unto these who has their thoughts so fixed on earthly things,
  To such, eternal noy and sturt and sorrow Death in-brings.[360]
And this, my woeful doleful death, for which thou has lament,

---

[357] These two lines appear to be the result of a misreading on Fowler's part. In Petrarch there is no second question on Laura's part; rather, the lover sees her as he had seen her with his youthful heart.
[358] This line is Fowler's addition.
[359] After the first 'thou', a word is missing, with a space left to fill it in.
[360] noy] annoy. sturt] discord.

For which thou has so many tears so vainly shed and spent,
I am assured should comfort thee, and quite efface thy noy, 55
If that thou felt the thousand part of this, my heav'nly joy.'

When thus she spoke she cast her eyes unto the highest heaven,
And then her rosy lips were closed, and I, to purpose driven:
'O dame,' said I, 'these tyrants strong, that ruled that last empire,
As Silla, Marius, Nero wild that set all Rome in fire, 60
Caligula, Maxentius with murder so acquent,[361]
That daily so to torture men all torments did invent;
The burning boiling fevers hot, the sickness in the breast,
The soreness in the limbs and nerves, that so does men molest,
Make Death for to accounted be with every one and all 65
Abhorrèd be, and so esteemed more bitter than the gall.'

'I cannot well deny', says she, 'but that the pain and woe
That goeth before or Death does come do make us think it so;[362]
But that which grieveth most of all it is that dreadful fear
To lose our long and lasting life, this is that most us dear. 70
But to the sprite that does in God his comfort all repose,
And to that heart that for his sins his weakness does disclose,
Unto that heart and to that sprite what Death can other be,
Than e'en a short and little sigh, as men do breathe, we see?
The proof thereof e'en by myself most plainly may be proven, 75
Who nearest was my latest course, or Death had me o'erthrown.[363]
When flesh was frail and body sick, and sprite more prompt again,
I heard with heavy sound a voice most heavily complain:
"O wretched he and miserable, that reckoneth Laura's days,[364]
To whom each one a thousand years appears to him always! 80
He every hour has such desire to visit her and see,
And if he see her not every hour, he cannot happy be!
He seeks for her through all the earth, but yet cannot her find,
And every hour and moment small he has her in his mind.
He seeks for her the foaming seas and searcheth all the banks, 85
The bays, the brayes, the brooks, the floods, the deep and watery stanks,[365]
Where'er he walks or holds his steps, ay holding still one style,

---

[361] acquent] acquainted.
[362] before or Death] before death.
[363] or] before.
[364] Laura's days] The days until the poet can see Laura again (Meikle, III. 15).
[365] brayes] hillsides. stanks] ponds. This line is not in the original, and well expresses Fowler's love for synonymic *copia*.

To think on her, to speak on her, and verse of her compile."
Then hearing thus, my fainting ee I turnèd to that side,[366]
90 From which that heavy sounding sound I heard and had espied;
And there perceived that gentle dame that long thy passions knew,
That thrust me forward in thy love, and backward thee withdrew.
The sugared words out from her mouth did make her known to me;
Her visage and her countenance did show the same was she
95 That oftentimes my woeful heart recomforted and glad,
When heaviness did it assail or sorrow made it sad.
She was acquent with our affairs, with wit she was replete,[367]
And faithful was she in our love, and at my death discreet.

And plainly now I will thee tell, e'en in my bravest state,
100 And in my green and growing years, to thee both brave and feat,
Which causèd has the thoughts and tongues of men to talk and think
In praise of that which was the chain that did in love us link,
That life which I that time then led more bitter was to me,
And sweeter then my gentle death, that has me made to die;
105 A thing most rare to mortal men, and strange it is to hear
That Death to me more better seemed than bitter did appear.
Because to me that passage was more joyful and content
Than he that from that exile is come and to his country went.[368]
The thing that only does me vex and most my mind does grieve
110 Is that thou in this wicked world so long, alas, shall live.'

Then answered I and spoke again: 'O precious pearl of praise,[369]
I thee adjure, by that same faith that all the world does blaze,
Which time, I trow, has manifest and openly does proclaim,
And now the more in sight of him that lives in lasting Fame,
115 Does more appear, whose eyes do pierce and see in every part,
Then tell me if thou ever had once pity on my smart,
Or on the pains that Love has lodged within my macered breast,[370]
Or of the thoughts that in such hudge did long my head molest,[371]
Not leaving of your chastely ways, nor honest enterprise,
120 Which you were wont for to oppone against my ruthful cries;[372]

---

[366] ee] eyes.
[367] acquent] acquainted.
[368] The use of the verb 'be' as an auxiliary of 'come' is common in Middle Scots.
[369] Thus Fowler renders Petrarch's *Madonna*.
[370] macered] macerated, tormented.
[371] hudge] *DOST* explains 'hudge' as a great quantity.
[372] oppone] oppose.

For that your pleasant, gracious ire, and these, your sweet disdains,
    So mixed with love and then with heat, redoubling so my pains,
Together with the platt of peace imprinted in your eyes,[373]
    The seals of grace, the nest of bliss that all my sorrow sees,
Did hold so long my hot desires in such uncertain sort,   125
    As ay my mind does stand in doubt, despairing of support.'
I scarcely had my woeful words out from my mouth declared,
    When, as I saw, a smirking smile with douce and sweet regard,[374]
Pass from the passage of her eyes which sometimes of my joy
    Was both the salve and medicine for to abate my noy.   130

So afterhend she sighing said: 'O Petrarch just and true,[375]
    Mark well my words, and credit give to that which does ensue.
My heart nor yet my lasting love did e'er from thee depart,
    Nor yet that Love my heart had once, Death ever shall subvert.
But warily I provided so to temper so thy flame,   135
    With coy regard to mitigate the fierceness of the same,
Because there were no other way to keep in honest fame[376]
    My chastity and thy renown of evil bruit and blame.
And so thou ought not for to think that Laura not thee loved,
    Or had not pity on thy plaints, or yet to ruth not moved;   140
For look how that a mother dear does chastise so her son,
    Corrects him for amendment to frame in better tone:
E'en so did I so use myself and to myself oft said:
    "Petrarca loves not but does burn; this fire must then be stayed.
It is my part for to foresee these evils before they grow,   145
    Less common bruit unto our shame our infamy forth blow".
But so to do it is very hard, for how can they provide
    Against these things for which they fear and earnestly abide?
Fain would ay, e'en as I did, thee to my love reclaim,[377]
    But slander made me ay mistrust and fear a greater shame.[378]   150
And to myself I oft have said: "He marks but outward things.
    Yet inwardly he sees it not that so me wounds and stings".

---

[373] platt] With reference to Fowler's translation, *DOST* explains 'platt' as a figurative use of the word, meaning 'A sketch of a piece of territory, a map; a plan or diagram of a building or the like, a draught or design'.
[374] douce] sweet, gracious.
[375] afterhend] afterwards. The insertion of the poet's name (repeated below, lines 144 and 199) is the translator's addition, as is the following line.
[376] there] The manuscript has 'they'.
[377] Fain] The original has 'Fame' (see Meikle, III. 16).
[378] These four lines are Fowler's addition.

I used this craft to draw thee back and spur thee thick again,
 E'en as a bridle backward bears the wanton horse and vain.
155 And yet this more I will confess: a thousand times has ire
 Depainted in my face what Love within had set on fire;
And thousand times my face has shown and thousand times expressed
 The sore conflicts and inward flames that brunt my heart and breast.
And look how much thy love appeared: so surely great was mine,
160 But will did not my reason rule, nor made from right repine.
And after, when I thee beheld o'ercome by love his rage,
 Then sweetly would I cast my eyes, thy sorrows to assuage,
With purpose and with full intent, and with a careful care,
 To save thy honour with my life that languished by despair.
165 And when the passions that thee pained so painful did appear,
 I purposed then to comfort thee with visage calm and clear,
So that my forehead and my voice did for thy safety move,
 Now full of woe, then full of joy, and dread full mixed with love.
170 This was the practice of my heart, these were my honest ways,
 That I through honour with thee used until my dying days,
Now showing forth a blithe aspect all gathered full of grace,
 And then again a coy disdain, and then a sourer face.
Thou know'st that all these things be true: thy sonnets this reveal,
 And all thy songs proclaim the same, which of thy woe bewail.[379]
175 In end I used such sundry salves to salve thy sore disease,
 That both my care and study was how thee to pain and please.
For when I saw thy watery eyes so full of streams of tears,
 Which trickling down in such a pace did wash thy cheeks and ears,[380]
Then would I say, "This man does run a course unto his death.
180 I see things: therefore must help prolong his lifely breath".
And therefore then I did provide some help and honest aid
 To ease thy woes, redress thy sores, and make thy state be stayed.
Then, when I saw so many spurs so forward in thy side,
 Then would I say, "An harder bit must make this man abide".
185 And thus when then I so espied how thou had hope of gain,
 "Convenient is", said I, "this hope be drownèd with disdain".[381]
So that amidst these contraries sometimes both hot and cold,
 Now white, now red, now blithe, now sad, I have, e'en as I would,
Conducted thee now to this point, though I now wearied be,
190 Wherethrough I lead a glorious life, and so shall all men see.'

---

[379] Petrarch alludes generically to putting these events in poetry, while Fowler, more specifically, refers to sonnets and songs.
[380] This line does not appear in the original.
[381] These two lines are Fowler's addition.

Then I replied with face besprent and visage weak with tears,[382]
    And tremblingly with trembling voice, all faint with thousand fears,
'O glorious dame of this my faith, great gain thou should me give,
    If that I could thy loving words so steadfastly believe'.
'O man, O man of little faith,' she answered in disdain, 195
    'If thou not knowest which that I speak to be both true and plain,
What reason is should me induce to tell these things to you,
    And thou nowise that which I speak will credit yet or trow?
I were unjust, O Petrarch mine, if I the truth should hide,
    Whilst as I lived thou in my heart and in my eyes did bide. 200
In truth that sweet and loving knot most pleasant was to me
    By which thou pressed by fervent love with me to coupled be.
That brave renown (if true I hear), which through the world does pierce,
    Which far and near thou has me won by thy immortal verse,
Does please me much, for that I knew thou had no other suit 205
    Than by a lawful honest means to reap thy wishèd fruit.
And this was it that only failed, this only did inlake,[383]
    For to perfect that perfect love which did not thine forsake:
For whilst that thou in heavy act thy sadness did bewray
    Thou made thy flames to published be through all the world, I say. 210
Hence came my zeal, to mollify and so thy flame to soft,
    But yet in all such other things such concord then was wrought,
As loyal love with honesty does temper and immixt,[384]
    So in my love both honesty and shamefastness was fixed.
This difference was twixt them both: thou published forth thy flame, 215
    When secretly I in my heart had buried up the same.

And when that thou for mercy cried, so that thy voice was hoarse,
    I held my tongue, yet in my heart I had on the remorse;
For shamefastness upon the one, on other side a fear,
    Did make my many hot desires far fewer more appear. 220
For neither is that dole the less that does another vex,
    Nor yet by moaning moan grows more that men does so perplex;
As neither things that are of truth and have by truth their stay,
    By feignèd fortune does increase or yet by it decay.

Yet did not I dissolve these doubts, when I with thee did sing 225
    Thy sugared songs, that with my pains thy praises all did ring;
And this much more I will thee tell: my heart was ay with thee,

[382] besprent] sprinkled.
[383] inlake] lack (attested in *DOST*).
[384] immixt] mix.

	Suppose my eyes were turned aside and seemed not thee to see.
	Of which thou very oft complained, as of these parts unjust,
230	That quenched thy hope and esperance and raisèd thy mistrust.[385]
	Yet so to do thou had no cause, for that of me the best
	Unto thy hands I did it yield, so that the worst but rest;
	And know when that my eyes sometimes were turned from viewing thee,
	That they a thousand times again with mercy did thee see.
235	And in this same persuade thyself they on thee ay had looked,
	Were not I fear that through their flames they had rekindled thy smoke.

Now somewhat more I am to say afore that I make end,
    That may thee please or I depart, or I to go intend:
It is that I in every point sufficiently am blissed,
240   And yet in one thing (to my grief) this happiness I missed.
It does me grieve my native soil and birthplace is so base,
    From which I had my living life in which I gendered was;[386]
And one thing more augments my woe: I was not born beside[387]
    That flowery nest, fair Florence town, in which thou did abide.[388]
245 And yet my country soil and ground contented much thy mind,
    If not the place, perhaps my love it was that made thee kind.

I wished this change because I feared that thy true, constant heart
    Through change to some unknown face and uncouth be convert,
And so that glorious, famous praise which thou to me procured
250   Should darkened be, so of less fame, and bruit it had endured.'

To this I said: 'Not so, O dame, such change could never chance;
    And then the third fair heav'nly sphere did so me far advance,
E'en with her whirling circled wheel to such a sort of love,
    As Venus stood immoveable, and I might not remove'.

255 Then answered she, 'Since so it is, such glore I have by thee
    That yet immortal thou dost lest and so shall follow me.
Grave therefore this within thy mind, and in thy heart imprint,
    The time does slip and through thy joy thou knowest not how is spent'.

---

[385] esperance] hope.
[386] gendered] engendered.
[387] beside] near, close to.
[388] In this line Fowler expands Petrarch's simple reference to the *fiorito nido*, the flowery nest, that is, Tuscany (the site of the poet's birth). Fowler plays on the paronomasia between 'flowery' and 'Florence'.

Already I Aurora saw rise from her golden bed,
    Re-bringing back the day to men, and all the clouds to shed;[389]   260
Already then fair Phoebus was mount in his golden cart,
    And out from the bosom wide of Neptune to depart,
When that my lady, Laura fair, from me was to resort,
    Whose going then renewed my woe, and prayed me to be short,
And with the time to distribute and all my speech divide,   265
    Because she was not long to stay, nor with me to abide.

Thus answered I, 'O thou, my dame, thy goodly words and sweet,
    So lovely, chaste, and pitiful, so wise and so discreet,
They make me take my painful pains, my martyrdom and smart,
    My lingering life and heavy loss far in a better part.   270
But this, alas, does most me grieve, and this does most me pain,
    That you no more in life shall live, and I but you remain.[390]
Now one thing therefore to me show: shall I thy footsteps trace,
    Or shall a longer space of time my lingering years increase?'
Then did my love, my gem and joy speak: 'So as I believe,   275
    Thou shall but me drive forth thy days, and long in earth shall live'.

The fourth Triumph called Fame

Chap. 1

Now afterhend that cruel Death had triumphed in her face,[391]
    Which oftentimes so over me triumphèd in like case,
And after that forth from this world my sun was ta'en away,
    And that despiteful wicked beast, which does all folk affray,
Pale, sad, in visage horrible, and in his countenance proud,[392]   5
    Had beauty's light extinguishéd, which did all brightness shroud;

Then, looking so me round about, upon the growing grass,
    I quickly on the other part espied a dame to pass,
And nearer me for to arrive, who draws men from their grave,
    And from their tomb, though being dead, in longer life does save.   10
And look how does the morning star at break of day appear,

---

[389] In the original, these lines (until line 266) are still part of Laura's speech.
[390] I but you] I without you.
[391] afterhend] afterwards.
[392] Fowler is alluding to Death.

And came from east before the sun, within her purpled sphere,
Who willingly does marrow her with all his light and flame;[393]
So in such sort and all alike approachéd them this dame.

15 Oh, shall I see now from what school a master shall proceed
That can at large describe what I do speak in simple leid?[394]
The heav'ns about her were so clear so that through great desire,
Wherewith my lingering heart was burnt and wasted in a fire,
My dazzled eyes, uncapable of such a splendent light,
20 Were then made less and could not well sustain such fair a sight.
Upon their foreheads were engraved the valour of these men,
Who were a people honourable; amongst them saw I then
Great sort of these whom Love before had with him captive led
As prisoners, and them enforced his tract to trace and tread.

25 And first unto my sight appeared to be in Fame's right hand
Great Caesar and brave Scipio about her then to stand;
But who of them was nearest her I could not well perceive,
For one of them to virtue was, and not to love, a slave,
The other subject was to both, and with them both endowed;
30 So after this beginning brave and glorious, ensued
A company and rank of men, a people warlike wight,
With valour and with armour armed, and full of force and might.
Like these who in the ancient times in high triumphant chair,[395]
To Capitol by Sacra street or Lata did repair,
35 These all so orderly, I say, with famous Fame them sped,
Where there, in every bree and brow might then his name be read,[396]
Who most through greatest glory too, this glorious world was friend
And by his valiancy and deeds obtainéd great commend.

As I did mark attentively their noble, secret talk,[397]
40 Their gesture, acts, and countenance, behold, I saw to walk
With them two other in array, the one one Neucis was,[398]
The other his son who through his deeds did all the world surpass;
There also these men I beheld, who by their valiant course

---

[393] This line refers to the sun, willingly joining with the star.
[394] in simple leid] with a plain speech.
[395] Fowler adds the reference to the 'high triumphant chair'.
[396] bree] eyelid, brow.
[397] Fowler uses the adjective 'secret' to translate Petrarch's *pispiglio* (a hapax, meaning solemn and sober talk, read by Fowler as *bisbiglio*, murmuring).
[398] Once again Fowler supplies the name that is missing in Petrarch.

Did close the passage to their foes, and stayed their force perforce.
Two fathers brave accompanied with the victorious sons,　　　　　　45
　　And one before and two behind so marchèd to their thrones,[399]
Of whose the last and hindmost was the chiefest first in glore,
　　Though not in march, yet far in praise the foremost was before.

Thereafter, like a carbuncle, great Claudius flamed and shined,
　　That by his counsel and his hands from Italy declined　　　　　50
The tempests of more great affairs that secretly at night,
　　As well the flood Metaurus yet can well record his might,
Came quickly there and did defeat Asdrubal's sacking host,
　　That threateningly the Roman arms so threatened and did boast,
Who there did purge the Roman fields of that most noisome seed,　55
　　And in this fact he had both eyes and wings to make more speed.

There old, great captain Fabius did second him next Fame,
　　Who by great craft fierce Hannibal and drift of Time o'ercame;
With him another Fabius, with them two Catos too,
　　Two Pauls with them, two Bruti also and eke Marcelli two,　　60
One Regulus that lovèd Rome and did himself more hate,
　　One Curio with Fabricius more fair in poor estate
Than Midas or yet Crassus too, for all their glancing gold,
　　Whose avarice their greedy minds from virtue did withhold;
With them did Cincinnatus march, with him Serianus walk,　　　　65
　　Not distant by a step or pace from them of whom we talk.
And there I saw Catullus go,[400] that great Camillus come,
　　That rather loath to live or that he did not good to Rome,
So that the gods him favouring so did bring him back again,
　　By his great proof of manful mind, and there for to remain,　　70
When that the blind and furious rage of vulgar people vile
　　Did banish him from native soil and chased unto exile.

So there I did Torquatus see to give command to kill
　　His valiant and victorious youth that disobeyed his will,
And chose rather to endure to live but child and son[401]　　　　75
　　Than that the discipline of wars by him should be undone.
Here one and other Decius who with their breasts made way

---

[399] Fowler alludes to three Scipios: Africanus Minor, Asiaticus and Nasica.
[400] Catullus, incongruous in the context (and already mentioned in the fourth chapter of *Triumphus Cupidinis*) is added by the translator.
[401] but] without.

Out through the thickest of their foes, them fiercely to assay.
O cruel vow, which with the son the father reft of breath,
80   And caused them both offer up their life unto one death![402]

Now Curtius with them does walk no less than those devote,[403]
    That to the cave did both himself and armour all alote[404]
And fillèd up that ugly den, alas, by horrible vow,
    In midst within the market place that trembling so did bow.
85 Levinus with Mummius, Attilius was with them,
    Flamminius who both by force and pity Greeks o'ercame.
There also was that Roman bold[405] who bounded with a wand
    The Syrian king within around to answer did demand,
And with his gesture and his brow, and with his tongue constrained
90   Unto his will and his desire which he afore disdained.
And him I spied who all inarmed alone did keep the hill[406]
    From whence he afterward was thrust and hurlèd by their will;[407]
With him also Horatius that did alone defend
    The bridge against the Tuscan force and brought them to their end.
95 And him I saw who in the midst and thickest of his foes
    In vain did thrust his hand in fire, his boldness to disclose,
And there so long did it retain till it was burnèd quite,
    For anger then effaced his pain and all his dole despite.[408]
With him was he who first o'ercame the Africans by sea,[409]
100   And with him had that man who twixt Sardinia and Sicily
Disparpled all their naval host and brought them all to sack,[410]
    And one part broke, another drowned, the rest did captive make.[411]

I Appius knew e'en by his eyes that heavy were and blind,
    Against the vulgar sort and folk unpleasant and unkind.
105 Then after there I did espy that chieftain good and great,
    The conqueror of many realms, which he did all defeat;
Sweet, courteous, douce in all his deeds who him behavèd so[412]

---

[402] Before 'offer', the word 'to' seems to be missing.
[403] devote] devoted.
[404] alote] assign.
[405] Marcus Popilius Laenas.
[406] inarmed] armed.
[407] Marcus Manlius Capitolinus.
[408] Caius Mutius Scaevola.
[409] Caius Duilius.
[410] Disparpled] dispersed, scattered.
[411] Quintus Lutatius Catulus.
[412] douce] sweet, benevolent.

That next to Fame and to renown he well deserved to go,
Were not his light was near at hand and glory in decay;
    And yet with us Italian folk he might been well, I say,   110
E'en he alone as all these three was unto Thebes town:
    Alcides, Bacchus, Epaminond, of fame and bruit renown,
But oh, alas, to live too long is to survive to shame,
    And longest life through length of years does shorten but our name.[413]

And him I saw who had his name for to be brave disposed   115
    And in his youth great valiancy and proofs of praise disclosed;
And look how raw and how severe he bloody was, and fierce,
    E'en far more courteous and benign was he whom I rehearse,
Whose manhood was so excellent as scarcely I can tell,
    Now whether he as chieftain did or soldier-like excel.   120

Then after came Volumnius who through well-known deeds
    Repressed the rankled swelling rage that weepeth sore men's heads,
And swells the blood and it infects maliciously with boils,
    And putrefying the corpse of man both plagueth and defiles.[414]
With him I spied Rutilius with Cossus, Phylon next,   125
    And afterhend to stand apart this thickest light betwixt,
Three valiant knights whose members were both lamed and hurt with wonder,
    Whose armour was both lost and cloven, and hinging all asunder:
Lucius Dentat and Mark Sergius and Cetius Scaeva named,
    Three thunderbolts, three fiery flaughts, three rocks of wars untamed;[415]   130
With them was cursèd Catiline that did from Sergius spring,
    Successor of a wrongous fame and cruel, un-benign.

Then Marius after there I spied, who Iugurth did subdue,
    And Cymbais with the Dutchmen's rage and fury overthrew.[416]
And Fulvius Flaccus there I saw, who purposely did err   135
    In heading of these thankless men that so ungrateful were.
Next him more noble Fulvius, with him I Gracchus spied,
    The father of these other two who did the town divide,
Whose clattering nest and cumbersome the Romans oft has rent,
    And was the cause that so great death and so much blood was spent.   140

---

[413] These two lines are highlighted by the scribe, as providing a moralizing epilogue to a long list of names.
[414] corpse] body.
[415] flaughts] flashes of lightning.
[416] Cymbais] Fowler's misreading of *Cimbri*, the Cimbrians. Dutchmen] Thus Fowler translates Petrarch's *tedesco*, German.

And him I saw who does appear to others blithe and blist,[417]
    But not to me who do not see such grace in him consist;
Or yet to be within his thoughts and secrecy enclosed
    A closèd heart on which all hap and mishap is reposed.
145 Hereby I do Metellus mean, his father and his heir,
    That from Numidia and from Spain the spoil and booting bare,
From Macedonia and Crete's Isle to Rome great riches brought,
    And from these towns wherein such loss and saccage he has wrought.[418]

Then afterhend Vespasian I spied to walk with Fame,
150   With him his son, both good and fair, who Titus hight by name,
And not that cursed Domitian, unworthy ay of praise;
    Good Nerva and Traianus eke, just princes in their days,
And Helius Adrianus I with Antonie Pius spied,
    Whose offspring and succession in Marius did abide,[419]
155 Who had at least to rule and ring a natural desire,
    And govern in justice and in right their noble large empire.
And whilst with wandering eyes I looked to spy the wandering way,
    I saw the first foundator of the Roman walls, I say;[420]
With him five other kings with Fame did forward march and step;
160   The seventh lay charged on the ground with ill and all mishap.
E'en as it oft befalls to these that virtue does forsake,
    To follow evil and wickedness and unto vice them take.[421]

The second chapter of the Triumph of Fame

When as with marvel infinite and such a noble sight
    I was surprised by deep desire to see these folk of might,
And that good martial people brave who were in world but pain,
    As such a race within the same shall ne'er appear again;
5 I then unto my scrolls and books re-joinèd so my eyes,
    Wherein their names were written all, which were in high degrees,
And these of greatest praise and price; but then I quickly knew
    My language was in naming them inferior to my view,
So that my speech their praise impaired, or all them not rehearsed;
10   And whilst my mind on this was set, another thought me pierced,
And turned my eyes another way, when as I saw encroach
    A trim consort of strangers stout, more nearer to approach.

---

[417] blist] blessed.
[418] saccage] havoc.
[419] Marius] Fowler's misreading of Marcus (Aurelius).
[420] foundator] founder.
[421] These two concluding lines are highlighted by the scribe.

Among the first was Hannibal, with him Achilles brave,
    Whose praise by Homer is depaint to free from death and grave;[422]
With freinyeis[423] he embroidered was of ever-living Fame   15
    These Trojans two who by their deeds demerited the same.
With them two Persians great I saw, one[424] Philip and his son,
    That to the Indies from Pella town establishèd his throne.

Not far from these I there did see another Alexander,[425]
    To whom dame Fortune in his fight such success did not render;   20
He ran not so as other did, he had like kind of stay,
    When fortune from true honour doth divide herself away.[426]

There in one knot the Thebans three I spied, as I have shown,
    There Diomed with Ajax and Ulysses might be known,
Who had to see this spacious world so great and deep desire,   25
    And Nestor who foresaw so much and knew all that empire.
I Agamemnon likewise viewed with Menelaus there,
    That threw this world by cursed wives in great debate and care;
Leonidas was them amongst, who did with merry cheer
    Propine a dinner hard and sharp unto his men of war.[427]   30
But harder and more horrible the supper he assigns,
    Who in a little part of ground did work great wondrous things.
Then Alcibiades I espied, that oft did Athens town
    E'en when it list him to revolt and turn upside down,
With sugared speech and language douce and with alluring words,[428]   35
    And with his brow and forehead clear restrainèd oft their swords.
With him was there Miltiades who took the yoke from Greece;
    With him his son Thunonus good was marching in that place,[429]
Who with a perfect pity and with a godly mind
    Did chain alive him with these chains that did his father bind.   40
With these who so were recompensed, Themistocles drew near,
    And Theseus with Aristide a Fabrice might appear,[430]
To whom, alas, was interdicted their kindly native grave,
    But yet the vice of these that so such malice did conceive

---

[422] depaint] painted.
[423] freinyeis] freezes, ornaments.
[424] The manuscript has 'and', a possible scribal mistake.
[425] Alexander I, King of Epirus, uncle of Alexander the Great.
[426] The scribe has highlighted the passage from 'he had like…' (line 20) to the end of line 21.
[427] Propine] offer.
[428] douce] sweet, persuasive.
[429] Thunonus] Miltiades' son was actually Cimon; this might be a scribal mistake (Petrarch does not mention his name).
[430] Fabrice] An allusion to Fabricius, to whom Aristides is compared because of his honesty.

45 Ennobled more their noble deeds, for nothing more makes known
        Two contraries than one by one by interspace is shown.
And Phocion with them was there, whom I above have named,
        Rewarded e'en with these alike, and equally defamed.
For so his thankless countrymen not caused him only die,
50   But banished e'en his boldest bones and made unburied be.

As I me turned, there Pyrrhus I among that troop espied,
        With Masinissa, that good king, besides him to abide,
Who seemed to be then malcontent and for to gotten wrong,
        Because he was not with his friends the Romans placed among.
55 With him I, looking there, did see the Syracusan king
        Called Hiero, and there then again with him prease to thrin,[431]
Hamilcar distant far from them, a man both fierce and raw,
        And him who naked from the flames escapèd there I saw;
Rich Croesus, king of Lidia, who teaches us this tale:
60   That no defence in fortune's spite nor buckler can prevail.[432]
I also Syphax then beheld, tormented in like sort,
        And Brennus under whom did fall full many a man athort,[433]
And he again yet afterward in spoiling Delphos temple
        Was beaten down and quite o'erthrown to serve for like example.

65 In strange attire and uncouth clothes and in that thickest band,
        This company was there amongst, and with them there did stand;
And whilst I backward turned my eyes I spied a sort of men[434]
        All gathered wholly in a round, where him I spied then,
Who first to God would build a house, and church to him erect,
70   To dwell among his creatures, and for the same effect.[435]
But he that did complete the same I saw him come behind,[436]
        To whom this work was destitute, as we in scripture find,[437]
Who from the lowest parts thereof, e'en to the highest tops,
        Did build the same and mounted up by many pins and props
75 And as I may conjecture well, and so the truth record,
        He was not such a master work, nor builder with his lord.

---

[431] prease to thrin] strive to press himself forward.
[432] This line is highlighted by the scribe.
[433] athort] A variant of 'athwart' (across).
[434] backward] upwards.
[435] Here the poet alludes to King David.
[436] Solomon.
[437] destitute] destined.

Then afterhend[438] I him espied to march within that place
    That with his God so homely was and spoke him face to face;
Few were they, yea, none ever was that hearing so might want
    Or with his God familiarly so long a time did haunt.   80
There him I spied who banned the sun e'en by his potent tongue,
    As beasts with their bands are bound and beaten, led and doung.[439]
So he did make the sun to stay, his foes to tract and trace,
    Till that he them o'ercoming all, did all by death deface.
O gentle trust! O noble faith of these that serve their God,   85
    That all which he created has, makes subject to their nod,
And does not only make the sun within his circle stay,
    But stable makes unstable heav'ns e'en by one word, I say.
Then after I our father saw,[440] to whom was given in charge
    For to depart out of his land, by wastes and deserts large,   90
And for to go unto that place which was by God elect[441]
    Unto the well of mankind's soul, and that for good respect.
With him his son and nephew was, who trumpèd by his wife,[442]
    And Joseph that was chaste and wise and honest all his life.
Extending then so far my eyes, as I had force and might,   95
    Beholding that which corporeal eyes cannot attain by sight,
I there just Hezekiah spied, and Samson there defaced,
    And him who first upon the seas the spacious Ark has placed;
And him I viewed who afterhend did build that stable tower
    That chargèd was with sin and shame by God his puissant power;   100
Then Judas good,[443] from whom could none draw from his father's laws,
    Who frankly for the love of truth did run in Death her claws.

Already was my great desire all wearied, e'en content,
    And satisfied by these brave sights that so with Fame then went,
When that a quick and gallant look did make me crave to see,   105
    And stay for to behold the troop that trimly drew to me.
I saw within that round and ring a sort of bravely dames:
    Antiope and Eurithea, and so were both their names;
Fair in their face, in armour clad, Hippolyta also,

---

[438] afterhend] afterwards.
[439] doung] cast down.
[440] our father] Abraham. In this section Fowler follows Petrarch in being less explicit with the names of the people he is describing, since, being biblical characters, they could be easily recognized by his readers.
[441] elect] elected, chosen.
[442] nephew] grandson (with the same ambiguity there is in the Italian *nipote*).
[443] Judas Maccabeus.

	Afflicted for Hippolytus, and pensive, full of woe;
110	And Menalippe there I saw, these dames so agile were,
	And ready to withstand that force that any would infer,
	That it was e'en a greatest proof of Theseus' manly might,
	And Hercules who them o'ercame by hard and doubtful fight.
115	I there that widow[444] saw who did securely see her son,
	Whose happy days of greatest hope were by his death undone:
	But she revenged the same with speed on Cyrus, who wrought the same,
	As she, in cutting of his head, has cut away his fame;
	For, seeing his unhappy end and also his shameless death,
120	It does appear that by his fault he hourly daily hath,
	So made himself to daily die, and all his former Fame
	To be suppressed and buried be, together with his name.
	Then saw I her[445] who happily did see the town of Troy,
	Together with that virgin[446] fair that did Aeneas annoy,
125	And that courageous valiant queen[447] with one tress of her hair
	Knit up when that the other hung e'en sparpled to her spair,[448]
	So soon she heard that Babylon revolted from her crown,[449]
	Did bring them back and stayed the rift begun within her town.
	With her I saw Cleopatra touched with unworthy flame,
130	And likewise saw I in that dance Zenobia of great fame,
	But very sparing of her glory and of her honour hard,
	In usage fair, and in her youth of comely sweet regard;
	And look how much she in her age and beauty praise possessed,
	So much her glory and renown by honesty increased.
135	Within her heart, though womanly, such constancy remained,
	That she them caused to stand in dread that others had disdained;
	Her visage fair, her face most sweet, her hair with helmet armed,
	Abased our emperor's heart and mind, and courage quelled and charmed.
	Although at last he sore assailed and captive took that queen,
140	And made his, to our brave Triumph a richer prey be seen.
	And now suppose upon these names I both be brief and short;
	Yet will I more discourse and of fair Judith make report,
	That bold and hardy widow chaste who brought unto the dead

---

[444] Tomyris, the queen of Scythia.
[445] Penthesilea.
[446] Camilla.
[447] Semiramis.
[448] sparpled] scattered. spair] Possibly a variant of *spear*.
[449] So soon she heard] as soon as she heard.

That drunken foolish Holofernes and cut from him his head.
And shall I now leave me behind, or Ninus shall forget, 145
From whom all histories begin and not with them him set?
Or yet is here in that empire, whose arrogance and pride
Conducted to a bestial life in it seven years to bide?
Or Belus yet shall I o'ersee, from whom did error spring,
Not by his fault but by his son, who did it first in bring? 150
Where now does lurk Zoroaster, that magic arts invent,
Or yet these men who of our dukes that in a curst ascent
And forward star did Euphrates pass with lose and shame also,
Whose evil conduct in Italy emplasters yet their woe.[450]
Where is Mithridates the great, a mortal foe to Rome, 155
And our eternal enemy, unto his death and doom,
Who soldering up his broken loss and his oft crazèd harms,
In summer and in winter fled before the Roman arms?

I many things of great report do in one bundle knit:
Where is he now, King Arthur, that at Table round did sit? 160
Where be these Augustus Caesars three, victorious, one of Spain,
Of Africa one other was, the last of Lorraine one?[451]
Whilst I so this victorious Fame triumphing so do see,[452]
I likewise spied twelve noble knights his Paladins to be.

Then Godfroy came since alone, a Duke of faith and trust, 165
Who made a holy enterprise whose steps and ways were just;
He, he alone, that valiant prince, did with his valiant hands
Rebuild that kept careless nest that in Jerusalem stands.[453]
This thing, alas, does cause my woe, this worketh my disdain,
This is the thing for which I cry and call so oft in vain: 170
Is prideful Christians miserable, go, go, yea, misers now,
And drink each one another's blood with settled oaths and vow!
Go work each one another's wrack, and others each destroy,
And every one against yourself does all your spite employ!
Ye careless are how that the grave of Jesus Christ remains 175
Within the hands of faithless dogs and Turks who it retain.
But after these whom I did see, if I be not deceived,
I saw but few or none at all that might renown have craved,

---

[450] emplasters] gives a medical remedy (compare Petrarch's *impiastro*).
[451] Theodosius, Septimius Severus and Charlemagne.
[452] This line is Fowler's addition.
[453] kept careless] carelessly guarded.

That by their art in planting peace, or skill in hardy fight,
180   Or doubtful yoke in hard combat appearèd to my sight.
Yet as the chosen men behind and chiefest oftest go,[454]
    I saw in end of all the troops that Saracen,[455] our foe,
That brought unto our Christians both skayith and blushing shame;[456]
    And Heguius son of Luria[457] did follow him with Fame.
185 The Duke of Lancaster was there,[458] who with his sword and lance
    A neighbour cursed and troublesome was to the realm of France.

Thus gazing on this famous sight I at that time and space
    Did look, like one who did advance his footsteps and his pace
To make some things he has not seen; so I did forward go,
190   To see if there were any more than these that I did know.
Where there I spied two noble wights who lately, oh, did die,
    Who of our countrymen were glory, and praise of Italy,
Who were enclosèd in that band and marchèd on with Fame:
    Good Robert of Sicily,[459] king of undefamed name,
195 Who in his knowledge most sublime and foresight most profound
    Did Argus-like see things far off, and well discerned their ground;
The other that did march with him was my Colonna great,
    Courageous, gentle, constant, large, and liberal in his state.

The third chapter of Fame

I could nowise return my eyes from such a famous sight,
    Nor yet convert them from these men of manhood, full of might,[460]
When that I heard one say again: 'Look on thine other side,
    Where fame and praise, and brave renown, with other folk do bide
5 By other means than use of arms'. So, turning to my left,
    I Plato first espied therein, with honour first infest,[461]
Who in that clear and comely band did nearest march these signs,
    To which he nearest does approach to whom the heav'ns these bring.
Then, next to Plato, there did go so godly and divine

---

[454] oftest] most often.
[455] Saladin.
[456] skayith] Attested in *DOST* as a variant of 'skath', damage.
[457] The use of Heguius is unclear. The allusion appears to be to the admiral Ruggero di Lauria.
[458] Henry of Lancaster, cousin of Edward III.
[459] Robert of Anjou.
[460] convert them] turn them (i.e. my eyes) away.
[461] infest] adorned.

Great Aristotle replenished with full and high engine,   10
And after him Pythagoras, that humbly first did name
    Philosophy, e'en by the same so worthy of great fame;[462]
Then Socrates with Xenophon, next him that agèd man
    To whom the Muses were his friends, as Troy and Argus can,
With Micen yet, resent his pen who sang the long astrayes,[463]   15
    And errors of Laertes' son, and bold Achilles' praise.[464]
In hand came singing on that Mantuan poet brave,[465]
    And striving which of them should first the way and passage have.
The one I spied whose steps the grass transformèd in a flower,
    Mark Cicero, who clearly shows what fruit, what force and power   20
His eloquence and ornate speech, so that these two be them
    Which were the eyes of Latin tongue has lightened much the same.

Then after came Demosthenes, all in a flame he went,
    Despairing of the foremost place, and not with next content.
Next him was Aeschines in press, who there might well have known   25
    In what respect his voice was hoarse, and by the other o'erthrown.
I cannot well in order tell whom first I saw and when
    To follow or yet go afore amongst these learnèd men;
For wondering at ten thousand things of that fair troop and band,
    My eyes and thoughts did both astray and were not at command.[466]   30

I Solon saw, who of good laws established first the plant,
    That now so well manurèd is, and does her fruit now want;[467]
With him these other learnèd six, the Grecian six and wise,
    Of whom does Greek so nobly vaunt, and yields them first the prize.
With these I also did behold him whom our countrymen   35
    As chieftain had for to conduct them, e'en with other ten:
I Varro mean, the third great light of Romans' high engine,
    Whom, more that I in face beheld, he seemèd more to shine.

---

[462] The scribe in this section highlights not only the names of the great persons of the past, but even key terms of philosophy, such as syllogism and dialectic.
[463] Micen] Mycenae. astrayes] wanderings.
[464] The allusion is to Homer.
[465] The poet is here alluding to Virgil. As with the biblical allusions in the previous chapters, Fowler is here faithfully following Petrarch's practice of not explicitly mentioning his characters' names.
[466] Contrary to usual practice, here Fowler condenses Petrarch's original.
[467] Fowler introduces an interesting change here: while Petrarch maintains that Solon's plant (i.e. his legislation) may produce bad fruit if it is badly cultivated, Fowler, perhaps as an act of homage to King James, takes it for granted that it is well cultivated, that is, that laws are justly applied.

Crisp. Sallust then appeared,[468] next with him I Livius spied,
40   Who forwardly did him regard, and greatly him envied.
Whilst I them then did see, behold, then quickly did I see
    Great Plinius, his neighbour next, and marrow for to be,[469]
Who took more care to write his books than to foresee his death,
    Whom Somma hill with brimstone blasts did stop his vital breath.[470]
45 Then after I Plotinus saw, one[471] learnèd of Plato's sect,
    Who trusting secretly to live, did for the same effect
Withdraw him quietly apart, with no man to be seen;
    But him his fierce and cruel fates and destinies did prevene,[472]
Which he contracted in her womb from whence he first did come,
50   So not his foresight him availed: this was his fatal doom.
Then Crassus, Galba I beheld, Calvus with Pollio,
    Hortensius with Antonius, who so in pride did go,
To arm their tongues and sharpen their mouths in Cicero's disgrace,
    And searching for unworthy fame did falsely theirs increase.
55 Thucydides I likewise saw, that well distings the place,[473]
    The time together with the feats, the quarrel and the case,
And truly tells by whose men's blood, so fiercely shed in store,
    The barren fields was fertile made, and fatter than before.
Herodotus I likewise saw, of all historians Greek
60   The father that their works full wrote and truly of them speak.

And Euclid geometrien that does depaint most sound[474]
    Triangles with the quadrat forms, the circles and the round;
And Porphir who against the truth became as hard as stone,[475]
    Who with his Syllogisms untrue and false he did compone,[476]
65 Assailed to shake the rocks of truth, but in Dialectic quick,
    And filled the same with arguments in number great and thick.
I also saw Hippocrates, both bred and borne in Co,[477]
    That more had made his works perfect and far more better so,
If that his subtle aphorisms had well been understand;
70   Apollo then with Aesculap I saw then, near at hand,

---

[468] Crisp. Sallust] Gaius Sallustius Crispus, Roman historian.
[469] marrow] companion, friend.
[470] Somma hill] A mountain of the Vesuvius group (the name does not appear in Petrarch).
[471] The manuscript has 'me'. I accept Meikle's emendation.
[472] prevene] prevent.
[473] distings] distinguishes.
[474] depaint] represent.
[475] Porphir] Porphyry, the Neoplatonic philosopher.
[476] compone] compose.
[477] Co] Cos.

But that way placed above my sight, with Time were worn away,
    So neither by their face nor name I could them know, I say.
Then Galen great, of Pergamum town, did follow next that band,
    On[478] whom did hinge that noble art on which our health does stand,
That now amongst us lies abused, so clean corrupt, and waste,   75
    Vile, abject and profanèd now, by everyone disgraced.
But in his days it was not so, though dark it was and short,
    Yet firstly he declared of it, and largely did report.
I fearless Anaxarchus saw, of manly port and mind,
    With him Zenocrates the chaste, that nowise him inclined,   80
Unto infamous wild attempts, but them withstood each one,
    So that in every point he did resemble a solid stone.
There followed Archimedes next, with visage base on ground,
    And Democrit, that pensive walked there, in that troop was found,
Who with his will and but constraint did with his sight inlake[479]   85
    The light, the gold, the riches great, which he did all forsake.
And Hippia I saw likewise, with him old Gorgias,
    That boldly vaunted that he knew all things that ever was;
And after him Archesilaus, of all things for to doubt,
    And Heraclitus within his sword more plainer spoken out.   90

Diogenes I also spied, so doggish in his words,[480]
    And plainer than more pleasanter a scoffer in his bwrdis.[481]
And Anaxagoras I beheld, who blithely did regard
    His fields to lie desert and wild, of which he little cared,
Which he did deem to bring envy, so that he them forsook,   95
    And charged with riches and with skill his riches he did brook.
There curious Dicearchus was, next him were other three,
    In discipline most different and distant in degree:
Quintilianus, Seneca, Plutarchus most renowned,
    That so in learning much excelled, as does their work resound.   100
I saw a rout of clattering men the seas of truth to storm,
    With contrary windy arguments, not to the truth conform,
Who through their erring, vaging thoughts were famous made and clear;[482]
    Yet rather by contention than wisdom they did learn.
They shulderingly rushed other out, together they did rail,   105

---

[478] My emendation; the manuscript has 'of'.
[479] inlake] lack.
[480] doggish] This is Fowler's translation of Petrarch's *cinico* (cynical, referring to the philosophy). Fowler here relies on the etymology of the word.
[481] bwrdis] jests.
[482] vaging] wandering.

As lions two together knit, and serpents tail by tail.
O now, what Bedlam men be these, what mad-like fools indeed,
    That are content with trifling toys, and further not proceed!
And then I saw Carneades, who was of such a wit,
110   And in his studies so expert, so ready, prompt and fit,
And in his speeches and brave discourse his tongue he had at will,
    That scarcely should one by him know the right almost from ill;
His life so long, his high engine and great abundant vein[483]
    Did make him then to undertake with travail great and pain,
115 For to accord these contrary sects, that then were at great jars,
    Whom literal furour did conduct unto such lasting wars.[484]
But this he could not well perform, for e'en as arts did grow,
    So likewise did envy and strife and discord with them flow,
And with their knowledge and their skill, and with their learnèd arts,
120   Arise likewise that poisoned spark within their emboldened hearts.
And Epicure, who would himself against that gracious man,
    Who raising up man's mortal hope, I there espied then,
Did prove his soul immortal; be that so, yet Epicure
    That boldly spoke against that man does now great shame endure.
125 But if he presses to challenge Fame, what can it else more be,
    Than borrowing it from Plato's strife, with whom he could not agree.

And Lippus there, likewise, I saw:[485] with him two were at hand,
    That to his master equal were, that progressed in that band.
I Methradore with Aristipp do mean, for these be they
130   That in the Epicurean sect were judgèd best that day.

Then did I spy Chrysippus so, e'en with a wondrous spindle,
    And with a large and broadest roll, his thread and webs to windle,[486]
Who by great Time and high engine did glorious works compose,
    And in the same much learnèd skill did learnedly disclose.
135 Then after, there I Zeno spied, the father of his sect,
    And for his ornate clearest speech above the rest erect,
Who for to give more proof of it, this song and show did give,
    Was opening up his hand and palm, and folding then his niwe.[487]
I saw Cleantes who, to stay and stable his intent,

---

[483] Thus Fowler translates *vena d'ingegno*, the vein of his wit.
[484] literal furour] literary fury, or literary contention.
[485] Lippus] This non-existent character is the result of Fowler's translation of *lippo*, 'bleary-eyed'.
[486] windle] spin.
[487] niwe] fist.

   Did gently weave his bravest webs on which he was most bent;   140
And curiously with earnest care to carefully provide
   To make their false opinions with Verity to bide.
But I him leave here with the rest, who did by Fame surmount,
   That I more grave and better things hereafter may recount.[488]

The fifth Triumph of Time

Forth from his golden inn and tent, afore Aurora fair,
   The sun, e'en belted in his beams, did from his place repair
And issued out with swifter course than one would e'en have said;
   He was above our hemisphere, uplifted with a braid,
And here a little staying; then he looks him round about,   5
   As does the wise and sagest men for things they stand in doubt,
And to himself within himself with rage beginning to say:
   'What thinkest thou how best now to be done? what will thou do this day?
Now is the hour that thou should have e'en of thyself more care,
   Because thou seest that mortal men, whose days does Death impair,   10
Yet being dead do nowise die, but by their Fame do live,
   And by their virtuous famous acts do far their death survive.
If it so be, as it does seem, that law shall be in vain,
   That so the heavens fixed with us so stable to remain;
And if the Fame of mortal men by Death does more increase,   15
   Which ought by Death to quenchéd be, and quickly brought to less,
Then of my glory and excellence must come my fall and end,
   And suddenly for which I rage shall all to ruin tend.
What greater wrong must I look for, what worser may befall,
   That I no more shall have in heav'n than man on earthly ball?   20
So far inferior is my state, and baser is my case,
   That I might equal be with man, I cry of special grace.
And yet four barded breathing horses with care I entertain,
   And in the Ocean them do feed, so long as I remain.
I with my spurs[489] do spur their sides and whip them with my wand,   25
   And yet against me does a man's undaunted Fame withstand.
If I were in the glorious heav'ns of stars not only he
   Who first is of the planets all, and highest in degree,
But e'en the second or the third, it were as I now say,
   An injury by hatred come, and not through sport and play.   30
So now it well beseemeth me to kindle all my zeal,

---

[488] This last line is Fowler's addition.
[489] My emendation; the manuscript has 'spous', possibly a scribal error.

    And to my flight join double wings, that I may more prevail;
Now do I grudge at mortal men, I bear them now envy,
    I hate and now despise them, nor can I this deny.
35 Whom all I see, yea, afterhend a thousand thousand years,[490]
    They flourish more than in their life, and famous more appears,
And I not more but to remain environèd with woe,
    And cannot get beyond my griefs, nor yet beyond them go.
I am e'en as I was at first, no better is my state,
40   Nor yet my glory more has grown, nor yet my fame more great;
And so I am as first I was, before the earth was placed,
    Ay turning in a circled street, day and night but end in haste.'[491]

When that the sun these words had said with grief and great disdain,
    He then resumed a swifter course, far speedier more again,
45 So that the same more sudden was than falcon in his flight
    That from the high descending down upon his prey do light.
The thought of man may not attain, far less his tongue and style,
    For to imagine what I saw with fear and dread this while.
Then did I reckon all our life most abject, vile and vain,
50   E'en by his swift and running course which nothing might restrain,
Whose solid course and movement did cause me judge much more
    The same to be contemptible which gentle I held before.
Where then I thought it vanity a vaness wondrous great,[492]
    That so our hearts should live to that whose stay and whole estate
55 Time dingeth and depresses down, and whilst we more do think,[493]
    To hold them fast, we least them hold, and passeth at a clink.
He therefore who has of his state once saucy care and fear,
    Let him provide and well foresee, that so it may appear,
Whilst as he may, through heav'nly grace his hope so founded be
60   And stablished in a stable place of long eternity.

For when I saw the turning Time so gallantly to go
    And lightly run behind his guide, that has no rest nor ho,[494]
Whose swiftness was so wonderful, so infinite and large,
    That for to tell my tongue nor thought be able of that charge.

---

[490] afterhend] after.
[491] circled street] The MS has 'scheit'; my emendation follows the original (*strada*) and presupposes a scribal error. This line, concluding the sun's meditation, has been highlighted by the scribe.
[492] vaness] vanity.
[493] dingeth] strikes, deals heavy blows.
[494] ho] halt.

For there without destruction at all, at any time, 65
    I saw the frost with roses mixt, the harvest with the prime,
And that which seemed more wonderful I saw, e'en at one point,
    The nipping cold with fervent hot and fiery flames conjoined.
And he who with a judgement firm does all these things regard,
    In time shall see them so to be, for which I little cared, 70
In these my reckless, youthless days, and in my lusty age,
    Which makes me now despite myself and with myself to rage:[495]
For then my hope did follow much my foolish vain desire,
    And both my hope and foolish thoughts to folly did aspire,
Where now in eild before my eyes of conscience is a glass,[496] 75
    Wherein myself and faultless I spy,[497] and what sometimes I was;
And as much as I may see me to my death decline,
    Remembering of my little life and of my latter fine,[498]
Where in the morning I see me a gallant child and light,
    And now a heavy, feeble, weak and agèd man at night. 80

What then is more man's mortal life, or longer than a day,
    Cold, cloudy, short and full of woe, that quickly wastes away?
It brave may seem, and long appear through outward show to be,
    But all that fair appearance is of little worth, we see.
What human hope, what mortal trust, what joy does men so blind, 85
    What makes these mortal folk to be so proud in mind?
Or yet so puftly lift their heads in vanity and pride,[499]
    And knowest not how, they soon shall die, or long in life shall bide?
I now behold e'en of my life the flight to be at hand,
    And with the same the days of all wherein men live and stand; 90
And in the swift and fleeing course of this resplendent sun,
    I see the world's wrack is come, and ruin is begun.

O lusty bloods, I see you now, your selves to comfort so,
    And in your folly all delight, and further therein go.
You all are careless of your death, you measure all the time, 95
    E'en with the largest, thinking it shall be ay in prime.
Live for to die, think on your death, for Death on you does call,
    The hurt foreseen brings lesser harm and dole when it doeth fall.[500]

---

[495] despite] The word is used as a verb, meaning despise or hate.
[496] eild] old age.
[497] I observe myself without flinching.
[498] fine] end.
[499] puftly] with inflated vanity (unattested in *OED* and *DOST*).
[500] These two lines have been highlighted by the scribe; the first is not in the original.

Perchance I sparple all my speech most vainly to the wind,[501]
100   But that I tell for truth it hold, and keep it in your mind.
If to my speech you take no heed, and not my counsel keep,
      Your brains do all oppressèd lie, with heavy deadly sleep.
For this much more you ought to mark, because the hours and days,
      The months, the years, together[502] goes, together all decays.
105 And we, with little interval and little distant space,
      Have all to search for other parts, for other rooms and place.
Do not against the truth, therefore, your hardened hearts indure,[503]
      As ye have done and practisèd unto this time and hour:
But turn your eyes unto yourself, and spy where ye offend,
110   And prease yourselves, whilst as ye may your faults and sins to mend.[504]
Abide while Death bend his bow, or yet delashe his shaft,[505]
      As does the most part of the world, which is a band most daft.

Then after that I had espied, as I now clear espy,
      The flight and chaise of Phoebus fair that rolleth in the sky,
115 From which by Time such heavy loss and harms I do sustain,
      I saw a sort and kind of folk in silence walked again;
But fear of Time, or of his rage, or of his furious faird,[506]
      Whom Poets and historians did keep within their guard.
The sun had more envy at them, and bore them more despite,
120   Who by their knowledge and their wit and virtues most perfyit[507]
Were mounted to such top of praise that never seemed decay;
      Who passèd from the vulgar trace and cage and common way;
In contrary them, he, only he, who only fair does shine,
      With greater force did him address to make them all decline.
125 So that he then began again a course more swift and great,
      And to his horses redoubled were their provender and meat,
And she of whom I wrote before, I mean the queen of Fame,
      Divorced herself from some of hers, who lie now but name.[508]

R. D. S. Jack comments thus on this addition: 'It is an intentional extension of the spiritual line in Petrarchism and goes along with similar additions to the Italian's descriptions of God and the Christian promise' ('Petrarch in English and Scottish Renaissance Literature', *Modern Language Review*, 71 (1976), 801–11 (p. 805)).
[501] sparple] waste, disperse.
[502] My emendation (the manuscript has 'to greter').
[503] indure] harden.
[504] prease yourselves] make an effort. sin] My emendation (the manuscript has 'sinnins').
[505] delashe] release.
[506] faird] attack.
[507] perfyit] perfect (meant to rhyme with 'despite').
[508] Some of Fame's favourite children are now reduced only to names. Significantly, here

I sometimes heard, but yet of whom I cannot tell nor say,
    And this much also have I read and ta'en the same away,   130
That all these human worldly works that primprint may be called[509]
    Are pits of blind oblivion, where darkly men are thralled.

Another sentence have I read, that Phoebus in his sphere
    Shall by his force revolt and turn, not once a single year,[510]
But lustres, and that longer age of hundred years' account   135
    Shall o'er the death of mortal men victoriously surmount;
And by this revolution we shall behold again
    Men's famous and illustrious fames to pass away in vain.

For look how much they were renowned, who were betwixt these floods
    Where Peneus runs and Hebrus slides, and all these folks includes,   140
Of Macedonia, of Thracia and of Thessalia,
    That borders with Boeotia and lands of Attica,[511]
Or yet so sunder distant be, as far as Zanthus runs,
    Where Trojans dwelt, and Tiber now wherein the Roman wins.
The Fame of all these people brave have hasted to their end,   145
    And if not yet, they yet shall soon all to that journey tend.

I heard likewise one say, 'Your fame no otherwise does bide
    Than does a pleasant changing blink shine in the winter tide,
Which soon a little cloud obscures and breaks and maketh dark;
    And to great names, great times to be a great and venomous spark.   150
Your triumphs and your prideful pomp shall all to dust decline;
    Your lordships shall all pass away, and then your kingdoms syne;[512]
Your health, strength, age, all mortal things, life, fame with fair renown,
    Time wastes, makes weak, defaces, kills, destroys and beated down.[513]
And also from these of meanest rank shall then be ta'en away   155
    Not only that which outwardly Time brought unto decay,
But e'en their knowledge, learning, skill, proportioned with their wit,
    Their eloquence and their engine shall quickly from them flit.

---

and in the next Triumph Petrarch avoids evoking famous names of the past.

[509] primprint] This is Fowler's translation of Petrarch's *ligustri* (literally, privet shrubs), poetically used as a symbol of candour and purity.

[510] revolt] revolve.

[511] These two lines are Fowler's addition, possibly in order to explain Petrarch's obscure reference to the rivers.

[512] syne] afterwards.

[513] These two lines have been highlighted by the scribe. Fowler transforms Petrarch's *ogni cosa mortal Tempo interrompe* ('Time stops every mortal thing') into two lists of synonyms.

Nor yet shall Time who does this world turn in his wandering flight,
  That never rests not yet returns, leave off to show his might
Afore all mortal men by him, both godly and unjust,
  Be all reduced to earthly ash and to a little dust.'
But some may say: 'Since humane glory and this, their famous pride,
  Has such a multitude of horns and pricks against her side,
No marvel is that it be pierced if it sojourn and dwell
  Beyond the common customed use; this does the vulgar tell.
But let them prattle: if that our life in haste did not consume,
  We soon should see all human glory to pass away like fume.'

I, hearing this, and now because none should the truth withstand,
  But thereto faith and credit give but doubt or more demand,
I saw our glory incontinent, our pomp and glorious show,
  To fade, to waste away, to melt, e'en as the sun does snow.
And then I saw that turning Time to have brought back again
  The spoil and prey of all your names, which I esteemed all vain,[514]
And to be of no importance, suppose the vulgar sort
  Believeth not, nor yet does know, but otherwise report.

O people blind, that so you plays and sports you with the wind,
  And does on false opinion feed, and errors of the mind,
With greater praise advancing more that Death that grows by age,
  Than that which in the cradle comes, and future griefs does swage!
How happy are already these, that Death in swaddling bands,
  How wretched more that through their age Death to their grave demands!
And some there be maintain this, and hold it for no scorn
  To deem them happy most and blessed, that never has been born.
But let this people answer me, with errors so acquaint,
  That through the lengthening of their life they seem so well content,
And think their growing age shall make their Fames more famous grow:
  What it is worth which they so prize, I pray them, let me know.
Confusèd dreams and puffs of wind, vain fables, sturt and strife:[515]
  This is the Fame that they do crave by long desired life.
So far is Time so covetous, and wars so much in wrath,
  That that which now is callèd Fame he makes a second Death,
For whose defence and steadfast stay there is no more remeid[516]

---

[514] your names] The original has *nostri nomi* (our names).
[515] This line has been highlighted by the scribe. This and the following line do not appear in the original.
[516] remeid] remedy.

Than was for our first former life, so swiftly time does speed,
For to triumph above the fame and glory of mortal men, 195
   And of this world miserable, a dungeon dark and den.[517]

The sixth and last Triumph of Immortality

When then I saw no mortal things so firm and stable stand,
   Now, whether the same in seas may be, in air or earth or land,
Or under heaven anything but totteringly decline,
   Unstable in their trustless course, I left these eyes of mine,
And with myself unto myself to speak I then began: 5
   'On whom has thou thy hope and faith now fixed, O[518] wretched man?'
My answer was then in this sort: 'E'en in that God and Lord
   Who faithful in his promise is, all falsity has abhorred,
Who in his truth most steadfast is, and in his doings just,
   And blessèd them of special grace that in him put their trust'.[519] 10

But now, alas, I know too well, and to my shame I see
   How that this blind deceitful world has blindly scorned me;
Now is the veil ta'en from my eyes: I see now what I am,
   And what in times past have I been, I now behold the same.
And now I look how that the time does pass, does go and fly, 15
   And knoweth none, but e'en myself for this should blamèd be,
For that the fault came by myself, who timely should foreseen[520]
   To open up the lowering lids and windows of my ene,[521]
And not so driftingly defer, nor tarry to this time,
   That has too long prolonged my age, so careless in his prime. 20

But when again I call to mind the goodness of our Lord,
   And how from age all ages do his mercies great record,[522]
Who of his heav'nly gracious grace was never late nor slow,
   On him I fix my confidence, that he shall make me show
Some worthy works of fervent faith, or I from hence do pass,[523] 25
   Or yet this caitiff encumbered corpse return to dust or ash.

---

[517] This final line is Fowler's addition.
[518] The manuscript has 'or'. I accept Meikle's emendation.
[519] The translation considerably amplifies Petrarch's five opening lines, transforming them into ten, and in the process exploring Petrarch's very compressed syntax and meaning.
[520] should foreseen] should have foreseen.
[521] ene] eyes.
[522] These two lines are not in the original.
[523] or] before.

Thus as I was within myself discoursing to and fro,
    'Now that all earthly mortal things do in their changing go,[524]
Who has their standing so unsure, what then their end shall be,
30   That thus the heaven's circled course do guide them, so we see?'

This pausing so, and whilst my mind the more on this was bent,
    Or it seemed to me that to this world a change in haste was sent,
In place thereof a new in age, not subject to decay,
    Eternal and immoveable, that shall no change assay.
35 There then appeared the splendent sun with all the heavens round,
    The twinkling stars, the spacious seas, and all this earthly ground,
With all their beauty and their grace so suddenly defaced,
    And in their room a merrier world and newer, bravely placed.[525]
What wonder and what marvel then did not my thoughts assay,
40   When that I saw the moving heav'ns upon one foot to stay,
That never wont to stable stand, but in their race and course
    Confusedly all things to change, reverse and to rebourse.[526]
And there the three parts of the sun[527] I saw all brought to one,
    And that same one not having course, nor motion having none,
45 Nor yet to be as it was wont to speed himself and haste,
    But for to be e'en like the earth, of herbs full bare and waste.

For neither shall nor 'was' nor 'is', 'afore' or yet 'behind';
    Nor such destruction of the times that by the heav'ns we find
Shall more have place, which wont to make the life of man withal
50   Weak, sickly, fragile and infirm, and bitterer than the gall.
And as the sun transparent is out through the glistering glass,
    So shall the thoughts of mortal men more through and swiftly pass;
For they no fancy shall retain wherein the glass is seen,
    Some object through the sunny beams that so resplendent been.
55 O, what a grace shall be to me if so that I could gain
    That high, that chief and sovereign good, and thereto might attain
Where is no evil, which only Time so mixes and inverts,
    And with the Time does only come, and with the Time departs.

Nor shall the sun more have his place or mansion in these signs
60   Of Pisces or the Hornèd Bull, which season change inbrings,[528]

---

[524] Now] The manuscript has 'thow'. I accept Meikle's suggestion (Meikle, III. 22).
[525] in their room] in their place.
[526] rebourse] reverse.
[527] The three divisions of time (past, present and future).
[528] change inbrings] brings in change.

Upon our labours and our works, in which they fade and grow,
    And gendered are, or else consumed, as we by proof do know.
O blessèd sprites that are so found within his holy choir,
    Or in that heav'nly company so happy do appear,
Who make themselves of mortal folk to be immortal men,   65
    And register their noble names by long eternal pen!
O happy he that finds the ford of this sharp, raging flood,
    That life is called, to worldly men both joyful, glad and good!
O, caitiff are these vulgar sorts, blind both in eyes and mind,
    That have their hope, their trust, their thought to these things all inclined,   70
Which eating and consuming Time so quickly does destroy,
    And nothing else does leave behind but sorrow and annoy.
O people deaf, in hearing hard, both naked, frail and weak,
    Of reason void, of counsel poor, that judgement does inlaik[529]
Sick everywhere, diseased in all, and destitute of grace,   75
    O, mortal misers miserable, that knowest not god this space,
That with the twinkling of his eye does rule this massive round,
    That calms and storms the elements, of contraries so compound;
Whose glory is so infinite none can it comprehend,
    No mortal wights, nor neither I, nor angels that attend   80
Upon his majesty divine who are with him acquent,[530]
    And of his glory to see one part for thousands are content.
O wandering minds that hinge in doubt, and hungry ay in end,
    To what effect do all your thoughts to trouble you intend,
When that a moment of an hour shall shadowless leave void   85
    That upon which so many years you have your pains employed?
For that which long time past, before, or present is in sight,
    Which was the strene or yet tomorrow, in morning or at night,[531]
Or any other course of time; all changèd soon shall be,
    And not one point shall pass away, as we a shadow see.   90

There shall no more hereafter then, 'is', 'was', nor 'shall' have place,
    But only all in present be in, nor this day and space,
And shall Eternity be gathered whole entire,
    And all such other obstacles shall from us far retire.
And all these marks united of 'before' or yet 'behind',   95
    Shall quickly there defacèd be, that occupied the mind;
Nor neither shall such object be, nor yet such sight remain,

---

[529] inlaik] lack.
[530] acquent] acquainted.
[531] the strene] yesterday.

On which our hope and memory shall thereto further strain.
Which variant view makes oftentimes impudent men to pense,[532]
100   And vainly in their vanity to take a foolish trance,
Whose thoughts are in themselves so vain, they think their life a play,
    In deeming surely they shall be tomorrow as the day.[533]

There shall be no division of less from less at all,
    But all shall jointly be conjoined and framèd in this ball;
105 Nor after that great trial day the summertime shall last,
    Nor winter with the sturdy storms and with her bustling blast:
But all shall change, and with the same e'en Time by Death shall die,
    And all this changeless solid place that day shall changèd be,
For neither then shall hasty Time that wastes away and wears,
110   And swiftly passes but returns, nor yet these present years,
Hereafter have within their hand the government of Fame,
    That does belong to mortal men and purchased has the same.
But that which once was pure and clear shall ay be clear and sure,
    And that which once so famous was eternal shall endure.

115 O blessèd souls and happy these, that are upon that way,
    Or yet hereafter are to come, that journey to assay;
Or to that end their lives address, on which I do indite
    And with such zeal and fervency thereof do speak and write!

And there amongst these glorious saints and pilgrims she shall be,
120   Whom Death afore her days defaced, and made untimely die;
Then shall be seen before these saints her angelic discourse,
    Her honest words, her chasteful thoughts, of honesty the source,
All which dame Nature to her praise, to make her more be graced,
    Within her young and tender heart for honour had emplaced.
125 These faces fair that Time with Death had so destroyed and slain,
    Shall to their flourishing state return back again,
Where then the visage of my dame most heav'nly shall be seen,
    Whose loyal love so long a space did so me bound detain.

And for that everything shall be unto the saints made known,
130   So there shall I amongst that band whom Love has so o'erthrown
Be pointed at with all their hands, and everyone shall say:

---

[532] pense] thing, consider.
[533] deeming] In believing that doubtlessly tomorrow they shall be as they are today. I accept Meikle's emendation (the manuscript has 'deuing').

'Behold the man for Laura's sake that plained both night and day,[534]
Yet notwithstanding all his plaints, his woe, his dole, his noy,[535]
    He happier is than any man that has enjoyed more joy'.
And then to her of whom I write and weepingly do sing,   135
    My constant faith and loyal heart great wonder shall inbring
And make her marvel at herself when all that heav'nly rout
    Shall have their tongues and all their voice forth in her praise break out.
When this shall be I know not well, but Laura well does ken,[536]
    For that the credit of these things belongs unto these men   140
And women who are of that troop and company elect,
    Companions with the faithful flock, whom God with crowns has decked.[537]
But since these secrets secret be, who thereto can attain,
    Or who shall then dissolve this doubt, or give an answer plain?
But yet so far as mortal men conjecture may or guess,   145
    E'en as the day does near approach, so does the world wax less.

Where then the conscience of all men shall give a just account
    Both of their false and justest gain before his throne, and mount
Where they their labours, pains and works, and travails all shall see,
    The instruments unto their wrack and spiders' webs to be.   150
There shall they likewise see and know how presently in vain
    They plunge themselves in vainest cares, to conquer worldly gain,
And how too long, most foolishly they tire themselves and sweat,
    When so in end they shall perceive them trumpèd by deceit;
And at that time and on that day no secret shall be then   155
    To cover or close, to hide or shut, the hearts and thoughts of man.
But every conscience then shall be dark, duskish, or else clear,
    And naked shall before the world and opened then appear;
And then that glorious God and judge, who well these things does know,
    Pronounce shall then his judgements just, and sentence forth shall show, 160
Whereafter it the godless men shall take them to their way,
    As do the wild dispersèd beasts, whom hounds do put in fray,
Return with speed unto the woods, to hide them in their hole,
    So wicked men shall haste to hell, there for their sins to thole.[538]
And at that time there shall be seen, and on that trial day,   165
    Possessions earthly, riches great, and glory without stay,

---

[534] plained] complained.
[535] noy] annoy, grief.
[536] ken] know.
[537] Lines 140–42 do not appear in the original, nor does the explicit mention of Laura.
[538] thole] suffer. Lines 163–64 are Fowler's addition.

High dignities and princely pomp, to which men did attain,
    No profit nor yet glory bring, but rather loss than gain.

But on the other side the just, whom God has ta'en to grace,
170   Shall be uplifted to the heav'ns, and there behold his face;
For they did bridle so their wills and used their fortune so,
    That it was reined with modesty, and did not higher go,
Where they shall joy in happiness and in eternal bliss;
    But pomp or pride or glory vain that so men leads amiss.[539]

175 These Triumphs five we on this earth have seen them both and known;
    The sixth, when it shall please our God, shall us above be shown,
Where Time that all things does undo and brings unto an end,
    And greedy Death that in her rage does on his prey intend,
Shall both together be defaced, and both to Death be brought,
180   Who by the force of their empire such spoil on all has wrought.
But these who merit lasting Fame though, while they livèd here,
    Time with despite consuming it, did waste away and wear,
And these fair looks and beauty brave, that gallant sight and hue
    That Death and Time did paleish make, shall brave again renew.
185 Oblivion and such ugly sights, so hideous, horrible, sad,
    Shall be again to them restored, so felon and so mad.
And in a far more fresher age our souls shall then reclaim
    Immortal beauty ay to last, with long eternal Fame.

Where then afore all other folk in that eternal glore,[540]
190   Madonna Laura,[541] lady fair, shall foremost be before,
Whom now this world does with his plaints and with my tongue require,
    And with my wearied pen to see does earnestly desire.
The heav'ns likewise do earnestly prease to have the same,[542]
    That they may her whole joined enjoy unto her former frame.

195 There is a flood from Giben flows,[543] upon whose bank and side
    There Love so long a lasting woe did unto me provide,
The memory whereof, alas, does make me yet to shrink,
    So that I tremble night and day, and faint thereon to think.

---

[539] These two lines are Fowler's addition.
[540] glore] glory.
[541] Once again Fowler inserts the name of Petrarch's beloved.
[542] prease] strive.
[543] Giben] Mont Ginèvre (*Gebenna* in the original).

O blessèd stone, O happy grave, that do within enclose
    The fairest face of feminine, yea, of the world the choice!   200
If I was happy then, esteemed or judge myself, then blist,[544]
    When I on earth beheld thy corpse, or Death had cut the twist[545]
That did prolong thy glorious life, whose wrack does work my woe,
    And causes so my sore laments, my pleasures to o'erthrow.
When shall I be, when I shall see thee in the heav'ns decored[546]   205
    With glory, and thy glorious corpse unto her soul restored?

Epilogue[547]

Now with this work my pains shall end, and here my pen shall stay,
    With earnest prayer to my God to lead me in that way
Of lasting life and living Fame, and that I may forsake
    These trifling toys and vain conceits that do my virtue shake.
And by example of this wight who first this work does write,
    My tongue may speak, my pen may oft the glory of God indite.

Finis

Deo honor et gloria[548]

Plurimum facere, nimium de se ipso loqui
prudentioris est.
                               Plautus[549]

---

[544] blist] blessed.
[545] twist] thread.
[546] decored] adorned.
[547] The epilogue is the translator's addition, and appears to be in Fowler's voice rather than Petrarch's.
[548] Finis. Deo honor and gloria] 'The end. All honour and glory be to God' (a customary formula at the conclusion of a literary effort).
[549] Although the manuscript indicates 'Plautus' at the end of the quotation, this passage seems to be closer to a sentence from Sallust's *De Bello Iugurthino*, § 6, a passage in which the writer describes Jugurtha ('Plurimum facere, [et] minimum ipse de se loqui': he did a lot, and spoke of himself very little). See Caio Sallustio Crispo, *Opere Complete*, ed. by Raffaele Ciaffi (Milan: Bompiani, 1983), p. 130. The scribe seems to have confused *minimum* with *nimium*, thus creating an apparently nonsensical phrase: 'it is wiser to do a lot and speak of oneself excessively'.

TRANSLATING THE *TRIUMPHUS MORTIS*

3.1. Henry Parker, Lord Morley

No manuscript survives of this translation. The printed version, according to its first modern editor, is extant in five copies in English or American libraries — two in the British Library, one in the Bodleian, one in Sion College and one in the Huntington Library.[1] Carnicelli collated all five copies for his 1971 edition, without noting any discrepancy among them. I have used the British Library copy of the 1555 edition (shelf mark C.13.a.7[1–2]), that is volume II bound together with Thomas Twyne's translation of *Phisicke against Fortune, aswell prosperous, as aduerse* (London: Richard Watkins, 1579). The frontispiece has no indication of place and year, and simply 'I. C.' for the printer. The excellent Carnicelli edition almost always maintains the original spelling, but adds punctuation, that seems to be almost completely absent in the 1555 edition.

---

[1] *TFP*, p. vii. The Sion College copy was probably transferred to Lambeth Palace Library with the rest of the collection on the closure of Sion College Library in June 1996.

3.1.1 Text

The Triumph of the excellent Poet Francis Petrarch, of fearful death most elegantly written; ye that read it, remember it.

This most noble and most glorious lady
That now is a spirit, and in the earth doth lie,
And sometime was the high pillar of valour
Turned from her war with laud and honour;
Glad to have o'ercome an enemy so great 5
That with his wit turneth all men under feet,
With none other armour she did this deed
But with a chaste heart at the time of need,
With a sweet face and with a clean thought,
And with an honest speech this hath she wrought. 10
It was a new wonder for to behold and see
Love to be o'ercome in such wise and degree:
His bow broken, his arrows cast aside,
That slain had so many men of pride,
And taken prisoners infinite of men. 15
This noble lady with her company then
Turned (as said is) from that high victory,
All together going under a fair canopy;[2]
There was but few, no marvel at all,
Virtuous glory is rath and ever shall.[3] 20
But those that were present in that place
Each one by themselves, it is a plain case,
Seemed well worthy of laud to rehearse,
Of poet or orator, in prose or verse.
Their victorious standard was this: 25
In a green field a white ermine is
With a chain of gold about his neck;
A fair topazium thereto did it deck.[4]
Nothing after mortal men's rate

---

[2] Here Morley misreads Petrarch's 'in un bel drappelletto ivan ristrette' ('they went together in a small group'), as noted by Carnicelli (*TFP*, p. 212). 'Morley sees with contemporary decorum' (Marie Axton 'Lord Morley's Tryumphes of Petrarcke: Reading Spectacles', in *'Triumphs of English': Henry Parker, Lord Morley: Translator to the Tudor Court. New Essays in Interpretation*, ed. by Marie Axton and James P. Carley (London: The British Library, 2000), pp. 171–200 (p. 185)). Compare Fowler's translation of the same word with 'cloth of state'.
[3] rath] Possibly a misprint for 'rare'.
[4] topazium] topaz.

30   Was neither their speech nor yet their gait,
     But all divine for to behold and see;
     Happy are those that have such destiny.
     They seemed all fair bright stars,
     The Sun in the midst that not debars
35   The light away, but giveth them light,
     Having on their fair heads on height
     Rose garlands and violets fresh and gay.
     And as a loving gentle heart always
     Getteth honour for his virtuous life
40   So passed this company without debate or strife;
     When that all suddenly there did appear
     A sad black banner that approached near,[5]
     And a woman wrappèd all in black,
     With such a fury and with such a wrack
45   That uneath I cannot the truth tell,[6]
     In the time of the great mighty giants fell,[7]
     Were any so loathsome for to behold and see.
     Unto this lady so ghastly movèd she,
     And said: 'O sweet and excellent maid,
50   That goest here most perfectly arrayed
     With youth and beauty, and dost not see
     The term that I shall present arrest thee:
     I am the same importune cruel beast[8]
     Callèd Death fearful, that doth arrest
55   All creatures with my great force and might
     Or the day's end, making it the night.[9]
     It is I that hath quite and clean wasted
     The great Greek nation, and also hasted
     The noble Trojans unto their decline,
60   And last of all hath made to end and fine
     The Romans' glory with this blade keen,
     That pricketh and cutteth all away clean,

[5] While Petrarch simply writes of a woman dressed in black, Morley explicitly contrasts Death's banner with the green banner carried by the ladies. On this point see Axton, p. 185.
[6] uneath] not easily, scarcely, hardly.
[7] Morley eliminates Petrarch's allusion to the Phlaegrean plain, the Thessalian peninsula where Zeus vanquished the giants.
[8] importune] importunate. cruel beast] Morley misunderstands *fiera* (ferocious).
[9] Or] Used, here and elsewhere, in the sense of 'before', i.e. 'ere'. making it the night] As noted in *TFP* (p. 213), here Morley misreads 'gente, a cui fa notte innanzi sera' ('people, for whom it is dark before evening comes'): Petrarch is alluding to people blinded in their perception of death.

And infinite of other barbarous nations,
Using evermore these ways and factions.
When that they look not for me at all   65
With sudden stroke I make them down to fall.
A thousand thoughts of men, frail and vain,
I have broken, this is true and certain;
And now to you, when life seemeth best,
Here am I come your body to arrest,   70
Or any hard fortune to you chance to fall.
I will you take and end not one but all.'
This excellent lady, having no peer
In all the world, with sad and wise cheer
Answered unto death there present again: 75
'In these chaste companies, this is true and plain,
Thou hast no reason nor yet no power.
And less of all other,[10] in me, at this hour,
Only the spoil that thou shalt have
It is my chaste body unto the grave.   80
That well knoweth one, as well as I,
That taketh well my death most heavily;
His life on my health all doth depend.
But unto thee this is thy small end;[11]
It shall be to me no displeasure at all   85
To depart the frail world. Lo, this is all.'
This cruel beast, with her wise reason,
Was no less marvelled at that time and season
Than one that doth a thing in sudden haste,
And when the deed is so done and passed   90
Doth blame himself of that that he hath done.[12]
E'en so did this terrible monster soon;
And when he had himself pausèd a while,[13]
With a more soft speech, and gentle style,
'Thou', says he, 'that present here dost guide   95

---

[10] A slight misreading on Morley's part: in the original, Laura says that Death has no power over these people, and little over her. Morley makes clear what in Petrarch is only alluded to: the only power Death has is over Laura's body.

[11] Meaning that for Laura this is a very small victory on the part of Death.

[12] Carnicelli speaks of 'extreme blurring' on the part of the translator here (*TFP*, p. 214); Morley in fact misreads 'cosa nova' and translates it as 'sudden haste', while Petrarch is talking of one who realizes that he is looking at something unexpected.

[13] *TFP* edits this line as 'And when she had her selfe paused a whyle'. Morley omits the two lines in which Death recognizes people it has already wounded with its cruelty.

This fair chaste band on every side,
That hast not yet my fearful stroke essayed,[14]
By my counsel be not so sore afraid,
For that I will now do is for the best:
100 To make thee flee (O maid) from age oppressed,
Which hath always longing thereunto,
Much grief and dolour with pain and long woe;[15]
And to this now present, disposed I am,
Thou fair creature and sweet woman,
105 To do thee such honour present in this place
That thy spirit shall from the body pass
Without fear, dolour, or grief at all.
Be of good comfort, O maid, I have said all.'
This angelic creature, when she had heard
110 What Death had said, again answered:
'As it pleaseth Christ our Lord almighty,
That ruleth and tempereth all things eternally,
Do thou unto her[16] as thou doest to all men'.
Thus this fair lady answered there and then;
115 And lo, e'en there present all suddenly,
Full of dead bodies that great place did lie,
In such a number that them for to rehearse
It cannot be counted in prose nor yet in verse:
Of Catay, of Morocco, of Spain and India,[17]
120 Innumerable dead of all mankind.
There were those that men happy did call,
Kings, emperors, and bishops all;[18]
Now be they poor, as poor as beggars be.
Where is their riches and honour, trow ye,[19]
125 Their sceptres, their crowns with their precious stones,
Their mitres of purple, deckèd for the nonce?
Gone is all their glory and their fresh lust:
A fool is he that to such things doth trust.[20]
But those that will needs hope thereunto
130 At length shall see the matter to be so:

[14] stroke] Morley's free translation of Petrarch's *tosco*, poison.
[15] This and the previous line are Morley's expansion of Petrarch's *fastidi* (troubles).
[16] *TFP* emends to 'unto me'.
[17] Catay] Cathay, the ancient name for the region of China.
[18] Morley uses 'bishops' to translate *pontefici* (popes).
[19] trow ye] do you think.
[20] fool] Thus Morley translates Petrarch's *misero* (desolate), adding a tinge of reproach.

Themselves utterly scornèd and beguiled,
When all their fancies shall be quite exiled.
O blind fools, e'en worse than mad,[21]
For all the pleasures and joys ye have had,
To your old mother ye must needs pass,   135
And your names forgotten and turned to was.[22]
What profit hath it then been unto you,
With sword and blood strong nations to subdue,
To muck up treasure and your souls to defile?
It had been better to have lived a while   140
Poorly in this world, with brown bread and water;[23]
But now will I return again to my matter.
I say then, when the extreme hour was come
Of this fair lady, this is all and some;
And that she must the doubtful pass assay   145
That puts all the world in dread and fray.[24]
There came to see her of women many one,
To know and see, or that the life were gone,
What pain the fair creature did abide,
Both friends and neighbours diverse on each side.   150
And lo, as they her great beauty did behold,
Death dissolvèd the fair hair of gold;[25]
And so the fairest flower that ever was
He did root up.[26] Alas, I say, Alas!
Not for no hate that he to her then had,   155
But in heaven for to make her spirit glad.
O, how many complaints and bewailing,
Sighs and tears and other lamenting
Were there then among the women all,
When that, that[27] fair bright eyes celestial,   160
For which many a sweet song I made,
Many a sonnet, many a fresh ballad,[28]
Were closèd and shut up. Alas, O woe is me!

---

[21] Again, the allusion to foolishness is Morley's addition.
[22] was] Presumably 'waste'.
[23] The homely detail of the *brown* bread is Morley's addition.
[24] fray] fear.
[25] Morley here misses the allusion to the classical myth of Death plucking a single hair from its victim's head (as in *Aeneid*, IV. 698–99).
[26] He] TFP emends to 'she'; but Morley here treats Death as masculine, in accordance with English usage.
[27] TFP emends to 'those'.
[28] Morley expands Petrarch's *cantai* into a list of various poetic forms.

This fair creature (what trow ye?), then, did she
Sit still and glad in quiet and peace,
And gather the fruit of her virtuousness.
Go thy ways, O dear goddess, well content,
In peace and quiet with all thy virtues excellent.[29]
But little it availed against Death's might
Than if she have against such a one right.
What shall it be, trow ye, of the rest?
O human hope, with all misery oppressed!
In a few nights[30] so sweet a maid
Gone and past in so short a braid;[31]
So many tears for her death spread;
Thou that seest it or hearest it read,
Think what it is the world for to trust,
When such a creature is turnèd unto dust.
It was for truth the sixth day of April
That love to love her did me compel;
And even that same-self hour and day
Death did take my love and joy away.
And now, as fortune is wont for to change,[32]
Hath broken the knot and eke the range,
With such sorrow unto my woeful heart
That I am afraid I say, as for my part,
To tell it either in verse or in rhyme.
It was to me so sorrowful a time;
'Virtue,' said they that were present there,[33]
'Excellent beauty and most womanly cheer,
Now is dead and gone. What shall we be,
When she is past the death, as we do see;
When shall her peer or like be seen again?
So great perfection in one for to remain,
So sweet a speech, so angelic a voice?'
This above all other was the choice,
And the spirit, when it should depart,
As they might see and perfectly advert,

---

[29] Morley omits Petrarch's *dicean*, which clarifies that these two lines were spoken by Laura's friends.
[30] Here I accept *TFP*'s emendation (the original reads 'myghtes').
[31] in so short a braid] suddenly.
[32] Here Morley omits two stanzas (*Triumphus Mortis*, I. 136–41).
[33] Once more Morley downplays the role of the women surrounding Laura, reducing them to a generic 'they'.

With all other virtues gathered in one
Where, as it went, the air most brightly shone.   200
None evil adversary was so hardy there,
Afore her presence to stand or appear
With foul semblaunt,[34] to put her in dread,
Till death his assault had done in deed.
But after that, when all the fear was past,   205
And by desperation they sure at the last,
Each one did behold that most sweet face,
How precious it was, how full of grace,
Not dissolved with no violent pain,
But passing away with an easy vain,[35]   210
Even as a sweet light that cometh to decay,
Little and little consuming away,
When that the birth liquor is past and gone,[36]
The flame extinct, then light is there none.
Not pale she lay, but whiter than the snow,   215
That the wind against the hill doth blow,[37]
As he that weary is, and would have rest;
So she lay when Death had her oppressed,
And as one that sleepeth soft and quietly,
So might they all then and there espy   220
Dreadful Death that fools have in disgrace,
Fair and beautiful in that sweetest face.

The second chapter of the Triumph of Death

The night following that this horrible chance
Fell, to my heart's joy and pleasance,
That made in manner the Sun lose his light,
And from the earth took also all delight;
And the fair flower in heaven on high set   5
My guide gone, and I with sorrow fret,[38]
And blind left from all joy and pleasure.
The sweet soft season, pleasant, be ye sure,
With the cold that spread was in the air,

---

[34] semblaunt] appearance.
[35] vain] Even if the general meaning of the sentence is clear, this word remains obscure.
[36] *TFP* interprets 'birth liquor' as 'life fluid'.
[37] Morley here misinterprets Petrarch, who evokes the gentle fall of the snow on a hill without wind.
[38] Lines 5–6 are Morley's addition.

10 Afore Aurora, most delicate and fair,[39]
    Taketh away with his[40] wholesome streams
    All untrue and feignèd false dreams.
    Even at that time to me did appear,
    Semblaunt to that season, a maid fair and clear,[41]
15 Crowned with rich orient pearls white;
    And for to increase the more my delight
    Her fair hand stretched forth; then did she,
    And softly sighing gently spoke to me.
    'Doest thou not know me,' sayeth she me tell,
20 'Her that sometime thou didst love so well,
    Of whom thy heart was all set on fire,
    And made thee forsake all foul and vile desire?'
    Thus saying, with a sad sombre countenance,
    She sat her down, my joy and my pleasance,
25 And made me sit by her, e'en there,
    Upon a bank — me thought we twain were —
    Which was shadowed with the laurel tree;
    A great beech thereby well might I see,
    And I so sat, much like in such a case
30 As he that speaketh and weepeth a great pace.
    So did I answer unto this lady dear:
    'O thou fair creature, without to have a peer,
    How should it be that I thee should forget,
    Sithen that ever my heart on thee was set.[42]
35 Art thou alive or dead? I long to know.'
    'I am alive,' says she, 'thou mayst me trow,
    And thou art dead, and so still shall be
    Till that the last hour that taketh thee
    From the earth. Now mark well what I say:
40 The time is short, and our will alway[43]
    Is long; and therefore I thee rede,[44]
    What thou wilt say, that is, be said with speed,
    Lest that the day that cometh at the hand
    Make thou shalt not here no longer stand.'[45]

---

[39] Afore] When.
[40] TFP emends to 'her'.
[41] Semblaunt] according.
[42] Sithen] since.
[43] alway] always.
[44] rede] advise.
[45] Unless daylight, that is arriving, makes it so that you will be unable to remain here.

Then said I: 'O lady sweet and peerless, 45
That hast proved, I see it doubtless,
That life and death are both certain,
Tell me if death be so great a pain'.
She answered forthwith, and to me said:
'Men's blind opinion makes it to be afraid; 50
But for to tell thee what it is in deed,
Death is dissolving of all doubt and dread,[46]
And clean delivers us from a prison dark,
Specially to him that gently doth work;
But unto him that hath done amiss, 55
And all on covetousness his heart set is,
It is a pain and dolour infinite.
But I, that from that am free and quite,[47]
For this death which I did essay,
For which thou hast mournèd to this day, 60
Would make thee merry and all thy sores heal
If half the joy[48] thou hadst that I do feel.'
Thus spoke she, and her celestial eyes
Devoutly she lift up unto the skies;
And that rosy lips, more sweet than rose, 65
She held them still, till I did purpose,
'Silla, Nero, Caius, and Marius,
With these tyrants put Maxentius,
Sicken in the breast and in the flanks,
Pain of burning, fevers and cranks, 70
Makes the death more bitter than gall'.
She answered me then forthwith all,
'I cannot', says she, 'for truth deny,
But that the pain most certainly
That goeth afore that the death doth come 75
Is wonder grievous; this is all and some.
But that which grieveth most of all
Is the fear of loss of the life eternal.[49]
But the spirit that comforts him in good,
And with his heart doth dread his rod,[50] 80

---

[46] Morley adds this definition of death; Petrarch only speaks of deliverance from a long prison.
[47] quite] requited.
[48] Petrarch talks about *la millesima parte*, 'a thousandth part'.
[49] Thus Morley translates Petrarch's *etterno danno*, 'eternal damnation'.
[50] Morley introduces the idea of the fear of divine punishment, absent in Petrarch.

Unto him I say, what is the death
But e'en a sigh, and a short stopping breath?
This by myself did I well know and see
At the last hour, when death did take me;
85 The body was sick, but the soul was well,
When that I heard one by me there tell,
"O how wretched and miserable is he
That counteth the days of the infinity
That Laura is in,[51] and thinketh every day
90 A thousand days, I dare right well say,
Her excellent person to see and to behold,
And never after see, his comfort should;
Seeks for her the water and the land,
And never for her in quiet doth stand;
95 But always following one manner of style,
How that he may in every time and while
On her to think, on her with penne to write,
On her to speak, on her for to endyte".[52]
This hearing, casting mine eyes aside,
100 Her among the other there I espied
That often moved me, thee for to love,
And kindled in thy heart far above
The love I bore always unto thee.
I know her well, that it was very she
105 That much comforted me or I died,
With her wise words on every side;[53]
And plainly to thee, when that I was
In my best time, and in that honest case,
In youth but tender, and unto thee most dear,
110 Which made many and diverse here and there
To speak both and often of thee and me.
The life wherein thou sawst me for to be
Was but bitter, I swear now on my faith,
To the respect of my most pleasant death
115 Which to men mortal is very rare;
So that when my life away did fare
E'en at that point I was most merry and glad,

---

[51] More explicitly than Petrarch, Morley mentions Laura's name.
[52] her] Here I accept *TFP*'s emendation; the original has 'hye'. to endyte] to compose poems.
[53] Morley's 'wise words' could be a free rendition of Petrarch's *grave e saggia*, 'grave and wise', referring to Laura's friend.

Saving that of the great pity I had
To depart this world, trust thou me,
As one in exile his own country to see.'⁵⁴ 120
Then said I to her, e'en there again:
'On the faith, Madam, which you are certain
That I ought you without for to change,⁵⁵
Tell me now and be not to me strange,
For you know all, seeing that glorious sight 125
Above our knowledge, the eternal light;
Had you ever pity in your heart⁵⁶
Of my great sorrows, and pains smart,
Not leaving apart your high chaste ways,
Which that you usèd with me always? 130
Now showing to me a sweet disdain,
Now a sweet anger to double my pain,
Now showing a peace written in your eyes,⁵⁷
That held me too tied, and in such wise
That doubtful I was in what case I stood. 135
Many years thus I in love abode.'
Scant had I these words to her said
When that I saw, e'en at a braid,⁵⁸
That sweet smiling and fair countenance
That sometime was my joy and pleasance, 140
My comfort, my lust, and my rejoicing,
In this wise to me most gracious speaking:⁵⁹
'From thee my heart was never divided,
Nor never shall, but that I provided
Diverse times with my wise regard; 145
I tempered thy love that well near thou had marred,
Because there was as then none other way
Our fervent love with honest⁶⁰ for to stay.

---

⁵⁴ Petrarch makes it clear that Laura's only regret is the pain Petrarch might be feeling; Morley makes this more generic.
⁵⁵ Petrarch has the lover ask Laura whether she had pity for him, and does so in the name of his love that was, at the time, apparent to her; Morley rather insists on a love that ought to be unchanged. The two lines may be read thus: 'For the sake of the love that I should have for you without change, Madam, as you well know'.
⁵⁶ Petrarch locates the possible thoughts of pity *nella testa*, in Laura's head; Morley prefers the more conventional heart.
⁵⁷ The anaphora is Morley's innovation.
⁵⁸ at a braid] suddenly.
⁵⁹ In Petrarch, Laura speaks with a sigh; Morley creates a rather more authoritative figure.
⁶⁰ *TFP* emends to 'honesty', which makes more sense, but halts the rhythm.

Therefore, in like case as thou seest a mother
150 Correct her dear child for no other
But all to bring her[61] to good frame,
E'en so did I then use the same,
And said to myself, "Full many a season
This man not loves but burns out of reason;
155 Wherefore it behoveth me for to provide[62]
In this hard, dangerous case on every side,
And surely full evil provideth he
That looketh outward and doth not see
What is inward in such a perilous case".
160 This in my pitiful heart took then place,
And this to thee as a bridle was then,
As thou seest by[63] a horse ruled by a man.
Wherefore sometime I showed me wonders glad,
Sometime again to be as sober and sad,
165 And yet I loved as hot and true as you,
Always saving the chosen honest due
Which so my will then and ever oppressed
That reason ruled my desire at the least;
And when that again I did behold and see
170 Thy sorrow so grievous and painful for to be,
Sweetly and gently on thee mine eyes I set,
Thy health and welfare again for to get.
This was ever my wise honest ways
That I honestly used with thee in those days.[64]
175 And when I saw the tears dropping avail
Down thy pale cheeks like unto the hail,
Then I did pray, and softly then I said,
"Here it is necessary I give anon an aid".
And when that thou were forthwith again
180 Into too much hope my love for to attain,
Anon unto myself e'en thus said I,
"Here of necessity must be had a remedy,
A hard and straight bit I must now put to".
This with diverse colours many mo,[65]

---

[61] *TFP* emends to 'it'.
[62] it behoveth me] it befits me.
[63] *TFP* eliminates 'by'.
[64] At this point Morley omits lines 106–11, in which Laura elaborates on Petrarch's sorrow.
[65] mo] more.

With hot, with green, with cold, with white,⁶⁶ 185
I kept thee always still in honest plight;
Thou knowest this well and hast it told,
And in many a sweet sonnet it enrol.'⁶⁷
When she had said these words to me plain,
With trembling voice I said to her again: 190
'Your words to me should be passing sweet,
For the great love and most fervent heat
That I have ever born my joy to you,
If I believed them faithfully to be true'.
'O unfaithful man,' then answered she, 195
'Why should I say these words unto thee,
If that my words were not true and just?
Now then, I tell thee, disclose my heart I must.⁶⁸
If in this world, living, to my sight
I took in thee just pleasure and delight 200
I kept it secret, where thou, I say again,
Thy love to all men didst make it plain.
There was no difference in our love at all,
But that my true love was joinèd all
In most honest wise so for to be; 205
But now one thing I will demand of thee:
When that thy sweet ballettes I did sing,⁶⁹
Didst thou then doubt of me in any thing?
I think plainly nay, and therefore thus,
Though for a time I was contrarious, 210
By loving strange, and seeming so to be,
A thousand times thou mayst trust me;
With my thought always so I fared,
Thou hadst of me an inward sweet regard,
And more thy mind at that time to appease 215
I will tell thee that thing that shall thee please.
It grieveth me sore that I was not borne

---

⁶⁶ cold] The original edition has 'golde', but it is almost certainly a misprint (compare Petrarch's *freddo*).
⁶⁷ Morley inserts here the reference to Petrarch's celebration of his state in his sonnets, after omitting Petrarch's earlier allusion.
⁶⁸ Carnicelli notes that 'from this point to the end of the chapter Morley's translation deteriorates' (*TFP*, p. 221). I would rather say that Morley here adopts a freer approach, changing the order of the various topics introduced in this final section.
⁶⁹ ballettes] ballads, simple songs. Morley here transforms Petrarch's precise reference to one of his poems to a more generic allusion.

By thy fair city; I say to thee therefore,
Although my country full pleasant be,[70]
220   I would my nest had been near to thee,
Lest that percase thy mind should change,[71]
And love some other among so great a range.'
To these words no word then I said.[72]
The third celestial sphere had so arrayed,
225   And lift in love so sore my loving thought,
That answer her at that time could I nought.
Then she to me, with a benign love and cheer:
'I have in this world by the great honour here,
And shall have always, mark well what I shall say:
230   The night is past, now cometh the bright day.[73]
If that to me thou wilt more say, sweet heart,
Be short, I bid thee, for I must hence depart.'
'O', said I, 'mine own sweet lady dear,
For all the sorrow and pain I have had here
235   In loving you, these words so fair and sweet
Doth recompense my love and makes all meet.
But from you thus for to be separate plain
Is unto me a deadly mortal pain.
But one thing now to me you must declare,
240   Or that ye from my woeful presence fare:
Shall I live long, tell me, after you,
Or shortly, as I would, O lady, you ensue?'
She answered gently, as far as she could tell,
Long after her on earth here should I dwell.[74]

---

[70] Morley may have misread here; Petrarch has Laura say that, although she grieves at being born in a humble village, she is pleased that she met Petrarch in a beautiful country (i.e. Provence).

[71] percase] perchance.

[72] In the original Petrarch does answer Laura, and the lines that follow are his answer. By having the poet unable to answer the woman, Morley creates a scene of singular pathos.

[73] Here Morley ignores the personification of Dawn rising from her bed that we find in Petrarch; 'he nevertheless stays true to the tenderness and intimacy of the scene and the sober grief of parting' (Axton, p. 188).

[74] While Petrarch has Laura deliver these final lines in a direct speech, Morley prefers a poignant reported speech.

3.2. 'E. D.'

This translation of *Triumphus Mortis*, I. 79–100, is included in *The prayse of Nothing. By E. D.* (London: H. Jackson, 1585). Approximately twenty-five copies of this book survive; the present transcription is based on Oxford, Bodleian Library, Douce D.199.[75] The text was reprinted in *Writings in Verse and Prose of Sir Edward Dyer*, edited by Alexander B. Grosart (1872), pp. 106–07 (the whole *Prayse of Nothing* appears on pp. 65–120). Grosart's transcription is extremely faithful. It is no more than a coincidence, albeit an intriguing one, that the same initials appear in two of the paratextual sonnets in Fowler's translation.

3.2.1 Text

But to return where I left, touching the contempt and abject use of worldly things, Petrarch in his Triumph of Death, newly speaking in our tongue, by an unlearned translator, maintaineth the same argument.

The popes (saith he), the kings, and who commanded have the world,
Are naked now, misers, and needy persons all;
Now treasures where? now honours where? and precious stones?
And sceptres where? and crowns, mitres, and purple shows?
He wretched is that lays his hope in mortal things.   5
But who doth not? and if he find himself at length
Deceived, 'tis reason great, and answereth well his act.
O senseless man,[76] so much to travail what avails?
To the ancient mother great all shall return at last,
And hardly shall the mention of your names be found.   10
Of a thousand labours not one a profit yields,
But each of them apparent vanities are known.
Your studies who doth understand can tell me this.
With minds inflamed, always to damage of your selves,
What profit is? so many countries to subdue,   15
And nations diverse tributaries make unknown,
And after enterprises perilous and vain,
With blood to conquer walled towns, and treasure get?
A way more sweet is found with water, and with bread.
With glass and wood, than with rich orient stone and gold.   20

---

[75] The Bodleian Library has another copy, Tanner 217(3), which is bound with other books and shows some marking and other signs of use; the frontispiece presents, under the date, the signature of Thom. Tanner. There are no variants between the two copies.
[76] Thus the translator avoids Petrarch's metaphor of blindness.

3.3 Mary Sidney, Countess of Pembroke

The text of Mary Sidney's translation of Petrarch's *Triumphus Mortis* is extant in a single manuscript, London, Inner Temple, Petyt MS 538.43. It is part of a large codex in a nineteenth-century binding, with the Inner Temple Library ex-libris on the guardsheet and the Library dry stamp in gold on the cover. The codex is a miscellany of late sixteenth- or early seventeenth-century material: a list of contents is pasted on the third guardsheet.[77] Section 14 is described as 'Copies in a small neat hand, of various poetical pieces, etc.', and this item as 'Versions of Psalms 51, 104, and 137, by Mary Sidney, Countess of Pembroke, and "The Triumph of Death," a poem translated by the same out of Italian'. The Petrarch translation appears as item 14.i (fols 284r–89v); item 14.xii (fol. 303v) contains a presentation letter to Lucy Countess of Bedford, from Sir John Harington, sending her the Countess of Pembroke's Psalms and his own epigrams, dated 29 December 1600. The very fine and clear hand is not Harington's, as can be seen if we compare this to his autograph manuscripts in the British Library. This manuscript is supposed to be a copy of a copy Harington made of the Sidney original;[78] Harington received the translation, presumably in December 1600, from Sidney herself. There is the possibility that this was just a sample of a longer translation, no longer extant, or that Mary Sidney was in the habit of having short translations written for friends.[79] The spelling is remarkably consistent and highlights the rhyme scheme; the punctuation is also quite accurate, often using question marks and brackets (which I have normally maintained here).

The text was first edited in 1912 by Frances Berkeley Young, in a diplomatic transcription, which unfortunately omitted twenty-four lines of text (I. 118–41).[80] More recent editions have been undertaken by Gary Waller, Gavin Alexander, Margaret Hannay and Danielle Clarke.[81]

---

[77] Listed also in Frances Berkeley Young, 'The Triumphe of Death Translated out of Italian by the Countesse of Pembroke', *PMLA*, 27 (1912), 47–75 (p. 48).
[78] See Frances Berkeley Young, *Mary Sidney, Countess of Pembroke* (London: David Nutt, 1912), p. 208. Young adds: 'There is no apparent reason, however, for doubting the authenticity of Lady Pembroke's authorship of the "Triumph of Death," especially since this translation is accompanied by a fragment of her very well-known metrical version of the Psalms' (p. 208).
[79] On this point see Gavin Alexander, 'The Triumph of Death: A Critical Edition in Modern Spelling of the Countess of Pembroke's Translation of Petrarch's Trionfo della Morte', *Sidney Journal*, 17 (1999), 2–18 (pp. 2–7).
[80] Young, 'The Triumphe of Death' and *Mary Sidney, Countess of Pembroke*.
[81] *The Triumph of Death and other Unpublished and Uncollected Poems by Mary Sidney, Countess of Pembroke (1561–1621)*, ed. by Gary F. Waller (Salzburg: Institut für Anglistik und Amerikanistik Universität Salzburg, 1977); Alexander, 'The Triumph of Death'; *The Collected Works of Mary Sidney Herbert, Countess of Pembroke: Volume I: Poems, Translations, and Correspondence*, ed. by Margaret P. Hannay et al. (Oxford: Clarendon Press, 1998); *Isabella Whitney, Mary Sidney and Aemilia Lanyer: Renaissance Women Poets*, ed. by Danielle Clarke (London: Penguin, 2000).

3.3.1 Text

The Triumph of Death translated out of Italian.
By the Countess of Pembroke

The first chapter

That gallant lady, gloriously bright,
    The stately pillar once of worthiness,
    And now, a little dust, a naked sprite,
Turned from her wars a joyful conqueress;[82]
    Her wars, where she had foiled the mighty foe,   5
    Whose wily stratagems the world distress.
And foiled him, not with sword, with spear or bow,
    But with chaste heart, fair visage, upright thought,
    Wise speech, which did with honour linkèd go.
And, love's new plight to see, strange wonders wrought   10
    With shivered bow, chaste arrows, quenched flame,
    While here some slain, and there lay others caught.
She, and the rest, who in the glorious fame
    Of the exploit her chosen mates did share,
    All in one squadronet close ranged came.[83]   15
A few, for nature makes true glory rare,
    But each alone (so each alone did shine),
    Claimed whole historians', whole poets' care;
Born in green field, a snowy ermiline[84]
    Collared with topazes, set in fine gold[85]   20
    Was this faire company's unfoilèd sign.[86]
No earthly march, but heav'nly, did they hold;
    Their speeches holy were, and happy those,
    Who so are borne, to be with them enrolled.
Clear stars they seemed,[87] which did a sun enclose,   25
    Who hiding none, yet all did beautify
    With coronets decked with violet and rose.
And as gained honour, filled with jollity

---

[82] The image of the conquering lady is Sidney's.
[83] squadronet] a small squadron.
[84] A diminutive of 'ermine'.
[85] Collared] The manuscript has 'coloured'; my emendation follows the Italian original.
[86] unfoiled] unmarred, or never vanquished.
[87] The manuscript has 'send'; this emendation is proposed by Alexander, 'The Triumph of Death' and Hannay (*Collected Works*, ed. by Hannay et al.).

	Each gentle heart, so made they merry cheer,
30	When lo, an ensign sad I might descry,
	Black, and in black, a woman did appear,
	Fury with her, such as I scarcely know
	If like at Phlegra with the giants were.
	'Thou dame', quoth she, 'that doeth so proudly go,
35	Standing upon thy youth, and beauty's state,
	And of thy life, the limits doest not know.
	Lo, I am she, so fierce, importunate,
	And deaf, and blind, entitled oft by you,
	You, whom with night ere evening I await.[88]
40	I, to their end, the Greekish nation drew,
	The Trojan first, the Roman afterward,
	With edge and point of this my blade I slew.
	And no barbarian my blow could ward,[89]
	Who stealing on with unexpected wound,
45	Of idle thoughts have many thousand marred.[90]
	And now no less to you-ward am I bound,
	While life is dearest, ere, to cause you moan,
	Fortune some bitter with your sweets compound.'
	'To this, thou right or interest hast none,
50	Little to me, but only to this spoil',
	Replied then she, who in the world was one.
	'This charge of woe on others will recoil,[91]
	I know, whose safety on my life depends;
	For me, I thank who shall me hence assoil.'[92]
55	As one whose eyes some novelty attend,
	And what it marked not first, it spied at last,
	New wonders with itself, now comprehends,
	So fared the cruel, deeply overcast[93]
	With doubt awhile, then spoke: 'I know them now;
60	I now remember when my teeth they past'.
	Then with less frowning, and less darkened brow,

---

[88] The manuscript has 'amate'.
[89] ward] resist.
[90] marred] deprived.
[91] Petrarch has *altri*, generally read as singular and taken to refer to the poet himself. Sidney's choice of the plural 'others' has been read as having a more general significance, and possibly alluding to the queen's refusal to name a successor (*Isabella Whitney, Mary Sidney and Aemilia Lanyer*, ed. by Clarke, p. 360). It might simply be a mistake.
[92] assoil] deliver.
[93] The manuscript has 'ouer-gast'.

'But thou that lead'st this goodly company,
    Didst never yet unto my sceptre bow.[94]
But on my counsel if thou wilt rely,
    Who may enforce thee, better is by far
    From age and age's loathsomeness to fly.
More honourèd by me, than others are
    Thou shalt thee find; and neither fear nor pain
    The passage shall of thy departure bar.'
'As likes that Lord, who in the heav'n doth reign,
    And thence, this all, doeth moderately guide;
    As others doe, I shall thee entertain.'
So answered she, and I withal descried[95]
    Of dead appear a never-numbered sum,
    Pestering the plain, from one to th'other side.[96]
From India, Spain, Cathay, Morocco, come,
    So many ages did together fall,
    That worlds were filled, and yet they wanted room.
There saw I, whom their times did happy call,
    Popes, emperors, and kings, but strangely grown,
    All naked now, all needy, beggars all.
Where is that wealth? Where are those honours gone?
    Sceptres, and crowns, and robes, and purple dye?
    And costly mitres, set with pearl and stone?
O wretch, who doest in mortal things affy;[97]
    (Yet who but doeth) and if in end they die
    Themselves beguiled, they find but right, say I.
What means this toil? Oh blind, oh more than blind;
    You all return to your great mother old,
    And hardly leave your very names behind.
Bring me, who doeth your studies well behold,
    And of your cares not manifestly vain,
    One let him tell me, when he all hath told.
So many lands to win, what boots the pain?
    And on strange lands tributes to impose,
    With hearts still greedy, their own loss to gain.
After all these, wherein you winning lose

---

[94] Sidney here proposes the image of bowing to the sceptre, while Petrarch refers to tasting poison.
[95] descried] saw, distinguished.
[96] The use of the word 'pestering' introduces the idea of contagion or epidemic, which is not present in Petrarch.
[97] affy] trust, confide.

>   Treasures and territories dear, bought with blood;
>   Water, and bread hath a far sweeter close.[98]
> 100 And gold, and gem, gives place to glass and wood.
>   But least I should too long digression make
>   To turn to my first talk[99] I think it good.
>   Now that short glorious life her leave to take
>   Did near unto the utmost instant go,
> 105   And doubtful step, at which the world doeth quake.
>   Another number than themselves did show
>   Of ladies, such as bodies yet did lade.[100]
>   If Death could piteous be, they fain would know.
>   And deep they did in contemplation wade
> 110   Of that cold end, presented there to view,
>   Which must be once, and must but once be made.
>   All friends and neighbours were this careful crew,
>   But death with ruthless hand one golden hair
>   Chosen from out those amber tresses drew.
> 115 So cropped the flower of all this world most faire,
>   To show upon the excellentest thing
>   Her supreme force, and for no hate she bore.
>   How many drops did flow from briny spring
>   In who there saw those sightful fountains dry,[101]
> 120   For whom this heart so long did burn and spring.[102]
>   For her in midst of moan and misery,
>   Now reaping once what virtues life did sow,
>   With joy she sat retired silently.
>   'In peace', cried they, 'right mortal Goddess, go.'
> 125   And so she was, but that in no degree
>   Could death entreat, her coming to forslow.[103]
>   What confidence for others? if that she
>   Could fry and freeze in few nights changing cheer:
>   Oh human hopes, how fond and false you be.
> 130 And for this gentle soul, if many a tear
>   By pity shed, did bathe the ground and grass,
>   Who saw, doeth know; think thou, that doest but hear.

---

[98] a far sweeter close] a far sweeter effect, or conclusion.
[99] Hannay emends to 'taske' (*Collected Works*, ed. by Hannay et al.).
[100] lade] burden.
[101] An interesting periphrasis for Petrarch's *occhi*. The 'briny spring' is the source of tears, where Petrarch simply has *lagrimosi*.
[102] Hannay emends to 'sing' (*Collected Works*, ed. by Hannay et al.).
[103] forslow] delay, slow.

The sixth of April, one o'clock it was[104]
> That tied me once, and did me now untie,[105]
> Changing her copy;[106] thus doeth fortune pass.   135

None so his thrall, as I my liberty;
> None so his death, as I my life do rue,
> Staying with me, who fain from it would fly.[107]

Due to the world, and to my years was due,
> That I, as first I came, should first be gone,   140
> Not her leaf quailed,[108] as yet but freshly new.

Now for my woe, guess not by't, what is shown,
> For I dare scarce once cast a thought thereto,
> So far I am off, in words to make it known.

'Virtue is dead; and dead is beauty too,   145
> And dead is curtesy, in mournful plight',
> The ladies said; 'and now, what shall we do?

Never again such grace shall bless our sight;
> Never like wit, shall we from woman hear,
> And voice, replete with angel-like delight.'   150

The soul now pressed to leave that bosom dear,
> Her virtues all uniting now in one,
> There, where it past did make the heavens clear.

And of the enemies so hardly none
> That once before her showed his face obscure   155
> With her assault, till death had thorough gone.

Past plaint and fear when first they could endure
> To hold their eyes on that fair visage bent,
> And that despair had made them now secure.

Not as great fires violently spent,   160
> But in themselves consuming, so her flight
> Took that sweet sprite, and passed in peace content.

Right like unto some lamp of clearest light,
> Little and little wanting nutriture,[109]

---

[104] As noted by Hannay (*Collected Works*, ed. by Hannay et al.), Sidney may have misunderstood Petrarch's *l'ora prima*, that is, the first hour of sunrise.
[105] tied] The manuscript has 'tyde'.
[106] Changing her copy] changing her style.
[107] William Kennedy notes that this version 'curiously alters the tense of this passage', from the past to the present; 'it also invests Petrarch's use of the word *libertade* with its echoes of Christian freedom and noble privilege'. See *The Site of Petrarchism: Early Modern National Sentiment in Italy, France, and England* (Baltimore: The Johns Hopkins University Press, 2003), p. 243.
[108] quailed] destroyed.
[109] nutriture] nourishment, fuel.

165   Holding to end[110] a never-changing plight.
Pale? no, but whitely; and more whitely pure,
      Than snow on windless hill, that flaking falls:
      As one, whom labour did to rest allure.
And when that heav'nly guest those mortal walls
170   Had left, it nought but sweetly sleeping was,
      In her fair eyes, what folly dying calls.
Death fair did seem to be in her fair face.

The second chapter of the Triumph of Death

That night, which did the dreadful hap ensue,
      That quite eclipsed, nay, rather did replace
      The sun in skies, and me bereave of view,
Did sweetly sprinkle through the airy space
5   The summer's frost, which with Tithon's bride[111]
      Cleareth of dream the dark-confusèd face.
When lo, a lady, like unto the tide[112]
      With orient jewels crowned, from thousands more
      Crowned as she; to me, I coming spied.
10 And first her hand, sometime desired so
      Reaching to me, at once she sighed and spake;
      Whence endless joys yet in my heart do grow.
'And know'st thou her, who made thee first forsake
      The vulgar path, and ordinary trade?
15   While her, their mark, thy youthful thoughts did make?'
Then down she sat, and me sit down she made.
      Thought, wisdom, meekness in one grace did strive,
      On pleasing bank in bay,[113] and beech's shade.
'My goddess, who me did, and doeth revive,
20   Can I but know?' (I sobbing answerèd)
      'But art thou dead? Ah speak, or yet alive?'
'Alive am I: and thou as yet art dead,
      And as thou art shalt so continue still
      Till by thy ending hour, thou hence be led.

---

[110] The manuscript has 'and'.
[111] Tithonus, lover of Eos, the goddess of the dawn. Sidney is the only translator who maintains the allusion to Tithon as we find it in the Petrarchan original.
[112] The season of spring.
[113] On pleasing] The manuscript has 'unpleasing'; I follow Hannay's emendation (*Collected Works*, ed. by Hannay et al.). bank in bay] Sidney uses the alliteration in lieu of Petrarch's pun between *Laura* and *lauro* (the laurel tree).

Short is our time to live, and long our will: 25
    Then let with heed, thy deeds, and speeches go,
    Ere that approaching term his course fulfil.'
Quoth I, 'When this our light to end doeth grow,
    Which we call life (for thou by proof hast tried)
    Is it such pain to die? That, make me know.' 30
'While thou' (quoth she) 'the vulgar make thy guide,
    And on their judgements (all obscurely blind)
    Doest yet rely, no bliss can thee betide.
Of loathsome prison to each gentle mind
    Death is the end; and only who employ 35
    Their cares on mud, therein displeasure find.
E'en this my death, which yields thee such annoy,
    Would make in thee far greater gladness rise,
    Couldst thou but taste least portion of my joy.'
So spake she with devoutly fixèd eyes 40
    Upon the Heavens; then did in silence fold
    Those rosy lips, attending their replies;[114]
'Torments, invented by the tyrants old;[115]
    Diseases, which each part torment and toss,
    Causes, that death we most bitter hold.' 45
'I not deny' (quoth she) 'but that the cross
    Preceding death, extremely martyreth,[116]
    And more the fear of that eternal loss.
But when the panting soul in God takes breath;[117]
    And weary heart affecteth heav'nly rest,[118] 50
    An unrepented sigh, not else, is death.
With body, but with spirit ready pressed,
    Now at the furthest of my living ways,
    There sadly uttered sounds my ear possessed:
"Oh hapless he; who counting times and days 55
    Thinks each a thousand years, and lives in vain
    No more to meet her while on earth he stays.
And on the water now, now on the main
    Only on her doeth think, doeth speak, doeth write,

---

[114] In Petrarch the reply is clearly assigned to the mourning lover.
[115] Sidney here eliminates Petrarch's list of tyrants. This, together with the slight confusion generated in the previous line, suggests a corrupted or imperfectly copied text.
[116] extremely martyreth] is very painful.
[117] The image of the *panting* soul is Sidney's, not Petrarch's; Clarke hypothesizes a link with Psalm 42 (*Isabella Whitney, Mary Sidney and Aemilia Lanyer*, ed. by Clarke, p. 363).
[118] affecteth] desires.

	And in all times one manner still retain."
60	

Herewith, I thither cast my failing sight,
    And soon espied, presented to my view,
    Who oft did thee restraining, me incite.
Well, I her face, and well her voice I knew,
65   Which often did my heart reconsolate;[119]
    Now wisely grave, then beautifully true.
And sure, when I was in my fairest state,
    My years most green, myself to thee most dear,
    Whence many much did think, and much debate
70 That life's best joy, was all most bitter cheer,
    Compared to that death, most mildly sweet,
    Which comes to men, but comes not everywhere:
For I, that journey passed with gladder feet,
    Than he from hard exile, that homeward goes,
75   (But only ruth of thee) without regret.'[120]
'For that faith's sake, time once enough did show,
    Yet now to thee more manifestly plain,
    In face of him, who all doeth see and know,[121]
Say, lady, did you ever entertain
80   Motion or thought more lovingly to rue
    (Not loving[122] honour's height) my tedious pain?
For those sweet wraths, those sweet disdains in you,
    In those sweet peaces written in your eye,
    Diversely many years my fancy drew.'
85 Scarce had I spoken, but in lightning wise
    Beaming,[123] I saw that gentle smile appear,
    Sometimes the sun of my woe-darkened skies.
Then sighing, thus she answered: 'Never were
    Our hearts but one, nor never two shall be:
90   Only thy flame I tempered with my cheer;
This only way could save both thee and me;
    Our tender fame did this support require,
    The mother hath a rod, yet kind is she.
How oft this said my thoughts: "In love, nay fire
95   Is he: now to provide must I begin,

---

[119] my heart reconsolate] bring comfort to my heart.
[120] She felt no regret at the idea of dying, but only compassion for him.
[121] Petrarch clearly attributes this tercet to the lover, while Sidney is more ambiguous. I have inserted inverted commas that follow Petrarch's choice.
[122] Hannay emends to 'Not leving' (*Collected Works*, ed. by Hannay et al.).
[123] Beaming like lightning.

                And ill providers are fear and desire.
Thou saw'st what was without, not what within."
                And as the brake the wanton steed doeth tame,
                    So this did thee from thy disorders win.
A thousand times wrath in my face did flame,   100
                    My heart meanwhile with love did inly burn;
                    But never will my reason overcame.¹²⁴
For, if woe-vanquished once, I saw thee mourn;
                    Thy life, our honour, jointly to preserve,
                    Mine eyes to thee sweetly did I turn.   105
But if thy passion did from reason swerve,
                    Fear in my words, and sorrow in my face
                    Did then to thee for salutation serve.
These arts I used with thee; now¹²⁵ ran'st this race
                    With kind acceptance, now sharp disdain,   110
                    Thou know'st, and hast it sung in many a place.
Sometimes thine eyes pregnant with teary rain
                    I saw, and at the sight; "Behold, he dies,
                    But if I help",¹²⁶ said I, "the signs are plain".
Virtue for aide, did then with love advise: 115
                    If spurred by love, thou took'st some running toy,
                    "So soft a bit" (quoth I) "will not suffice".
Thus glad, and sad, in pleasure, and annoy;
                    Hot¹²⁷ red, cold pale; thus far I have thee brought
                    Weary, but safe, to my no little joy.'   120
Then I with tears, and trembling: 'What it sought
                    My faith hath found, whose more than equal meed
                    Were this; if this, for truth could pass my thought'.
'Of little faith' (quoth she) 'should this proceed,
                    If false it were, or if unknown from me';   125
                    The flames withal seemed in her face to breed.
'If liking in mine eyes the world did see
                    I say not, now, of this, right fain I am,
                    Those chains that tied my heart¹²⁸ well likèd me.

---

¹²⁴ But my will never overcame my reason.
¹²⁵ My emendation (the manuscript has 'thou') to preserve an analogy with the original.
¹²⁶ Unless I help, he dies.
¹²⁷ The manuscript has 'whot'.
¹²⁸ This has often been seen as a translation mistake on the part of Sidney, who translates *avei* ('you had', second person singular) as if it were a first person singular, referring to Petrarch. For a discussion of this point, see Ilona Bell, *Elizabethan Women and the Poetry of Courtship* (Cambridge: Cambridge University Press, 1998), pp. 102-03.

130 And well me likes (if true it be) my flame,[129]
        Which far and near by thee related goes,
        Nor in thy love could ought but measure blame.
That only failed; and while in acted woes
        Thou needs wouldst shew, what I could not but see,
135   Thou didst thy heart to all the world disclose.
Hence sprang my zeal, which yet distempereth thee,
        Our concord such in every thing beside,
        As when united love and virtue be.
In equal flames[130] our loving hearts were tried,
140   At least when once thy love had notice got,
        But one to shew, the other sought to hide.
Thou didst for mercy call with weary throat
        In fear and shame, I did in silence go,
        So much desire became of little note.
145 But not the less becomes concealèd woe,
        Nor greater grows it uttered than before,
        Through fiction, truth will neither ebb nor flow.
But cleared I not the darkest mists of yore?
        When I thy words alone did entertain
150   Singing for thee? my love dares speak no more.
With thee my heart, to me I did restrain
        Mine eyes; and thou thy share canst hardly brook
        Leasing by me the less, the more to gain.
Not thinking if a thousand times I took
155   Mine eyes from thee, I many thousands cast
        Mine eyes on thee; and still with pitying look.
Whose shine no cloud had ever overcast:
        Had I not feared in thee those coals to fires
        I thought would burn too dangerously fast.
160 But to content thee more, ere I retire
        For end of this, I something will thee tell,
        Perchance agreeable to thy desire:
In all things fully blest, and pleasèd well,
        Only in this I did myself displease:
165   Born in too base a town for me to dwell.
And much I grieved, that for thy greater ease,

---

[129] Hannay emends to 'fame' (*Collected Works*, ed. by Hannay et al.).
[130] Sidney eliminates Petrarch's *quasi* (in the original, the flames of love are *almost* equal), so that Laura's love is on the same level as Petrarch's (Kennedy, *The Site of Petrarchism*, p. 243).

  At least, it stood not near thy flowery nest.
    Else far enough, from whence I did thee please.
So might the heart on which I only rest
    Not knowing me, have fit itself elsewhere,   170
    And I less name, less notice have possessed.'
'Oh no' (quoth I) 'for me, the heav'ns' third sphere
    To so high love advanced by special grace.
    Changeless to me, though changed thy dwelling were.'
'Be as it will, yet my great honour was,   175
    And is as yet' (she said) 'but thy delight
    Makes thee not mark how fast the hours do pass.
See[131] from her golden bed Aurora bright
    To mortal eyes returning sun and day
    Breast-high above the ocean, bare to sight.   180
She to my sorrow calls me hence, away.
    Therefore thy words in time's short limits bind,
    And say in brief, if more thou have to say.'
'Lady' (quoth I) 'your words most sweetly kind
    Have easy made, whatever erst I bare   185
    But what is left of you to live behind.
Therefore to know this, my only care,
    If slow or swift shall come our meeting day.'
    She parting said, 'As my conjectures are,
Thou without me long time on earth shalt stay'.   190

---

[131] The manuscript has 'shee' (probably in imitation of what happens in line 181).

3.4. Anna Hume

Anna Hume's translation of the first three *Triumphi* survives in its first (and only) printed edition, published in Edinburgh in 1644 by Evan Tyler; in 2006, the publisher Ashgate printed a facsimile of this edition, with an introduction by Thomas P. Roche.[132] Roche used the copy now held at the Houghton Library at Harvard, but he also checked ten other surviving copies in British and American libraries, and concluded that all the examined copies were similar. The only exception was the British Library copy (now with the shelfmark E.1164(2)), 'which includes at the end, after a printer's errata page, a full-page emblem showing a broken tomb with mysterious figures almost apocalyptic in intensity (sig. G7v), and on the facing page (sig. G8) a poem'.[133] Here is the text of that poem, transcribed from the same British Library copy:

When first my *light* did shine, you lik'd me well.
Now that is gone; you hate my loathsome smell;
You with prolongers made me live, and art
Preserv'd my *light*; but now *Time* acts his part,
Triumphant *Time*, shews now my glasse is run
And all must end, that ever was begun:
Envy hath playd its part, and I do go
To *Coffin*: as I do, all must do so.
Time breaths a shrewd and life-bereaving blast,
Yet upward flyes my *light*, where it shall last.
I'me glad to part from *body*, which I lov'd
So deer, that many wayes and arts I prov'd
This mudwall to maintain, and body save,
But yet in spight of me 'twill go to grave.
This is my comfort, *Body*, that thy tombe
Which is thy *grave*, shall be thy mothers womb
To bring thee once again unto the *light*,
And *life*, which *death* shall never know, or night:
Then be content, though you and I depart:
Yet *Soul* and *Body* still shall have one heart.
    And upward flyes my *soul*, where it shall dwell,
    Beyond the reach of *Envy*, *Death*, or *Hell*.

The imagery appears to be the standard fare of early seventeenth-century

---

[132] Anna Hume, *The Triumphs of Love: Chastitie: Death: Translated out of Petrarch by Mris Anna Hume* (Edinburgh: Evan Tyler, 1644); *Anna Hume: The Triumphs of Love: Chastitie: Death*, ed. by Thomas P. Roche (Farnham: Ashgate, 2006).
[133] *Anna Hume*, ed. by Roche, p. xvi.

religious texts that insist on the mortification of the flesh (the most splendid example probably being John Donne's *Deaths Duell*). As noted by Roche, the poem is not Hume's, apart from the last two lines: 'I am happy to report that the poem is the work of another Scottish poet, Robert Farley, and is found in his *Lychnocausia, sive moralia facum emblemata. Lights Morall Emblems* (1638)'.[134] The present edition of Hume's translation of the 'Triumph of Death' is based on the British Library copy, which is also the one available in EEBO. It is a very small octavo, but a very clear copy (clearer than the Ashgate facsimile). I have also included Hume's argument and notes appended at the end of each chapter. I have maintained italics as used in the original.

3.4.1 Text

The Triumph of Death. Chapter I

The Argument.
Lauretta *meeting cruel death,*
Mildly resigns her noble breath.

The glorious maid, whose soul to heav'n is gone,[135]
And left the rest cold earth; she who was grown
A pillar of true valour, and had gained
Much honour by her victory, and chained
That God which doth the world with terror bind, 5
Using no armour but her own chaste mind;[136]
A fair aspect, coy thoughts, and words well weighed,
Sweet modesty to these gave friendly aid;[137]
It was a miracle on earth to see
The bow and arrows of the deity[138] 10
And all his armour broke, who erst had slain[139]
Such numbers, and so many captive tain:[140]
The faire dame from the noble fight withdrew

---

[134] *Anna Hume*, ed. by Roche, p. xvii.
[135] whose soul to heaven is gone] This is Hume's addition, and gives the whole translation a strongly religious and moralizing overtone.
[136] armour] As will happen in line 11, Hume translates Petrarch's *arme*, weapons, as 'armour'.
[137] The 1644 edition at this point inserts a full stop, which helps the reading but not the syntax. By omitting the main verb (in the original *tornava*, line 3), and moving it to line 13 ('withdrew'), Hume creates a rather convoluted sentence.
[138] deity] Petrarch refers, more explicitly, to *amor*, love.
[139] erst] first.
[140] tain] taken.

With her choice company; they were but few,
15 and made a little troop (true virtue's rare),
Yet each of them did by herself appear
A theme for poems, and might well incite
The best historian: they bore a white
Unspotted ermine, in a field of green,
20 About whose neck a topaz chain was seen
Set in pure gold; their heav'nly words and gait
Expressed them blest were born of such a fate.
Bright stars they seemed, she did a sun appear,
Who darkened not the rest, but made more clear
25 Their splendour: honour in brave minds is found.[141]
This troop, with violets and roses crowned,
Cheerfully marched, when lo, I might espy
Another ensign dreadful to mine eye:
A lady clothed in black, whose stern looks were
30 With horror filled, and did like hell appear,[142]
Advanced, and said, 'You who are proud to be
So fair and young, yet have no eyes to see
How near you are your end, behold, I am
She, whom they, fierce, and blind, and cruel name,
35 Who meet untimely deaths;[143] 'twas I did make
Greece subject, and the Roman Empire shake;
My piercing sword sacked Troy; how many rude
And barbarous people are by me subdued?
Many ambitious, vain, and amorous thought[144]
40 My unwished presence hath to nothing brought:
Now am I come to you, whiles yet your state
Is happy, ere you feel a harder fate.'
'On these you have no power', she then replied,
Who had more worth than all the world beside,
45 'And little over me; but there is one
Who will be deeply grieved when I am gone;
His happiness doth on my life depend,

---

[141] While not substantially deviating from Petrarch's original, Hume uses specific syntactic choices, and occasional inversion of the lines, to highlight such moralizing reflections, as she had done in line 15.
[142] Hume eliminates Petrarch's classical allusion to the *giganti*, the mythological giants, substituting it with the image of the Christian hell.
[143] Hume simplifies the original — Petrarch spoke of those who are met by night before they see the evening.
[144] 'Ambitious' and 'amorous' are Hume's additions.

I shall find freedom in a peaceful end.'
As one who glancing with a sudden eye
Some unexpected object doth espy,   50
Then looks again, and doth his own haste blame;
So, in a doubting pause, this cruel dame
A little stayed,¹⁴⁵ and said, 'The rest I call
To mind, and how I have o'ercome them all'.
Then, with less fierce aspect, she said, 'Thou guide   55
Of this fair crew, hast not my strength assayed;¹⁴⁶
Let her advise, who may command, prevent
Decrepit age, 'tis but a punishment;¹⁴⁷
From me this honour thou alone shalt have,
Without or fear or pain, to find thy grave.'   60
'As he shall please, who dwelleth in the Heaven
And rules on earth, such portion must be given
To me, as others from thy hand receive',
She answered then. Afar we might perceive
Millions of dead heaped on th'adjacent plain;   65
No verse nor prose may comprehend the slain
Did on Death's triumph wait: from India,
From Spain, and from Morocco, from Cathay,
And all the skirts of th'earth they gathered were.¹⁴⁸
Who had most happy lived, attended there;   70
Popes, emperors, nor kings, no ensigns wore
Of their past height, but naked showed and poor.¹⁴⁹
Where be their riches, where their precious gems,
Their mitres, sceptres, robes and diadems?
O miserable men, whose hopes arise   75
From worldly joys, yet be there few so wise
As in those trifling follies not to trust;¹⁵⁰
And if they be deceived, in end, 'tis just.
Ah, more than blind, what gain you by your toil?
You must return once to your mother's soil,   80
And after times your names shall hardly know,
Nor any profit from your labour grow;

---

¹⁴⁵ Death, surprised by Laura's words, remains silent for a moment.
¹⁴⁶ Hume simplifies Petrarch's allusion to *tosco* (poison).
¹⁴⁷ Hume may have misunderstood Petrarch here; the Italian poet has Death say that it is best to escape old age and its ailments.
¹⁴⁸ skirts] outskirts.
¹⁴⁹ height] magnificence.
¹⁵⁰ Hume's addition.

All those strange countries by your warlike stroke
Submitted to a tributary yoke;
85 The fuel erst of your ambitious fire,
What help they now? the vast and bad desire[151]
Of wealth and power at a bloody rate[152]
Is wicked; better bread and water eat
With peace; a wooden dish doth seldom hold
90 A poisoned draught, glass is more safe than gold.
But for this theme a larger time will ask,[153]
I must betake me to my former task.
The fatal hour of her short life drew near,
That doubtful passage which the world doth fear;
95 Another company, who had not been
Freed from their earthy burden there were seen,
To try if prayers could appease the wrath,
Or stay th'inexorable hand of death.
That beauteous crowd convened to see the end
100 Which all must taste; each neighbour, every friend
Stood by, when grim death with her hand took hold,
And pulled away one only hair of gold.[154]
Thus from the world this fairest flower is tane
To make her shine more bright, not out of spleen.
105 How many moaning plaints, what store of cries
Were uttered there, when fate shut those fair eyes
For which so oft I sang; whose beauty burned
My tortured heart so long.[155] Whiles others mourned
She pleased, and quiet did the fruit enjoy
110 Of her blest life. 'Farewell, without annoy,

---

[151] Hume's addition (as in 'a poisoned draught' below), underlining once more her moralizing strain.

[152] At a bloody cost.

[153] for] since.

[154] Sarah Dunnigan comments on this passage: 'In general, Hume's attentiveness to textual detail rather than emotive power grants her greater verbal precision than Fowler in these passages. She renders "un aureo crine" as "one onely hair of gold" (III, i, 96) in contrast to Fowler's "hair as fyne as gould", retaining Petrarch's emblematic significance'. See 'Scottish Women Writers, c.1560–c.1650', in *A History of Scottish Women's Writing*, ed. by Douglas Gifford and Dorothy McMillan (Edinburgh: Edinburgh University Press, 1997), pp. 15–43 (p. 36). Hume's note at the end of this chapter shows her understanding of the classical allusion. In general, Hume follows the original closely when describing actions or reproducing dialogue, while, as we have seen, she is freer when translating more meditative or sententious passages.

[155] Here Hume expands Petrarch's simple *arsi* ('I burned').

True saint on earth', said they; so might she be
Esteemed, but nothing bates Death's cruelty.
What shall become of others, since so pure
A body did such heats and colds endure,
And changed so often in so little space? 115
Ah worldly hopes, how blind you be, how base?
If since I bathe the ground with flowing tears
For that mild soul, who sees it witness bears;
And thou who read'st mayst judge she fettered me,
The sixth of April, and did set me free 120
On the same day and month: O! how the way
Of fortune is unsure! none hates the day
Of slavery, or of death, so much as I
Abhor the time which wrought my liberty,
And my too-lasting life; it had been just 125
My greater age had first been turned to dust,
And paid to time, and to the world the debt
I owed, then earth had kept her glorious state.
Now at what rate I should the sorrow price
I know not, nor have art that can suffice 130
The sad affliction, to relate in verse
Of these faire dames, that wept about her hearse;
'Courtesy, virtue, beauty, all are lost,
What shall become of us? none else can boast
Such high perfection, no more we shall 135
Hear her wise words, nor the angelical
Sweet music of her voice.' Whiles thus they cried
The parting spirit doth itself divide
With every virtue from the noble breast,
As some grave hermit, seeks a lonely rest;[156] 140
The heav'ns were clear, and all the ambient air
Without a threatening cloud, no adversair[157]
Durst once appear, or her calm mind affright;
Death singly did herself conclude the sight.
After, when fear, and the extremest plaint 145
Were ceased, th'attentive eyes of all were bent
On that fair face, and by despair became
Secure; she who was spent, not like a flame
By force extinguished, but as lights decay,

---

[156] This line expands Petrarch's simple *romito* (hermit).
[157] adversair] adversary.

150   And undiscernèd waste themselves away:
      Thus went the soul in peace, so lamps are spent
      As the oil fails which gave them nourishment;
      In sum, her countenance you still might know,
      The same it was, not pale, but white as snow,
155   Which on the tops of hills in gentle flakes
      Falls in a calm, or as a man that takes
      Desired rest, as if her lovely sight[158]
      Were closed with sweetest sleep, after the sprite
      Was gone. If this be that fools call to die,
160   Death seems in her exceeding fair to be.[159]

The end of the first chapter

Annotations upon the Triumph of Death

Noble fight, line, 13.] Her fight with *Cupid*: see above in the *Triumph of Chastity*.
Choice company, 14. *line*.] The ladies that had been virtuous before her time, and now waited on her Triumph, *Lucrece*, *Penelope*, &c.
They bore a white, 18. *line*.] Their ensign, a white ermine in a green field, with a chain of topazes set in pure gold. The white ermine was an emblem of innocence; the topazes of chastity: and the pure gold of tried virtue.
On these 43. *line*.] Meaning the other ladies that waited on her, because they were all dead long before.
There is one, 45. *line*.] *Petrarch*, whom she thought would be more hurt by her death than herself, in regard of his extreme affection.
Another company, 95. *line*.] The former company who were dead, could not be sorry for her death, because she would be nearer them, but another company of ladies, her friends and neighbours, came to pray that death would let her stay longer amongst them.
One only hair, 102. *line*.] Alluding to the purple hair on the head of *Nisus*, which his daughter stole, because he could not die whiles he wore it, as if *Lauretta* had had such another: or as if everybody had one. See above in the *Triumph of Love*, 2. Chap. 155. line.
No adversair, 142. *line*.] No wicked spirit, meaning, that she was troubled with no apparitions at her death.

---

[158] sight] Here the word refers to Laura's eyes.
[159] In these last two lines, Hume transforms Petrarch's calm statement into a sententious pronouncement.

Chapter II

The Argument.
The happy spirit doth descend
To comfort her afflicted friend.

That night which followed the too-sad decay
Of my best sun, whiles it was yet full day
(Whence I remain as blind), the summer dew
Slides through the Aire, and fair *Titonia* now[160]
Bestows true dreams, when, like the growing year,   5
A lady (crowned with orient gems) drew near
(With whom a thousand other crowns did move);[161]
And stretching forth that object of my love,
Her hand, she spoke, from whose sweet words did flow
Joy to my soul, and said, 'Do you not know   10
Her, who hath raised your thoughts above the strain
Of the low vulgar, as her love did gain
Place in your heart?' Then with a sober look
She sat herself and me, close by a brook
O'ershadowed with a laurel and a beech.   15
Like one whose weeping interrupts his speech:
'Must I not know the soul maintains my breath;[162]
But do you live, or are ta'en hence by death?',
I answered, 'Pray, instruct'; 'I live', said she,
'And you are dead, till you be joined with me: 20
But time is short, though we desire it long,
Take my advice, and curb your flowing tongue:
The day approacheth fast'. My sad reply
Was this: 'Ah say, is it much pain to die?[163]
You lately tried and knew.' 'You'll ne'er obtain   25
True happiness', she said, 'if you remain
In this so blind and common error; know,
Death is the end of prison and dark woe

---

[160] Unlike Petrarch, Hume passes from the past to the present tense to give vividness to the scene. She uses the name Titonia for sunrise, referred to in Petrarch as 'Tithon's friend'.
[161] Here the translator renders, somewhat confusedly, the idea that Laura moves among a thousand stars.
[162] Do I not recognize the soul that keeps me alive?
[163] The translation here is surprisingly similar to Sidney's ('Is it such pain to die?', line 30), while Morley and Fowler choose the more convoluted form of the indirect question. Note also that here Hume shortens the original, making the question more urgent and effective.

        To well-bred souls, doth only terror prove
30   To those that place on earthy dross their love;
        And e'en my death, which doth my soul annoy,[164]
        Could you conceive the least part of my joy,
        Would make you happy' (having fixed her eye,
        Whiles thus she spoke, devoutly on the sky).
35   Then closed her rosy lips, and silent stayed.
        'Sickness and tyrants' cruelties have made
        Death bitter', I replied.[165] ''Tis true,' said she,
        'The pains we feel before death bitter be,
        And hellish torments worse;[166] but he whose mind
40   Is stayed by heav'nly hopes, shall truly find,
        Though weak and wearied, this last step a short
        Sigh, and no more. As I drew near the port,
        My body weak, my soul did much rejoice;
        Yet heard the whispering of mourning voice:
45   "Alas, for him who reckons every day
        A thousand years, and still in vain doth stay
        On earth, and never more must see her face
        On sea or land, and filleth every place
        With that one theme, and findeth no delight
50   Of ought but her, to think, or speak, or write".
        My sight I that way turned, from whence mine ear
        Received the sound, and saw 'twas she whose care
        Used to incite my love, and temper thine:
        Her face and speech I knew, oft her divine
55   Wise counsels, healing cordials were to me,
        With honest mirth and cheerful gravity.
        When I with most felicity was blest
        In my first prime, and when thou lov'dst me best;
        When thy praise famed me most, e'en then my life
60   Was little better than a bitter strife,
        Compared with that sweet death, which few obtain;
        No banished man called to his home again
        Is more joyed, than this passage pleasèd me:

---

[164] Petrarch, more logically, attributes the 'annoy' to the lover, not to Laura. 'My soul' might be a misprint for 'thy soul'.
[165] Hume eliminates the list of Roman tyrants, and the comparison between the bitterness of death and of absinth, thus substantially reducing the original.
[166] Hume here misreads the Italian original. Petrarch states that the fear of hell, rather than the actual hellish torment, is painful.

But for the pity that I had of thee.'[167]
'I do adjure thee, by that faithful love
Thou knewst on earth, but better knowst above;
Did ever love', said I, 'beget in thee
One thought to pity my long misery,
Not wronging thy great mind? the sweet disdain,
Sweet mildness of your looks in doubtful pain,
Hath held my wishes long.' Ere I had said
The words, a lightning smile, such as oft paid
And eased the sadness of my wounded heart
I saw. Then she replied:[168] 'Nothing could part
My soul from thine, nor shall; but it did behove
With outward coldness to restrain thy love,
No other way would have preserved our fame;
A rod destroys not a kind mother's name.
I studied to conceal my love, such care
And providence dwell not with hope and fear;[169]
My countenance you saw, but not my heart:
I turned and stayed thy course with heedful art,
As one would tame a horse. My cheeks have been
Oft dyed with feigned wrath, when my heart within
Was a whole fire of love; yet reason still
Kept her own place, and did command my will.
But when I found thee overcharged with woe,
I used my milder looks, preventing so
Thy death, and my reproach; when I observed
Thy passion grow too strong, I then reserved
Myself, as if with grief or fear oppressed.
These were my ensigns,[170] and I found it best
To mix disdains with favours, this your songs
Have made already pass through many tongues.
When I beheld the tears swim in thine eye,
I said, "Without my help, I fear he'll die".
Then gave some modest aid; when you were bold,
I said, "He must be curbed": now pale and cold,
Now warm and fresh, now sad, now full of joy,

---

[167] Following the syntax of the original, I have added a full stop and concluded Laura's speech here, while the printer of the 1644 edition appears to think that this line belongs to the sentence that follows, spoken by the lover.
[168] In the original, Laura replies *sospirando*, with a sigh.
[169] Here Hume simplifies the original, eliminating Laura's meditation on Petrarch's love.
[170] Possibly a misprint for 'engines' (Petrarch has *ingegni*).

100 I kept thee safe, not without much annoy.'
'Glad t'have thus finished, 'twere enough reward
Could I believe 't'; thus trembling, as affeared,
Not with dry eyes, I said. She made reply,
'Do you distrust, for what end should I lie?'
105 A little blushing, then went on, 'If to
My partial eye, the world esteemèd you,
I held me quiet, being thoroughly blest
In that true-love knot locked within my breast;
The fair report (if it be truth) I hear,
110 The praises have acquired me far and near,
I much esteem, and never more did crave
But moderation in thy love to have;
That only wanted; whiles with signs of woe
You would persuade what I did throughly know,[171]
115 To open view you did your heart expose.
My coldness hence, hence your distemper rose:
In other things we did like friends agree,
Joined by a love, from all base passions free.
My heart was burnt with almost equal fire,
120 At least, when once I knew thy strong desire;
But mine I hid, whiles yours was open laid.
When you were hoarse, with having often prayed
For pity, I was silent: shame and fear
Were cause my great love did but small appear.
125 Grief is of no less weight, because concealed,
Nor more when by impatience 'tis revealed;
Deceit[172] doth not increase, nor yet impair
A truth. But say, was not my love then clear
When I received the lines you sent before
130 Your face and song? *My love dares say no more.*[173]
My heart was still with thee, though I restrained
My looks; and you, as having wrong, complained,
Because I gave the most part, and withdrew
The least, yet was not that withheld from you.
135 A thousand and a thousand times mine eye
Was turned with pity on thy misery;

---

[171] throughly] thoroughly, wholly.
[172] Petrarch has the very ambiguous *ficzion* (invention?), which has prompted much debate. Hume opts for 'deceit', a word which has decidedly negative connotations.
[173] As highlighted in the commentary, Hume and the printer make it clear that this is an allusion to one of Petrarch's poems.

And ever had continued still the same
But that I feared a danger in thy flame.
And not to leave you in suspense, I'll show
What I believe you will be glad to know: 140
In all the rest I found a pleasing fate,
Only for one cause I disliked my state;
My place of birth did to my thoughts appear
Too mean, and I still grieve 'twas not more near
Thy flowery seat; yet do I well approve 145
Of any country where I had thy love.
Besides, the heart in which I place most trust,
If me thou hadst not known, 'tis like it must
Have elsewhere loved, so had I got less fame.'
'You do mistake, my love had been the same 150
Where ever you had lived, my stars did raise
Me to so high a flame', I said.[174] 'Much praise
And honour have attended me', she said,
How e'er it be; but I too long have stayed:
Thy joy makes thee forget the wings of time. 155
Aurora now brings day, the sun doth climb
Above the ocean, from her golden bed,
At last, about to part and leave me sad',
She said. 'If you have ought besides, make haste
And end your speech before the time be past.' 160
'All my past suff'rings your kind words make light',
I answered, 'But I grieve without your sight,
And wish to know, if I am like to be
Long here, or if I soon may follow thee'.
She, going, thus replied: 'I do believe, 165
That without me on earth you long must live'.

The end of the Triumph of Death

Annotations upon the second chapter of the Triumph of Death

Best sun, 2. *line.*] Meaning *Lauretta*, who died in the midst of her age, being but 33 years old.
Titonia, 4. *line.*] Aurora the morning, called Titania from Titan, the Sun, who lodgeth with her.[175]

---

[174] Hume simplifies Petrarch's reference to the *rota terza* (the third heaven, devoted to Venus) with a simple allusion to stars.
[175] Here Hume confuses Tithon (Tithonus, lover of Eos, the goddess of the dawn) with a

True dreams, 5. *line.*] The morning dreams are held true, because the fancy is then most free from vapours.

A lady, 6. *line.*] *Lauretta* crowned, because she was now a Saint.

Other crowns did move, 7. *line.*] Other crowned saints that came along with her, belike he thought they must dote on her, as he did.[176]

Do you live, &c. 18. *line.*] The *Italian Commentary* makes a long and needless discourse to defend the congruity of this place, as if all did not know that those who dream they see a dead person appear, as if alive, do ordinarily make such a doubt in their sleep.

When I received, 129. *line.*] He had one time, as he used, sent her some of his verses, and coming himself just as they were presented to her, she received them in his presence, *Italian Commentary*.

My love dares say no more, 130. *line.*] She sang a song, beginning thus, for an undirect excuse of her reservation.

Flowery seat, 145. *line.*] Florence.

Of any country, &c. 146. *line.*] The sense here seemed clear to me, that *Lauretta* being well descended, but borne in Cabriers, an obscure village,[177] she was only displeased with that particular; yet the honour of his love was recompense enough for that misfortune, and any place good enough where she had that honour: and if she had been born near Florence, where he had his birth,[178] she might have been unknown to him who had left it, his parents being chased from thence by a contrary faction; and if he had not seen her, it is like he might have loved another, so should she have missed that honour, to which *Petrarch* answers, that wherever she had been born, he must needs have loved her, by the influence of his stars. But when I look on the *Italian Commentary*, I find he takes the meaning quite otherwise, which I have expressed as near his sense as I can, thus:

> *Thy flowery seat, for though I well approve*
> *Of that fair country where I had thy love:*
> *Yet might that heart, in which I trusted, stray*
> *To other beauties, and be turned away*
> *By this defect, so had I got less fame, &c.*

As if she had said her greatest misfortune was fear or jealousy, that he disliking

---

Titan (Hyperion, father of Aurora).

[176] A misreading on the part of Hume. In Petrarch Laura moves away from a company of other blessed souls to approach the poet.

[177] The actual place Laura refers to has been the cause of much scholarly debate, and different villages close to Avignon have been proposed. Hume might be referring to the village now known as Cabrières-d'Avignon.

[178] Petrarch was actually born in Arezzo, but is commonly associated with Florence. His parents were from Florence, and had been exiled due to their political beliefs, as Hume notes.

the place in which she lived (though she thought it sweet enough) might change his affection, and be drawn to love some other: let him that reads or compares, take the sense he approveth most.

OTHER PETRARCHS: FRAGMENTARY TRANSLATIONS OF THE *TRIUMPHI*

4.1 Henry Howard, Earl of Surrey, 'Such wayward ways hath love'

This poem survives in four manuscripts: London, British Library, MS Additional 36529, fol. 53r; London, British Library, MS Additional 28635, fols 26r–27r; Dublin, Trinity College, MS 160 (the Blage Manuscript), fol. 178; Arundel Castle, Arundel Harington MS, fols 50r–51r. It was also printed in *Tottel's Miscellany*.[1] The first two manuscripts are considered the most reliable witnesses.

Additional 36529 is described in the twentieth-century catalogue as 'Poems, by Henry Howard, Earl of Surrey (d. 1547), Sir Thomas Wyat (d. 1542), and others, apparently collected by Sir John Harington of Kelston (d. 1612)'.[2] John Harington is known as the first English translator of Ariosto's *Orlando Furioso*, and played a large part in the editing of the so-called Arundel-Harington manuscript, the only source we have for the translation of the *Triumphi* attributed to Queen Elizabeth.[3] In paper, composed of 82 folia, Additional 36529 can be dated to the late sixteenth century, and, together with the Arundel-Harington manuscript, is the largest source we have for Surrey's poems. These appear on fols 50 to 57, followed on fols 58v to 65v by his paraphrases of the Psalms. The father of Sir John Harington copied the lyric 'Suche waiwarde wais hath love' into a manuscript owned by George Blage, his fellow courtier at Henry VIII's court (now Dublin, Trinity College, MS 160, also known as the Blage Manuscript).[4] Additional 28635 is described in these words:

> Exact transcript of a manuscript belonging to Dr. Harington of Bath, His father, and others; some of which were printed in 'Nugae Antiquae,' by Henry Harington and Thomas Park, 1804. At the beginning is a note by P[ark], transferred from the original MS., in which it is stated that the

---

[1] *Songes and sonettes, written by the right honorable Lorde Henry Haward late Earle of Surrey, and other* (London: Richard Tottel, 1557), sig. Aiiiv.

[2] *Catalogue of Additions to the Manuscripts in the British Museum in the Years MDCCCC-MDCCCCV* (London: British Museum, 1907), p. 128.

[3] Now at Arundel Castle, this manuscript is fully transcribed in *The Arundel Harington Manuscript of Tudor Poetry*, ed. by Ruth Hughey, 2 vols (Columbus: The Ohio State University Press, 1960). See also A. S. G. Edwards, 'Manuscripts of the Verse of Henry Howard, Earl of Surrey', *Huntington Library Quarterly*, 67 (2004), 283–93. I describe the manuscript more fully in the section dedicated to the translation attributed to Elizabeth.

[4] 'It is possible that the original body of Surrey's verse in the manuscript was originally much larger, since eleven leaves have been lost before folio 49, where the group of Surrey's poems begins' (Edwards, 'Manuscripts of the Verse of Henry Howard', p. 286).

printer made use of the original leaves, whereby the MS. was in many places rendered imperfect. Paper; XIXth cent. The present copy belonged to George Frederick Nott, D. D., Prebendary of Winchester, who has added a note at the beginning. Folio.[5]

It restores two lines (lines 31–32) not appearing in Additional 36259. My edition is based on the latter, along with the restored lines from Additional 28635.[6]

4.1.1 Text

Such wayward ways hath love,[7] that most part in discord
Our wills do stand whereby our heart but seldom doth accord.
Deceit is his delight, and to beguile and mock
The simple heart which he doth strike with forward diverse stroke,
He causeth heart to rage with golden burning dart,   5
And doth allay with leaden cold against the other's heart.
Hot gleams of burning fire and easy spark of flame
In balance of unequal weight, he pondereth by aim.[8]
From easy ford where I might wade and pass full well
He me withdraws, and doth me drive into the dark deep well,   10
And me withholds where I am cold and offered place,
And will that still my mortal foe I do beseech of grace.
He lets me to pursue a conquest well-near won,
To follow where my pains were spilt or that my suit begun.
Lo,[9] by these rules I know how soon a heart can turn   15
From war to peace, from truce to strife, and so again return.
I know how to convert my will in others' lust
Of little stuff unto myself, to weave a web of trust,
And how to hide my harm with soft dissembled cheer,
When in my face the painted thoughts would outwardly appear.   20
I know how that the blood forsakes the face for dread,

---

[5] *Catalogue of Additions to the Manuscripts in the British Museum in the Years MDCCCLIV–MDCCCLXXV*, 3 vols (London: British Museum, 1877), II, p. 522.
[6] The modern edition by Jones (*Henry Howard, Earl of Surrey: Poems*, ed. by Emrys Jones (Oxford: Clarendon Press, 1964), pp. 8–10) is based on Additional 36259 and preserves the original spelling.
[7] Lines 1–14 are based on Ludovico Ariosto's *Orlando Furioso*, II. 1 (see Ludovico Ariosto, *Orlando Furioso e cinque Canti*, ed. by Remo Ceserani and Sergio Zatti, 2 vols (Turin: UTET, 2015)). Lines 5–6 echo Ovid, *Metamorphoses*, I. 468–71 (see *Metamorphoses*, ed. by Miller and Goold).
[8] by aim] by hazard, or by guess (see *Henry Howard*, ed. by Jones, p. 113).
[9] The remainder of the poem, with the anaphoric series 'I know...', translates *Triumphus Cupidinis*, III. 151–87, presenting a meditation on the symptoms of love.

And how by shame it stains again the cheek with flaming red.[10]
I know under the green the serpent how he lurks;[11]
The hammer of the restless forge I know eke how it works.[12]
25 I know, and can be sooth, the tale that I would tell,
But oft the words come forth awry of him that loveth well.
I know in heat and cold the lover, how he shakes,
In singing how he can complain, in sleeping how he wakes,
To languish without ache, sickless for to consume
30 A thousand things for to devise, resolving all in fume.[13]
And though he likes to see his lady's face full sore,
Such pleasure as delights his eye doth not his health restore.
I know to seek the track of my desired foe,
And fear to find that I do seek; but chiefly this I know,
35 That lovers must transform into the thing beloved,
And live, alas (who could believe), with sprite from life removed.[14]
I know in hearty sighs and laughter of the spleen[15]
At once to change my state, my will, and eke my colour clean.
I know how to deceive myself without help,
40 And how the lion chastised is by beating of the whelp,[16]
In standing near my fire I know how that I freeze;
Far off, to burn; in both to waste, and so my life to lose.
I know how love doth rage upon the golden mind,
How small a net may take and mash a heart of gentle kind,
45 Which seldom tasted sweet to seasoned heaps of gall,
Revivèd with a glint of grace, old sorrows to let fall.
The hidden trains I know, and secret snares of love;
How soon a look may print a thought that never will remove.
That slippery state I know, those sudden turns from wealth,
50 That doubtful hope, that certain woe, and sure despair of health.[17]

---

[10] The lover's sudden paling and blushing face is a topos of Petrarchan love, appearing also in the sonnet 'Amor, che nel pensier mio', translated by both Wyatt ('The Long Love') and Surrey ('Love That Doth Reign').
[11] The image comes from Virgil (*Eclogues*, III. 93), and recurs in Dante's *Divina Commedia*.
[12] This image does not appear in Petrarch, but rather belongs to the English tradition (*Henry Howard*, ed. by Jones, p. 114); it shows Surrey's love for strikingly domestic metaphors, giving new life to the sometimes conventional Petrarchan images.
[13] Jones reads 'resolving all hys fume', and explains the image as 'allaying his anguish' (*Henry Howard*, ed. by Jones, p. 114). I rather read this passage as a wry commentary on the uselessness of the lover's efforts.
[14] sprite] spirit.
[15] The line presents a double adynaton: the heart, the seat of blood, produces sighs, while the spleen, associated with melancholy, produces laughter.
[16] It was a commonplace that lions could be domesticated by forcing them to witness the beating of a little dog. Jones (*Henry Howard*, ed. by Jones, p. 115) connects this line to the coat of arms of the Howards, which included a lion.
[17] The list of paradoxes that concludes this chapter of Petrarch's *Triumphi* is enriched by an

4.2. John Florio, *Second Frutes*

Florio's translation of Petrarch's *Triumphus Pudicitie* (lines 174 and 76-90) appears in chapter twelve of his *Second Frutes*.[18] The whole book presents the Italian text and its English translation on facing pages, setting each chapter in the form of a dialogue; chapter twelve, the last and by far the longest, discusses love and women, presenting a dialogue between Pandolpho, Siluestro, Nicodemo and Dormiglione, in which each interlocutor makes use of proverbs and literary allusions to defend his feminist or anti-feminist stance. Silvestro is given both the first reference to the *Triumphus* (line 174), and the second (lines 76-90) within his argument on women's chastity.

The text is extant in the 1591 edition (the copy I am consulting, available in *EEBO*, comes from the Huntington Library). There is no modern edition. Following the 1591 text, I am printing only the English version.

4.2.1 Text

The poor cannot, the rich will not, buy gold too dear. So, as we may say in honour of beauty, as Petrarch wrote in the triumph of chastity,

> The chastest there of all, the fairest was of all,[19]
> And only for in work she spent her days,
> Penelope's renown doth match Ulysses' praise.

But all this appertains to courtesans, called common women, not to the better, though the fewer sort. But if you will view their muster, read Petrarch in his triumph of chastity, who, as their provost marshal, ordereth them thus:[20]

> With her the virtues all, O glorious band,
> Resplendent in their complete armour paced,
> And two by two they marchèd hand in hand.[21]
> First honesty with bashfulness was placed,
> A noble pair of virtues most divine;
> Which, her above, the highest ladies graced.
> Wisdom and modesty with them combine;
> Delight with seemliness kept heart's possession,
> Perseverance and glory came in fine.

echo of *Triumphus Cupidinis*, IV. 139-53.

[18] *Florios second frutes to be gathered of twelue trees, of diuers but delightsome tastes to the tongues of Italians and Englishmen. To which is annexed his Gardine of recreation yeelding six thousand Italian prouerbs* (London: Thomas Woodcock, 1591). Chapter twelve is on pp. 164-205.

[19] In the Italian section, Florio has 'La più casta era iui la piu bella', which corresponds with what we find in Vellutello; in the modern Italian edition by Marco Ariani it is 'e la più casta v'era la più bella'.

[20] In this section, too, the transcription of the Petrarchan original corresponds to the text in the Vellutello edition.

[21] The passage evokes the topos of the chaste lady 'armed' with her virtues, which are listed as if following the lady in a military formation.

Without, fair entertainment and direction.[22]
About about, pure mind and courtesy;[23]
Sole care of honour, fear of fame's oppression,
Grey-headed thoughts in youthful jollity,
And that consent which in the world is rare,[24]
Their rarest beauty was with chastity.

4.3. The translation attributed to Elizabeth I

The translation of the first ninety lines of Petrarch's *Triumphus Eternitatis*, attributed to Queen Elizabeth I, is extant in one manuscript, now Arundel (West Sussex), Arundel Castle, Arundel Harington MS, fols 219v to 220v. The manuscript is currently preserved in an early nineteenth-century binding, in bad repair, with gold tooling on back and sides. The codex includes a number of blank pages at the beginning and at irregular intervals throughout. It is on sturdy paper, ruled in red (there are normally thirty-eight lines to a page), with the poems clearly written and divided one from the other; most of them have the word *Finis* at the end, followed by blank lines. On fol. 144v there is a poem by Queen Elizabeth, 'The lowest trees have toppes', with no indication of the author (there are none throughout). The Petrarch translation is towards the end of the codex: 'Triumphe Petrarcke' is written at the very top of the page, in the same hand and ink as the rest; the hand has been ascribed to the early years of Elizabeth's reign.[25] After this translation the manuscript has six blank pages, which suggests that the compiler hoped to complete this version of the *Triumphus Eternitatis*.

The first modern editor was Ruth Hughey, who first rediscovered and studied the manuscript in 1934, then published a complete description and annotated edition of the codex in 1960.[26] Hughey calculated that of the original 228 leaves of the manuscript, 145 now survive. As concerns the Petrarch translation, she offered a very faithful and accurate transcription, preserving the original punctuation, which is surprisingly modern and thorough. A few years later, the text was edited by Leicester Bradner for his edition of the poems of Elizabeth;[27] in recent years, Janel Mueller and Joshua Scodel inserted it in their complete

---

[22] These virtues are outside ('without') the group, as they represent exterior qualities. fair entertainment] In Petrarch, *Bella Accoglienza*, corresponding to *Bel Acueil* in the *Roman de la Rose*. direction] The practical application of wisdom.
[23] About about] all around.
[24] consent] concord, agreement.
[25] AHM, I, p. 457.
[26] AHM, I, pp. 360–63.
[27] *The Poems of Queen Elizabeth I*, ed. by Leicester Bradner (Providence: Brown University Press, 1964).

edition of Elizabeth's works.[28] In both cases the editors slightly modernized punctuation and spelling, and introduced some capitalization. The present text is based on the manuscript; I have indicated significant choices or emendation on the part of other editors in the footnotes.

4.3.1 Text

Triumph Petrarch

Amazed to see, naught under heaven's cope[29]
Steady and fast, thus to myself I spoke:[30]
'Advise thee well: on whom doth hang thy hope?'
'On God (said I) that promise never broke
With those that trust in him. But now I know   5
How erst the fickle world abusèd me,[31]
Eke what I am and was,[32] and now to go
Or rather fly the nimble time I see.
Blame would I, wist I whom:[33] for all the crime
Is mine that should (not slacking till the last)   10
Have erst unclosed mine eyes before this time.
For, truth to say, old wax I all too fast.
But over-late God's grace came never yet;[34]
In me also I trust there shall be wrought
Works wonderful and strange by means of it.'[35]   15
This said, and answer made thus, more I thought:
If none of all these things do stand in stay
That heaven turns and guides, what end at last
Shall follow of their ever-turning sway?
While deeper yet my searching mind I cast,   20
A world all new e'en then it seemèd me,
In never-changing and ever-living age,
The sun, the sky with all her stars to see
Dissolvèd quite with earth and seas that rage;[36]

---

[28] *Elizabeth I: Translations 1544–1589*, ed. by Janel Mueller and Joshua Scodel (Chicago: University of Chicago Press, 2009). The text appears on pp. 469–74.
[29] cope] cover, canopy.
[30] fast] firm, fixed.
[31] erst] first.
[32] My reading of this line, following Petrarch's original, is: I also know what I am and was.
[33] I would blame somebody, if I knew whom.
[34] over-late] too late.
[35] These two lines clarify Petrarch's rather convoluted meaning.
[36] The last two words in this line are the translator's addition.

25 One made more fair and pleasant in his place,
When him[37] that never stayed but erst to change
Each thing was wont, wandering in diverse race
Stand on one foot[38] I saw: how seemed it strange!
All his three parts,[39] brought into only one,
30 And that one fast, so that as wont it was
No more so swift it hasted to be gone,
But had one show as earth despoiled of grass;[40]
There were not 'shall be', 'hath been', 'after', 'erst'[41]
To irksome,[42] weak, and diverse state that brought
35 Our life. As sun doth pierce the glass,[43] so pierced
My thought, yea more, for nothing stoppeth thought.
What grace find I, to see if I attain,
E'en face to face, the greatest god[44] of all
(No ill, which only time gives, and again,
40 As first it came, with time eke part it shall).
The Bull or Fish[45] lodge shall no more the sun,
Whose change doth make our toil[46] now die, now spring,
Now waste, now grow. Oh, happy spirits that won,
Or shall hereafter stand in the chief ring
45 Whose names aye memory writes in her book!
Oh, happy he to find (whose hap shall be)
The deep channel of this swift running brook[47]
Whose name is life, that many wish to see!
Wretched and blind the common sort, that stay[48]

---

[37] The agent is variously interpreted, even by early commentators, as Time, or the sun.
[38] Modern editions of Petrarch's text have *in un punto*, in one point, while sixteenth-century editions have *in un pie*, on one foot, as translated here.
[39] Past, present and future.
[40] Showed itself only as naked earth.
[41] The translator has omitted from this series *mai* (never), perhaps for metrical reasons.
[42] As Mueller and Scodel conjecture (*Elizabeth I*), this word translates the *amara* to be found in early editions (modern editions have *umana*, human).
[43] This image appears in the *Canzoniere*, but also in Ovid (*Metamorphoses*, IV. 348–49), and Dante (*Inferno*, XXIV. 12; *Purgatorio*, XXXI. 121; *Paradiso*, II. 89, and elsewhere).
[44] Both Bradner (*The Poems of Queen Elizabeth I*) and Mueller and Scodel (*Elizabeth I*) emend to 'good'. I prefer to leave the original spelling, aware that there might be a deliberate ambiguity, playing on the concept of *summum bonum*.
[45] Taurus or Pisces (referring to the constellations in whose 'houses' the sun resides, respectively from late April to late May and from late February to late March).
[46] I have here emended the manuscript, which has 'a toil'.
[47] The point where the swift torrent of life can be forded.
[48] stay] set.

Their hope on things which time reaves in a trice;[49] 50
All deaf, naked, and subject to decay,
Quite void of reason and of good advice,
And wretched mortal men throughout diseased![50]
Whose beck doth guide the world, by whom at jar[51]
Are set the elements and eke appeased; 55
Whose skill doth stretch beyond my reach so far
That e'en the angels are content and joy
Of thousand parts but one to see, and bend
Their wits to this, and this wish to enjoy.
Oh, happy wandering mind, ay hungering to the end,[52] 60
What mean so many thoughts? one hour doth reave
That many years gathered with much ado:
Tomorrow, yesterday, morning and eve,[53]
That press our soul and it encumber so,
Before him pass shade-like, at once away; 65
For 'was' or 'shall be' no place shall be found,
But for the time of 'is', 'now', and 'today',
Only eternity knit fast and sound.
Huge hills[54] shall be made plain, that stoppèd clean
Our sight, nor shall there anything remain 70
Where one may hope or our[55] remembrance lean;
Whose change make others do that is but vain,
And life to seem a sport. E'en with this thought,
'What shall I be, what was I heretofore?'
All shall be one, no piecemeal parted ought 75
Summer shall be, no winter any more
But time shall die, and place be changed with all;
And years shall bear no rule on mortal fame,
But his renown for ever flourish shall
That once achieved to be of flowering name.[56] 80
Oh, happy souls that now the path doth tread,
Or henceforth shall, when it so haps to be,

---

[49] reaves] plunders, lays waste.
[50] Thoroughly diseased (Petrarch has *egri del tutto*, 'wholly sick').
[51] beck] An excellent rendering of *ciglio*, the divine brow that gives assent or denies.
[52] happy] Translator's addition, perhaps used in the sixteenth-century meaning of 'fortuitous'.
[53] The translator omits *dianzi, adesso* (before, now), possibly for metrical reasons.
[54] Petrarch simply has *poggi*, hills.
[55] This translates the *nostro* to be found in early editions, while modern editions have *vostro* (your).
[56] Shall flourish forever.

Which to the end whereof I speak doth lead.
Of fair and wandering sprites yet happiest she
85 Whom death hath slain far short of nature's bound.[57]
The heav'nly talk, good words, and thoughts so chaste,
Open shall lie, unfolded in that stound[58]
Which kind within a youthful heart hath placed.[59]

---

[57] This allusion to Laura introduces the second part of the triumph, which the translator omits.
[58] stound] hour.
[59] kind] nature. The text ends here, with 'E. R.', written in a different ink and hand, on the margin of the last three lines. Beneath these initials is a contraction which might be *scr* (scripsit) or *sec* (secundus): 'the latter reading might refer to the second year of the Queen's reign, but this is not certain' (*Poems of Queen Elizabeth I*, ed. by Bradner, p. 79). The verso of the folio, and fols 221, 222 and 223r are blank, but they are ruled, so evidently the scribe expected to fill them.

FURTHER READING

AXTON, MARIE, and JAMES P. CARLEY, eds, *'Triumphs of English': Henry Parker, Lord Morley: Translator to the Tudor Court. New Essays in Interpretation* (London: The British Library, 2000)
BERGERON, DAVID, *English Civic Pageantry, 1558-1642* (London: Edward Arnold, 1975)
BOSWELL, JACKSON CAMPBELL, and GORDON MCMURRY BRADEN, *Petrarch's English Laurels 1475-1700* (Farnham: Ashgate, 2012)
BRADEN, GORDON MCMURRY, *Petrarchan Love and the Continental Renaissance* (New Haven: Yale University Press, 1999)
CLARKE, DANIELLE, '"Lover's Songs Shall Turne to Holy Psalmes": Mary Sidney and the Transformation of Petrarch', in *Mary Sidney, Countess of Pembroke*, ed. by Margaret P. Hannay (Farnham: Ashgate, 2009), pp. 137–49
COOGAN, ROBERT, 'Petrarch's "Trionfi" and the English Renaissance', *Studies in Philology*, 57 (1960), 306–27
DUNNIGAN, SARAH M., 'Daughterly Desires: Representing and Reimagining the Feminine in Anna Hume's *Triumphs*', in *Woman and the Feminine in Medieval and Early Modern Scottish Writing*, ed. by Sarah M. Dunnigan, C. Marie Harker and Evelyn S. Newlyn (Basingstoke: Palgrave Macmillan, 2004), pp. 120–35
EDWARDS, A. S. G., 'English Poems', in *The Complete Works of St. Thomas More: Volume 1*, ed. by A. S. G. Edwards, Katherine Gardiner Rodgers and Clarence H. Miller (New Haven: Yale University Press, 1997), pp. xvii–xxxvi
EISENBICHLER, KONRAD, and AMILCARE A. IANNUCCI, eds, *Petrarch's Triumphs: Allegory and Spectacle* (Ottawa: Dovehouse, 1990)
FOWLER, ALASTAIR, *Triumphal Forms: Structural Patterns in Elizabethan Poetry* (Cambridge: Cambridge University Press, 1970)
HAINSWORTH, PETER, MARTIN MACLAUGHLIN and LETIZIA PANIZZA, eds, *Petrarch in Britain: Interpreters, Imitators, and Translators over 700 Years: Proceedings of the British Academy* (London: The British Academy, 2007)
HANNAY, MARGARET PATTERSON, *Philip's Phoenix: Mary Sidney, Countess of Pembroke* (Oxford: Oxford University Press, 1990)
HODDER, MIKE, 'Petrarch in English: Political, Cultural and Religious Filters in the Translation of the *Rerum vulgarium fragmenta* and *Triumphi* from Geoffrey Chaucer to J. M. Synge' (unpublished doctoral thesis, University of Oxford, 2013)
KENNEDY, WILLIAM J., *Authorizing Petrarch* (Ithaca: Cornell University Press, 1994)
—— *The Site of Petrarchism: Early Modern National Sentiment in Italy, France, and England* (Baltimore: The Johns Hopkins University Press, 2003)
—— *Petrarchism at Work: Contextual Economies in the Age of Shakespeare* (Ithaca: Cornell University Press, 2016)
MANN, NICHOLAS, 'La prima fortuna del Petrarca in Inghilterra', in *Il Petrarca ad Arquà. Atti del convegno di studi nel VI centenario (1370-1374)*, ed. by Giuseppe Billanovich and Giuseppe Frasso (Padua: Antenore, 1975), pp. 279–89
—— 'Il Petrarca e gli inizi del Rinascimento inglese', *La Cultura*, 15 (1977), 3–18

—— 'Petrarch and Humanism: The Paradox of Posterity', in *Francesco Petrarca, Citizen of the World*, ed. by Aldo S. Bernardo (Padua: Antenore, 1980), pp. 287–99

MARTIN, CHRISTOPHER, 'Retrieving Jonson's Petrarch', *Shakespeare Quarterly*, 45 (1994), 89–92

MELZI, ROBERT C., 'A Contribution to the History of Petrarchism in England: Robert Tofte and The Blazon of Jealousy', *Rivista di Studi Italiani*, 15 (1997), 1–32

PETRINA, ALESSANDRA, 'Translation and Language Learning: The English Version of Petrarch's *Triumph of Eternity* Attributed to Elizabeth I', in *Early Modern Exchanges: Dialogues Between Nations and Cultures, 1550–1750*, ed. by Helen Hackett (Farnham: Ashgate, 2015), pp. 55–71

—— 'Approaching Petrarch's *Trionfi*: Paratexts in the Early Modern Scottish Translations', in *Thresholds of Translation: Paratexts, Print, and Cultural Exchange in Early Modern Britain (1473–1660)*, ed. by Marie-Alice Belle and Brenda M. Hosington (Cham: Palgrave Macmillan, 2018), 161–82

REES, D. G., 'Petrarch's "Trionfo della Morte" in English', *Italian Studies*, 7 (1952), 82–96

SARGENT, RALPH M., *At the Court of Queen Elizabeth: The Life and Lyrics of Sir Edward Dyer* (London: Oxford University Press, 1935)

SESSIONS, WILLIAM A., *Henry Howard: The Poet Earl of Surrey: A Life* (Oxford: Oxford University Press, 1999)

TRAPP, J. B., 'More and the Visual Arts', in *Saggi sul Rinascimento*, ed. by Sergio Rossi (Milan: Unicopli, 1984), pp. 27–54

—— 'Petrarch's *Triumph of Death* in Tapestry', in *Studies of Petrarch and his Influence* (London: The Pindar Press, 2003), pp. 171–200

VAN HEIJNSBERGEN, THEO, 'Coteries, Commendatory Verse and Jacobean Poetics: William Fowler's Trivmphs of Petrarke and its Castalian Circles', in *James VI and I, Literature and Scotland: Tides of Change, 1567–1625*, ed. by David J. Parkinson (Leuven: Peeters, 2013), pp. 45–64

VERVEIJ, SEBASTIAAN, *The Literary Culture of Early Modern Scotland: Manuscript Production and Transmission, 1560–1625* (Oxford: Oxford University Press, 2016)

WALLER, GARY F., *Mary Sidney, Countess of Pembroke: A Critical Study of her Writing and Literary Milieu* (Salzburg: Institut für Anglistik und Amerikanistik Universität Salzburg, 1979)

WILKINS, ERNEST HATCH, 'The Fifteenth-Century Editions of the Italian Poems of Petrarch', *Modern Philology*, 40 (1943), 225–39

YATES, FRANCES A., *John Florio: The Life of an Italian in Shakespeare's England* (Cambridge: Cambridge University Press, 1934)

YOUNG, FRANCES BERKELEY, *Mary Sidney, Countess of Pembroke* (London: David Nutt, 1912)

BIBLIOGRAPHY

6.1. Manuscript sources

Arundel, Arundel Castle, MS Arundel Harington
Cambridge, Cambridge University Library, MS Ii.VI.39, fols 177v-88v
Dublin, Trinity College, MS 160 (Blage Manuscript), fol. 178
Edinburgh, Edinburgh University Library, MS Drummond De.1.10
Edinburgh, Edinburgh University Library, MS Drummond De.3.68
Edinburgh, National Library of Scotland, MS 2061
Edinburgh, National Library of Scotland, MSS Hawthornden 2063-67
London, British Library, MS Additional 24195, fol. 35r
London, British Library, MS Additional 28635, fols 26r-27r
London, British Library, MS Additional 36529, fol. 53r
London, British Library, MS Additional 60544 (Winchester Anthology), fols 8r-22v
London, British Library, MS Royal 19 C.vii
London, Inner Temple Library, MS Petyt 538.43
Munich, Bayerische Staatsbibliothek, MS Ital. 81
York, Minster Library, MS XVI.N.2.

6.2 Printed sources

6.2.1. Editions and translations of Petrarch's works[1]

[*Princeps* of *Rerum Vulgarium Fragmenta* and *Triumphi*] incipit: A Pie decolli ove labella vesta (Venice: Vindelinus de Spira, 1470)

[*Triumphi* with Ilicino's commentary and RVF 1-136 with Filelfo's commentary] incipit: AD Illustrissimum Mutinae Ducem Diuum Borsium estensem Bernardi glicini Medicinae ac philosophiae discipuli in triumphorum. CL[arissimi] P[oetae] Fra[ncisci] Petrarce expositio incipit (Bologna: Hannibal Malpiglius, 1475-76)

[*RVF* with Filelfo's and Squarciafico's commentaries and *Triumphi* with Ilicino's commentary] incipit: Prohemio del prestante Oratore & poeta Messer Francesco Philelpho al illustrissimo & i[n]victi simo principe Philippo Maria Anglo Duca

---

[1] This section, with entries listed in chronological order, makes no attempt at listing all the early editions of Petrarch's works, a task that goes beyond the scope of the present volume. For a census of Petrarch manuscripts and early printed editions, I refer the reader to the PERI database: *Petrarch's Exegesis in Renaissance Italy,* prepared by Giacomo Comiati and Lorenzo Sacchini with Francesco Venturi (overseen by Simon Gilson and Federica Pich) <https://petrarch.mml.ox.ac.uk> (last accessed 21 January 2020).

de Milano circa la interpretatione per lui sopra gli sonetti & ca[n]zone de messer Francesco Petrarcha facta (Venice: Bernardinus Rizus Novariensis, 1488)

Le cose volgari di Messer Francesco Petrarcha (Venice: Aldus Manutius, 1501)

Petrarcha con doi commenti (Venice: Albertino da Lissona, 1503)

Le volgari opere del Petrarcha con la espositione di Alessandro Vellutello (Venice: Giovanni Antonio Nicolini da Sabbio, 1525)

Il Petrarcha col commento di m. Sebastiano Fausto da Longiano (Venice: Francesco Bindoni and Maffeo Pasini, 1532)

Il Petrarcha con l'espositione di m. Giovanni Andrea Gesualdo (Venice: Giovanni Antonio Niccolini da Sabbio, 1533)

Sonetti, canzoni, e triomphi di messer Francesco Petrarcha con la spositione di Bernardino Daniello (Venice: Giovanni Antonio Niccolini da Sabbio, 1541)

Il Petrarcha. Con l'espositione d'Alessandro Vellutello di novo ristampato con le figure ai triomphi (Venice: Gabriel Giolito, 1547)

Sonetti canzoni e Triomphi di m. Francesco Petrarca con breve dichiaratione e annotatione di Antonio Brucioli (Venice: Antonio Brucioli, 1548)

The tryumphes of Fraunces Petrarcke, translated out of Italian into English by Henrye Parker knyght, Lorde Morley. The tryumphe of loue. Of chastitie. Of death. Of fame. Of tyme. Of diuinitie (London: John Cawood, 1555)

Phisicke against fortune, aswell prosperous, as aduerse conteyned in two books [...] now first Englished by Thomas Twyne (London: Richard Watkyns, 1579)

The Triumphs of Love: Chastitie: Death: Translated out of Petrarch by Mris Anna Hume (Edinburgh: Evan Tyler, 1644)

A Dialogue between Reason and Adversity: A Late Middle English Version of Petrarch's De Remediis, ed. by F. N. M. Diekstra (Assen: Van Gorcum, 1968)

Tryumphes of Fraunces Petrarcke: Translated by Lord Morley, ed. by D. D. Carnicelli (Cambridge: Harvard University Press, 1971)

Canzoniere, ed. by Gianfranco Contini (Turin: Einaudi, 1975)

Triumphi, ed. by Marco Ariani (Milan: Mursia, 1988)

Trionfi, ed. by Marco Santagata (Milan: Mondadori, 1996)

Rerum senilium Libri IV–VII, ed. by Elvira Nota (Paris: Les Belles Lettres, 2003)

Rerum familiarium Libri XVI–XIX, ed. by Ugo Dotti (Paris: Les Belles Lettres, 2005)

Anna Hume: The Triumphs of Love: Chastitie: Death, ed. by Thomas P. Roche (Farnham: Ashgate, 2006)

Rerum memorandarum Libri, ed. by Marco Poletti (Florence: Le Lettere, 2014)

Rerum familiarium Libri XX–XXII, ed. by Vittorio Rossi and Ugo Dotti (Paris: Les Belles Lettres, 2015)

A Middle English Translation from Petrarch's Secretum, ed. by Edward Wilson and Daniel Wakelin (Oxford: Oxford University Press, 2018)

6.2.2. Other printed sources

ARIOSTO, LUDOVICO, *Orlando Furioso e cinque Canti*, ed. by Remo Ceserani and Sergio Zatti, 2 vols (Turin: UTET, 2015)

The Arundel Harington Manuscript of Tudor Poetry, ed. by Ruth Hughey (Columbus: The Ohio State University Press, 1960)

ASCHAM, ROGER, *The Scholemaster*, in *English Works*, ed. by William Aldis Wright (Cambridge: Cambridge University Press, 1904), pp. 171–302
BEMBO, PIETRO, *Prose della volgar lingua*, ed. by Carlo Dionisotti (Turin: UTET, 1966)
CHURCHYARD, THOMAS, *A Pleasant conceite penned in verse* (London: Roger Warde, 1593)
CICERO, *The Speeches*, ed. by N. H. Watts (Cambridge, Mass.: Harvard University Press, 1953)
[CICERO] MARCO TULLIO CICERONE, *Le Orazioni: Volume II. Dal 69 al 59 a.C.*, ed. by Giovanni Bellardi (Turin: UTET, 1981)
The Collected Works of Mary Sidney Herbert, Countess of Pembroke: Volume I: Poems, Translations, and Correspondence, ed. by Margaret P. Hannay, Noel J. Kinnamon and Michael J. Brennan (Oxford: Clarendon Press, 1998)
The Complete Works of Sir Thomas Wyatt the Elder: Volume I: Prose, ed. by Jason Powell (Oxford: Oxford University Press, 2016)
DANIEL, SAMUEL, *A Defence of Ryme* (London: Edward Blount, 1603)
DRUMMOND OF HAWTHORNDEN, WILLIAM, *The Works* (Edinburgh: James Watson, 1711)
DU BELLAY, JOACHIM, *The Regrets with The Antiquities of Rome, Three Latin Elegies, and The Defense and Enrichment of the French Language*, ed. by Richard Helgerson (Philadelphia: University of Pennsylvania Press, 2006)
DYER, EDWARD, *The Writings in Verse and Prose of Sir Edward Dyer, Knt. (1540 (?)-1607)*, ed. by Alexander B. Grosart (Blackburn: printed for private circulation, 1872)
ELIZABETH I, *The Poems*, ed. by Leicester Bradner (Providence: Brown University Press, 1964)
—— *Selected Works*, ed. by Steven May (New York: Washington Square, 2004)
—— *Translations 1544-1589*, ed. by Janel Mueller and Joshua Scodel (Chicago: The University of Chicago Press, 2009)
FLORIO, JOHN, *Florio his firste fruites* (London: Thomas Woodcocke, 1578)
—— *Florios Second Frutes, to be Gathered of Twelve Trees* (London: Thomas Woodcock, 1591)
—— *A Worlde of Wordes* (London: Blount, 1598)
Henry Howard, Earl of Surrey: Poems, ed. by Emrys Jones (Oxford: Clarendon Press, 1964)
HENRYSON, ROBERT, *The Poems*, ed. by Denton Fox (Oxford: Clarendon Press, 1981)
HUME OF GODSCROFT, DAVID, *The History of the House of Douglas*, ed. by David Reid (Edinburgh: The Scottish Text Society, 1996)
Isabella Whitney, Mary Sidney and Aemilia Lanyer: Renaissance English Poets, ed. by Danielle Clarke (London: Penguin, 2000)
JAMES VI, 'Ane Schort Treatise Conteining Some Reulis and Cautelis to be Observit and Eschewit in Scottis Poesie', in *The Mercat Anthology of Early Scottish Literature 1375-1707*, ed. by R. D. S. Jack and P. A. T. Rozendaal (Edinburgh: Mercat Press, 1997), pp. 460–73
Letters and Papers, Foreign and Domestic, of the Reign of Henry VIII, ed. by James Gairdner and R. H. Brodie (London: Eyre and Spottiswoode, 1864)
Lydgate's Fall of Princes, ed. by Henry Bergen (London: Oxford University Press, 1924–27)

The Minor Poems of John Lydgate: Part II, ed. by Henry Noble MacCracken (London: Oxford University Press, 1934)
MINTURNO, ANTONIO, *L'Arte Poetica* (Venice: Giovanni Antonio Valvassori, 1564)
MOFFETT, THOMAS, *The silkewormes, and their flies: lively described in verse, by T. M. a countrie farmar, and an apprentice in physicke. For the great benefit and enriching of England* (London: Nicholas Ling, 1599)
Original Letters, Illustrative of English History: Third Series, Volume II, ed. by Henry Ellis (London: Richard Bentley, 1846)
OVID, *Metamorphoses: Books I–VIII*, ed. by Frank Justus Miller and G. P. Goold (Cambridge, Mass.: Harvard University Press, 1977)
PARKER, HENRY, LORD MORLEY, *Forty-Six Lives Translated from Boccaccio's De claris mulieribus*, ed. by Herbert G. Wright (London: Oxford University Press, 1943)
The Poems of Henry Howard, Earl of Surrey, ed. by F. M. Padelford (Seattle: University of Washington Press, 1928)
Le Prince de Nicolas Machiavelle secretaire et citoien de Florence. Traduit d'Italien en Françoys Par Guillavme Cappel (Paris: Charles Estienne, 1553)
PUTTENHAM, GEORGE, *The Art of English Poesy*, ed. by Frank Whigham and Wayne A. Rebhorn (Ithaca: Cornell University Press, 2007)
Records of Early English Drama: Norwich 1540–1642, ed. by David Galloway (Toronto: University of Toronto Press, 1984)
The Riverside Chaucer: Third Edition, ed. by Larry D. Benson (Oxford: Oxford University Press, 1987)
The Riverside Shakespeare, ed. by G. Blakemore Evans (Boston: Houghton Mifflin, 1974)
[SALLUST] CAIO SALLUSTIO CRISPO, *Opere Complete*, ed. by Raffaele Ciaffi (Milan: Bompiani, 1983)
Songes and sonettes, written by the right honorable Lorde Henry Haward late Earle of Surrey, and other (London: Richard Tottel, 1557)
SPENSER, EDMUND, *The Poetical Works*, ed. by J. C. Smith and E. de Selincourt (London: Oxford University Press, 1912)
[SUETONIUS] CAIO SVETONIO TRANQUILLO, *Le vite di dodici Cesari. Volume I: Cesare — Augusto — Tiberio — Caligola*, ed. by Guido Vitali (Bologna: Zanichelli, 1973)
THOMAS, WILLIAM, *The historie of Italie* (London: Thomas Bertelet, 1549)
Tho. wyatis translatyon of Plutarches boke, of the quyete of mynde (London: Richard Pynson, 1528)
TREVISA, JOHN, 'Dialogue between a Lord and a Clerk', in *A Book of Middle English: Third Edition*, ed. by J. A. Burrow and Thorlac Turville-Petre (Oxford: Blackwell, 2005), pp. 235–42
The Triumph of Death and other Unpublished and Uncollected Poems by Mary Sidney, Countess of Pembroke (1561–1621), ed. by Gary F. Waller (Salzburg: Institut für Anglistik und Amerikanistik Universität Salzburg, 1977)
VIRGILIO, *Eneide*, ed. by Rosa Calzecchi Onesti (Turin: Einaudi, 1967)
—— *Bucoliche*, ed. by Luca Canali (Milan: Rizzoli, 1978)
WATSON, THOMAS, *The Complete Works*, ed. by Dana F. Sutton (Lewiston: The Edwin Mellen Press, 1996)
The Works of Gabriel Harvey, D. C. L., ed. by Alexander B. Grosart, 3 vols (London: The Huth Library, 1884)

The Works of William Fowler, Secretary to Queen Anne, Wife of James VI, ed. by Henry W. Meikle (Edinburgh: Blackwood, 1914, 1936, 1940)

6.3 Studies

ADORNO, THEODOR W., *Essays on Music* (Berkeley: University of California Press, 2002)

ALEXANDER, GAVIN, 'Mary Sidney Herbert: The Psalmes, The Triumph and The Scribes', *Sidney Journal*, 16 (1998), 16–30

—— 'The Triumph of Death: A Critical Edition in Modern Spelling of the Countess of Pembroke's Translation of Petrarch's Trionfo della Morte', *Sidney Journal*, 17 (1999), 2–18

ARMSTRONG, GUYDA, 'Boccaccio and Dante', in *The Cambridge Companion to Boccaccio*, ed. by Guyda Armstrong, Rhiannon Daniels and Stephen J. Milner (Cambridge: Cambridge University Press, 2015), pp. 121–38

—— 'Coding Continental: Information Design in Sixteenth-Century English Vernacular Language Manuals and Translations', *Renaissance Studies*, 29 (2015), 78–102

—— 'Re-materialising the Incunable Petrarch: Ernest Hatch Wilkins and the Politics of Bibliographical Description', *Italian Studies*, 75 (2020), 55–70

ATIĆ, SVJETLANA, 'An Analysis of William Fowler's Translation of Petrarch's "Trionfi"' (unpublished MA thesis, University of Padua, 2009)

AXTON, MARIE, 'Lord Morley's *Tryumphes of Petrarcke*: Reading Spectacles', in *'Triumphs of English': Henry Parker, Lord Morley: Translator to the Tudor Court. New Essays in Interpretation*, ed. by Marie Axton and James P. Carley (London: The British Library, 2000), pp. 171–200

BAKER-SMITH, DOMINIC, 'Spenser's "Triumph of Marriage"', *Verbal/Visual Enquiry*, 4 (1988), 310–16

BARAŃSKI, ZYGMUNT G., 'The Triumphi', in *The Cambridge Companion to Petrarch*, ed. by Albert Russell Ascoli and Unn Falkeid (Cambridge: Cambridge University Press, 2015), pp. 74–84

BARTLETT, KENNETH, 'The Occasion of Lord Morley's Translation of the *Trionfi*: The Triumph of Chastity over Politics', in *Petrarch's 'Triumphs': Allegory and Spectacle*, ed. by Konrad Eisenbichler and Amilcare A. Iannucci (Ottawa: Dovehouse, 1990), pp. 325–34

BASSNETT, SUSAN, 'Daring to Show Discontent: Queen Elizabeth I as Poet and Translator', in *Under Construction: Links for the Site of Literary Theory: Essays in Honour of Hendrik Van Gorp*, ed. by Dirk de Geest, Ortwin de Graef, Dirk Delabastita et al. (Leuven: Leuven University Press, 2010), pp. 211–23

—— 'Translation and Creativity', in *La traduction comme création: Translation and Creativity*, ed. by Martine Hennard Dutheil de la Rochère and Irene Weber Henking (Lausanne: Centre de Traduction Littéraire, 2016), pp. 39–61

BATTAGLIA RICCI, LUCIA, 'Immaginario Trionfale: Petrarca e la tradizione figurativa', in *I Triumphi di Francesco Petrarca*, ed. by Claudia Berra (Milan: Cisalpino, 1999), pp. 255–98

BAWCUTT, PRISCILLA, 'James VI's Castalian Band: A Modern Myth', *The Scottish Historical Review*, 80 (2001), 251–59

—— 'The "Library" of Gavin Douglas', in *Bards and Makars: Scottish Language and Literature: Medieval and Renaissance*, ed. by Adam J. Aitken, Matthew P. McDiarmid and Derick S. Thomson (Glasgow: University of Glasgow Press, 1977), pp. 107–26

BAYERLIPP, SUSANNE, '"All gentilmen dooe speake the courtisane": Negotiations of the Italian *Questione della lingua* in William Thomas and the Florios', in *Elizabethan Translation and Literary Culture*, ed. by Gabriela Schmidt (Berlin: Walter de Gruyter, 2013), pp. 147–65

BEILIN, ELAINE V., *Redeeming Eve: Women Writers of the English Renaissance* (Princeton: Princeton University Press, 1987)

BELL, ILONA, *Elizabethan Women and the Poetry of Courtship* (Cambridge: Cambridge University Press, 1998)

BELLONI, GINO, *Laura tra Petrarca e Bembo: studi sul commento umanistico-rinascimentale* (Padua: Antenore, 1992)

BENNETT, J. A. W., *Chaucer's Book of Fame: An Exposition of 'The House of Fame'* (Oxford: Clarendon Press, 1968)

BERGERON, DAVID, *English Civic Pageantry, 1558–1642* (London: Edward Arnold, 1975)

BERNARDO, ALDO S., *Petrarch, Laura, and the Triumphs* (Albany: State University of New York Press, 1975)

BIRRELL, THOMAS ANTHONY, *English Monarchs and their Books: From Henry VII to Charles II* (London: The British Library, 1987)

BISHOP, MORRIS, *Petrarch and his World* (London: Chatto and Windus, 1964)

BOITANI, PIERO, *Chaucer and the Imaginary World of Fame* (Cambridge: Brewer, 1984)

BONDANELLA, JULIA CONAWAY, *Petrarch's Visions and their Renaissance Analogues* (Madrid: José Porrúa Turanzas, 1978)

BOSWELL, JACKSON CAMPBELL, and GORDON MCMURRY BRADEN, *Petrarch's English Laurels 1475–1700* (Farnham: Ashgate, 2012)

BOUTCHER, WARREN, '"A French Dexterity, & an Italian Confidence": New Documents on John Florio, Learned Strangers and Protestant Humanist Study of Modern Languages in Renaissance England from c. 1547 to c. 1625', *Reformation*, 2 (1997), 39–109

—— 'Humanism and Literature in Late Tudor England: Translation, the Continental Book and the Case of Montaigne's Essais', in *Reassessing Tudor Humanism*, ed. by Jonathan Woolfson (Basingstoke: Palgrave Macmillan, 2002), pp. 242–68

BRADEN, GORDON MCMURRY, *Petrarchan Love and the Continental Renaissance* (New Haven: Yale University Press, 1999)

BRADNER, LEICESTER, 'From Petrarch to Shakespeare', in *The Renaissance: A Symposium. February 8–10, 1952* (New York: The Metropolitan Museum of Art, 1953), pp. 63–76

BRANCA, VITTORE, *Boccaccio Medievale* (Florence: Sansoni, 1956)

—— 'Per la genesi dei "Trionfi"', *La Rinascita*, 4 (1941), 681–708

BRAUDY, LEO, *The Frenzy of Renown: Fame and its History* (New York: Oxford University Press, 1986)

BRIGDEN, SUSAN and JONATHAN WOOLFSON, 'Thomas Wyatt in Italy', *Renaissance Quarterly*, 58 (2005), 464–511

CALCATERRA, CARLO, *Nella selva del Petrarca* (Bologna: Cappelli, 1942)
CAMPBELL, HEATHER, 'Petrarch's *I Trionfi* in the English Renaissance' (unpublished doctoral thesis, York University, Ontario, 1990)
CARLEY, JAMES P., *The Books of Henry VIII and his Wives* (London: The British Library, 2004)
—— ed., *The Libraries of Henry VIII* (London: The British Library, 2000)
—— 'Marks in Books and the Libraries of Henry VIII', *Papers of the Bibliographical Society of America*, 91 (1997), 583–606
CARLEY, JAMES P., and MYRA D. ORTH, '"Plus que assez": Simon Bourgouyn and his French Translations from Plutarch, Petrarch and Lucian', *Viator*, 34 (2003), 328–63
CARNICELLI, D. D., 'Bernardo Illicino and the Renaissance Commentaries on Petrarch's *Trionfi*', *Romance Philology*, 23 (1969), 57–64
Catalogue of Additions to the Manuscripts in the British Museum in the Years MDCCCLIV–MDCCCLXXV, 3 vols (London: British Museum, 1877)
Catalogue of Additions to the Manuscripts in the British Museum in the Years MDCCCC–MDCCCCV (London: British Museum, 1907)
CATTANEO, ARTURO, *L'ideale umanistico: Henry Howard, Earl of Surrey* (Bari: Adriatica, 1991)
CLARKE, DANIELLE, '"Lover's Songs Shall Turne to Holy Psalmes": Mary Sidney and the Transformation of Petrarch', in *Mary Sidney, Countess of Pembroke*, ed. by Margaret P. Hannay (Farnham: Ashgate, 2009), pp. 137–49
—— *The Politics of Early Modern Women's Writing* (Edinburgh: Pearson, 2001)
CLEMENT, JENNIFER, 'The Queen's Voice: Elizabeth I's *Christian Prayers and Meditations*', *Early Modern Literary Studies*, 13 (2008), 1–26
COOGAN, ROBERT, 'Petrarch and Thomas More', *Moreana*, 6 (1969), 19–30
—— 'Petrarch's Latin Prose and the English Renaissance', *Studies in Philology*, 68 (1971), 270–91
—— 'Petrarch's *Liber Sine Nomine* and a Vision of Rome in the Reformation', *Renaissance and Reformation / Renaissance et Réforme*, 7 (1983), 1–12
—— 'Petrarch's "Trionfi" and the English Renaissance', *Studies in Philology*, 57 (1960), 306–27
DOMENICHELLI, MARIO, 'La lingua affinata e la percezione di sé', *In forma di parole*, 24 (2004), 447–60
—— 'Sonnets as Triumphi', *Memoria di Shakespeare*, 6 (2008), 61–75
DONAWERTH, JANE, 'Women's Poetry and the Tudor-Stuart System of Gift Exchange', in *Women, Writing, and the Reproduction of Culture in Tudor and Stuart Britain*, ed. by Mary E. Burke, Jane Donawerth, Linda L. Dove and Karen Nelson (Syracuse: Syracuse University Press, 2000), pp. 3–18
DUNCAN-JONES, KATHERINE, 'Review of Carnicelli, *Tryumphes of Fraunces Petrarcke*', *The Review of English Studies*, 23 (1972), 528–29
DUNNIGAN, SARAH M., 'Daughterly Desires: Representing and Reimagining the Feminine in Anna Hume's *Triumphs*', in *Woman and the Feminine in Medieval and Early Modern Scottish Writing*, ed. by Sarah M. Dunnigan, C. Marie Harker and Evelyn S. Newlyn (Basingstoke: Palgrave Macmillan, 2004), pp. 120–35
—— 'Scottish Women Writers, c.1560–c.1650', in *A History of Scottish Women's Writing*, ed. by Douglas Gifford and Dorothy McMillan (Edinburgh: Edinburgh University Press, 1997), pp. 15–43

EDWARDS, A. S. G., 'English Poems', in *The Complete Works of St. Thomas More: Volume 1*, ed. by A. S. G. Edwards, Katherine Gardiner Rodgers and Clarence H. Miller (New Haven: Yale University Press, 1997), pp. xvii–xxxvi

—— 'Manuscripts of the Verse of Henry Howard, Earl of Surrey', *Huntington Library Quarterly*, 67 (2004), 283–93

EISNER, MARTIN, 'Petrarch Reading Boccaccio: Revisiting the Genesis of the *Triumphi*', in *Petrarch and the Textual Origins of Interpretation*, ed. by Teodolinda Barolini and H. Wayne Storey (Leiden: Brill, 2007), pp. 131–46

ELLIS, ROGER, 'The Juvenile Translations of Elizabeth Tudor', *Translation and Literature*, 18 (2009), 177–79

ERASMI, GABRIELE, 'Petrarch's *Trionfi*: The Poetics of Humanism', in *Petrarch's 'Triumphs': Allegory and Spectacle*, ed. by Konrad Eisenbichler and Amilcare A. Iannucci (Ottawa: Dovehouse, 1990), pp. 161–74

EVANS, JOHN, 'Extracts from the Private Account Book of Sir William More', *Archaeologia: or, Miscellaneous Tracts Relating to Antiquity*, 36 (1855), 284–310

FIENBERG, NORA, 'Mary Wroth and the Invention of Female Poetic Subjectivity', in *Reading Mary Wroth: Representing Alternatives in Early Modern England*, ed. by Naomi J. Miller and Gary F. Waller (Knoxville: University of Tennessee Press, 1991), pp. 175–90

FINOTTI, FABIO, 'The Poem of Memory: *Triumphi*', in *Petrarch: A Critical Guide to the Complete Works*, ed. by Victoria Kirkham and Armando Maggi (Chicago: The University of Chicago Press, 2009), pp. 63–83

FLÜGEL, EWALD, 'Verschollene Sonette', *Anglia*, 13 (1891), 72–76

FORSTER, LEONARD WILSON, *The Icy Fire: Five Studies in European Petrarchism* (Cambridge: Cambridge University Press, 1969)

FOSTER, KENELM, *Petrarch: Poet and Humanist* (Edinburgh: Edinburgh University Press, 1984)

FOWLER, ALASTAIR, *Triumphal Forms: Structural Patterns in Elizabethan Poetry* (Cambridge: Cambridge University Press, 1970)

FRECCERO, JOHN, 'The Fig Tree and the Laurel: Petrarch's Poetics', *Diacritics*, 5 (1975), 34–40

FREER, COBURN, 'Mary Sidney: Countess of Pembroke', in *Women Writers of the Renaissance and Reformation*, ed. by Katharina M. Wilson (Athens: University of Georgia Press, 1987), pp. 481–521

GATTI, HILARY, 'Petrarch, Sidney, Bruno', in *Petrarch in Britain: Interpreters, Imitators, and Translators over 700 Years: Proceedings of the British Academy*, ed. by Peter Hainsworth, Martin MacLaughlin and Letizia Panizza (London: The British Academy, 2007), pp. 149–60

GODI, CARLO, 'La "Collatio Laureationis" del Petrarca nelle due redazioni', *Studi Petrarcheschi*, 5 (1988), 1–58

GOLDBERG, JONATHAN, 'The Countess of Pembroke's Literal Translation', in *Desiring Women Writing: English Renaissance Examples*, ed. by Jonathan Goldberg (Stanford: Stanford University Press, 1997), pp. 114–31

GREER, GERMAINE, ET AL., eds, *Kissing the Rod: An Anthology of Seventeenth-Century Women's Verse* (London: Virago Press, 1988)

GUARDIANI, FRANCESCO, 'The Literary Impact of the Trionfi in the Renaissance', in *Petrarch's 'Triumphs': Allegory and Spectacle*, ed. by Konrad Eisenbichler and Amilcare A. Iannucci (Ottawa: Dovehouse, 1990), pp. 259–68

HADFIELD, ANDREW, *Shakespeare and Renaissance Politics* (London: Thomson, 2004)

HANNAY, MARGARET PATTERSON, *Philip's Phoenix: Mary Sidney, Countess of Pembroke* (Oxford: Oxford University Press, 1990)

HIGGITT, JOHN, ed., *Scottish Libraries* (London: The British Library, 2006)

HODDER, MIKE, 'Petrarch in English: Political, Cultural and Religious Filters in the Translation of the *Rerum vulgarium fragmenta* and *Triumphi* from Geoffrey Chaucer to J. M. Synge' (unpublished doctoral thesis, University of Oxford, 2013)

HOSINGTON, BRENDA, 'Tudor Englishwomen's Translations of Continental Protestant Texts: The Interplay of Ideology and Historical Context', in *Tudor Translation*, ed. by Fred Schurink (Basingstoke: Palgrave Macmillan, 2011), pp. 121–42

HUGHEY, RUTH, 'The Harington Manuscript at Arundel Castle and Related Documents', *The Library*, 15 (1935), 388–444

—— *John Harington of Stepney, Tudor Gentleman: His Life and Works* (Columbus: Ohio State University Press, 1971)

HULL, SUZANNE W., *Chaste, Silent & Obedient: English Books for Women 1475–1640* (San Marino: Huntington Library, 1982)

IANNUCCI, AMILCARE A., 'Foreword', in *Petrarch's 'Triumphs': Allegory and Spectacle*, ed. by Konrad Eisenbichler and Amilcare A. Iannucci (Ottawa: Dovehouse, 1990), pp. xi–xv

—— 'Petrarch's Intertextual Strategies in the *Triumphs*', in *Petrarch's 'Triumphs': Allegory and Spectacle*, ed. by Konrad Eisenbichler and Amilcare A. Iannucci (Ottawa: Dovehouse, 1990), pp. 3–10

JACK, R. D. S., 'Petrarch in English and Scottish Renaissance Literature', *Modern Language Review*, 71 (1976), 801–11

—— 'Petrarch and the Scottish Renaissance Sonnet', in *Petrarch in Britain: Interpreters, Imitators, and Translators over 700 Years: Proceedings of the British Academy*, ed. by Peter Hainsworth, Martin MacLaughlin and Letizia Panizza (London: The British Academy, 2007), pp. 259–73

—— 'William Fowler and Italian Literature' *Modern Language Review*, 65 (1970), 481–92

JAMES, THOMAS, *Catalogus librorum bibliothecae publicae quam vir ornatissimus Thomas Bodleius eques auratus in Academia Oxoniensi nuper instituit* (Oxford: Joseph Barnes, 1605)

JAYNE, SEARS, *Library Catalogues of the English Renaissance: Reissue with New Preface and Notes* (Godalming: St Paul's Bibliographies, 1983)

JAYNE, SEARS, and FRANCIS R. JOHNSON, eds, *The Lumley Library: The Catalogue of 1609* (London: The Trustees of the British Museum, 1956)

JOHNSTON, ALEXANDRA F., 'English Civic Ceremony', in *Petrarch's 'Triumphs': Allegory and Spectacle*, ed. by Konrad Eisenbichler and Amilcare A. Iannucci (Ottawa: Dovehouse, 1990), pp. 395–402

JORDAN, CONSTANCE, 'Representing Political Androgyny: More on the Siena Portrait of Queen Elizabeth I', in *The Renaissance Englishwoman in Print: Counterbalancing the Canon*, ed. by Anne M. Haselkorn and Betty S. Travitsky (Amherst: The University of Massachusetts Press, 1990), pp. 157–76

JOSSA, STEFANO, 'Bembo and Italian Petrarchism', in *The Cambridge Companion to*

Petrarch, ed. by Albert Russell Ascoli and Unn Falkeid (Cambridge: Cambridge University Press, 2015), pp. 191–200

KEITH, ROBERT, ed., *History of the Affairs of Church and State in Scotland, from the Beginning of the Reformation to the Year 1568* (Edinburgh: Spottiswoode, 1844–1850)

KENNEDY, WILLIAM J., *Authorizing Petrarch* (Ithaca: Cornell University Press, 1994)

—— 'Petrarchan Poetics', in *The Cambridge History of Literary Criticism, III: The Renaissance*, ed. by Glyn P. Norton (Cambridge: Cambridge University Press, 1999), pp. 119–26

—— *Petrarchism at Work: Contextual Economies in the Age of Shakespeare* (Ithaca: Cornell University Press, 2016)

—— *The Site of Petrarchism: Early Modern National Sentiment in Italy, France, and England* (Baltimore: The Johns Hopkins University Press, 2003)

—— 'Versions of a Career: Petrarch and his Renaissance Commentators', in *European Literary Careers: The Author from Antiquity to the Renaissance*, ed. by Patrick Cheney and Frederick A. de Armas (Toronto: University of Toronto Press, 2002), pp. 146–64

KING, JOHN N., 'Queen Elizabeth I, Representations of the Virgin Queen', *Renaissance Quarterly*, 43 (1990), 30–74

—— *Tudor Royal Iconography: Literature and Art in an Age of Religious Crisis* (Princeton: Princeton University Press, 1989)

KINGSLEY-SMITH, JANE, *Cupid in Early Modern Literature and Culture* (Cambridge: Cambridge University Press, 2010)

KIRKPATRICK, ROBIN, *English and Italian Literature from Dante to Shakespeare* (London: Longman, 1995)

LABRIOLA, ADA, 'Da Padova a Firenze: l'illustrazione dei Trionfi', in *Francesco Petrarca. I Trionfi, Commentario*, ed. by I. Giovanna Rao (Castelvetro di Modena: Artcodex, 2012), pp. 59–115

LAMB, MARY ELLEN, 'The Countess of Pembroke and the Art of Dying', in *Women in the Middle Ages and the Renaissance: Literary and Historical Perspectives*, ed. by Mary Beth Rose (Syracuse: Syracuse University Press, 1986), pp. 207–26

—— 'The Myth of the Countess of Pembroke: The Dramatic Circle', *Yearbook of English Studies*, 11 (1981), 194–202

LAWRENCE, JASON, *'Who the devil taught thee so much Italian?': Italian Language Learning and Literary Imitation in Early Modern England* (Manchester: Manchester University Press, 2005)

LEWIS, C. S., *English Literature in the Sixteenth Century Excluding Drama* (Oxford: Clarendon Press, 1954)

LIEVSAY, JOHN L., *The Englishman's Italian Books 1550–1700* (Philadelphia: University of Pennsylvania Press, 1969)

LINDEMAN, YEHUDI, 'Translation in the Renaissance: A Context and a Map', *Canadian Review of Comparative Literature*, 8 (1981), 204–16

LOADES, DAVID, 'The Personal Religion of Mary I', in *The Church of Mary Tudor*, ed. by Eamon Duffy and David Loades (Aldershot: Ashgate, 2006), pp. 1–29

MACARTHUR, JANET, 'Ventriloquizing Comfort and Despair: Mary Sidney's Female Personae in *The Triumph of Death* and *The Tragedy of Antony*', *Sidney Newsletter & Journal*, 11 (1990), 3–13

MacDonald, Robert H., *The Library of Drummond of Hawthornden* (Edinburgh: Edinburgh University Press, 1971)

Mackenzie, Elizabeth, 'What about Petrarch?', *The Review of English Studies*, 34 (1983), 458–63

Mann, Nicholas, 'Dal moralista al poeta: appunti per la fortuna del Petrarca in Inghilterra', in *Atti dei convegni Lincei: Convegno internazionale Francesco Petrarca* (Rome: Accademia Nazionale dei Lincei, 1976), pp. 59–69

—— 'Il Petrarca e gli inizi del Rinascimento inglese', *La Cultura*, 15 (1977), 3–18

—— 'Petrarch and Humanism: The Paradox of Posterity', in *Francesco Petrarca, Citizen of the World*, ed. by Aldo S. Bernardo (Padua: Antenore, 1980), pp. 287–99

—— 'Petrarch Manuscripts in the British Isles', *Italia Medioevale e Umanistica*, 18 (1975), 139–509

—— 'Petrarch's Role in Humanism', *Apollo*, 94 (1971), 176–83

—— 'La prima fortuna del Petrarca in Inghilterra', in *Il Petrarca ad Arquà. Atti del convegno di studi nel VI centenario (1370–1374)*, ed. by Giuseppe Billanovich and Giuseppe Frasso (Padua: Antenore, 1975), pp. 279–89

Martin, Christopher, 'Retrieving Jonson's Petrarch', *Shakespeare Quarterly*, 45 (1994), 89–92

Martinez, Ronald L., 'Francis, Thou Art Translated: Petrarch Metamorphosed in English, 1380–1595', *Humanist Studies & the Digital Age*, 1 (2011), 80–108

May, Steven W., 'Early Courtier Verse: Oxford, Dyer, and Gascoigne', in *Early Modern English Poetry: A Critical Companion*, ed. by Patrick Cheney, Andrew Hadfield and Garrett A. Sullivan (New York: Oxford University Press, 2007), pp. 60–69

—— 'Recent Studies in Elizabeth I', *English Literary Renaissance*, 23 (1993), 345–54

—— 'Tudor Aristocrats and the Mythical "Stigma of Print"', in *Renaissance Papers 1980*, ed. by A. Leigh Deneef and M. Thomas Hester (Durham, NC: The Southeastern Renaissance Conference, 1981), pp. 11–18

Mazzotta, Giuseppe, *The Worlds of Petrarch* (Durham, NC: Duke University Press, 1993)

McClure, J. Derrick, 'Translation and Transcreation in the Castalian Period', *Studies in Scottish Literature*, 26 (1991), 185–98

Melzi, Robert C., 'A Contribution to the History of Petrarchism in England: Robert Tofte and The Blazon of Jealousy', *Rivista di Studi Italiani*, 15 (1997), 1–32

Minta, Stephen, *Petrarch and Petrarchism: The English and French Traditions* (Manchester: Manchester University Press, 1980)

Mommsen, Theodor E., 'Petrarch and the Decoration of the *Sala Virorum Illustrium* in Padua', *Art Bulletin*, 34 (1952), 95–116

—— 'Petrarch's Conception of the "Dark Ages"', *Speculum*, 17 (1942), 226–42

Mueller, Janel, 'Textualism, Contextualism, and the Writings of Queen Elizabeth I', in *English Studies and History*, ed. by David Robertson (Tampere: University of Tampere Press, 1994), pp. 11–38

Muir, Kenneth, 'Surrey Poems in the Blage Manuscript', *Notes and Queries*, 205 (1960), 368–70

Mumford, Ivy L., 'Petrarchism in Early Tudor England', *Italian Studies*, 19 (1964), 56–63

Norbrook, David, 'The Rhetor', *New Republic*, 223 (2000), 41

PELLEGRINI, CARLO, 'Il Petrarca nella cultura francese', *Rivista di letterature moderne*, 1 (1946), 75–84
PERRY, MARIA, *Elizabeth I: The Word of a Prince: A Life from Contemporary Documents* (London: The Folio Society, 1990)
PETRINA, ALESSANDRA, 'Approaching Petrarch's Trionfi: Paratexts in the Early Modern Scottish Translations', in *Thresholds of Translation: Paratexts, Print, and Cultural Exchange in Early Modern Britain (1473–1660)*, ed. by Marie-Alice Belle and Brenda M. Hosington (Cham: Palgrave Macmillan, 2018), 161–82
—— 'The Humanist Petrarch in Medieval and Early Modern England', *Journal of Anglo-Italian Studies*, 12 (2013), 45–62
—— *Machiavelli in the British Isles: Two Early Modern Translations of the Prince* (Farnham: Ashgate, 2009)
—— 'Translation and Language Learning: The English Version of Petrarch's *Triumph of Eternity* Attributed to Elizabeth I', in *Early Modern Exchanges: Dialogues Between Nations and Cultures, 1550-1750*, ed. by Helen Hackett (Farnham: Ashgate, 2015), pp. 55–71
PIRILLO, DIEGO, 'Republicanism and Religious Dissent: Machiavelli and the Italian Protestant Reformers', in *Machiavellian Encounters in Tudor and Stuart England: Literary and Political Influences from the Reformation to the Restoration*, ed. by Alessandro Arienzo and Alessandra Petrina (Farnham: Ashgate, 2013), pp. 121–40
PLANT, MARGARET, 'Patronage in the Circle of the Carrara Family: Padua, 1337–1405', in *Patronage, Art and Society in Renaissance Italy*, ed. by F. W. Kent and Patricia Simons (Oxford: Clarendon Press, 1987), pp. 177–99
POZONE, ANGELA, 'Un commentatore quattrocentesco del Petrarca: Bernardo Ilicino', *Atti della Accademia Pontaniana*, 23 (1974), 371–90
PUGH, SYRITHE, 'Sidney, Spenser, and Political Petrarchism', in *Petrarch in Britain: Interpreters, Imitators, and Translators over 700 Years: Proceedings of the British Academy*, ed. by Peter Hainsworth, Martin MacLaughlin and Letizia Panizza (London: The British Academy, 2007), pp. 243–57
REES, D. G., 'Petrarch's "Trionfo della Morte" in English', *Italian Studies*, 7 (1952), 82–96
RELLE, ELEANOR, 'Some New Marginalia and Poems of Gabriel Harvey', *The Review of English Studies*, 23 (1972), 401–16
RICHARDSON, BRIAN, *Print Culture in Renaissance Italy: The Editor and the Vernacular Text 1470–1700* (Cambridge: Cambridge University Press, 1994)
RIDDEHOUGH, GEOFFREY B., 'Queen Elizabeth's Translation of Boethius' *De consolatione philosophiae*', *Journal of English and Germanic Philology*, 45 (1946), 88–94
ROBERTS, JOSEPHINE A., 'Recent Studies in Women Writers of Tudor England Part II: Mary Sidney, Countess of Pembroke', *English Literary Renaissance*, 14 (1984), 426–39
ROCHE, THOMAS P., *Petrarch in English* (London: Penguin, 2005)
ROE, JOHN, 'Petrarch in England', in *The Routledge Research Companion to Anglo-Italian Renaissance Literature and Culture*, ed. by Michele Marrapodi (London: Routledge, 2019), pp. 269–87
SARGENT, RALPH M., 'The Authorship of *The Praise of Nothing*', *The Library*, 12 (1931), 322–31

—— *At the Court of Queen Elizabeth: The Life and Lyrics of Sir Edward Dyer* (London: Oxford University Press, 1935)

SAUNDERS, J. W., 'The Stigma of Print: A Note on the Social Bases of Tudor Poetry', *Essays in Criticism*, 1 (1951), 139–64

SCHURINK, FRED (ed.), *Plutarch in English, 1528–1603*, 2 vols (London: Modern Humanities Research Association, forthcoming).

SCODEL, JOSHUA, 'Lyric', in *The Oxford History of Literary Translation in English: Volume 2: 1550–1660*, ed. by Gordon McMurry Braden, Robert Cummings and Stuart Gillespie (Oxford: Oxford University Press, 2010), pp. 212–47

SCOTT, JANET G., *Les Sonnets élisabéthains: les sources et l'apport personnel* (Paris: Champion, 1929)

SCOTT-WARREN, JASON, *Early Modern English Literature* (Cambridge: Polity Press, 2005)

—— *Sir John Harington and the Book as Gift* (Oxford: Oxford University Press, 2001)

SESSIONS, WILLIAM A., *Henry Howard: The Poet Earl of Surrey: A Life* (Oxford: Oxford University Press, 1999)

SEZNEC, JEAN, 'Petrarch and Renaissance Art', in *Francesco Petrarca, Citizen of the World*, ed. by Aldo S. Bernardo (Padua: Antenore, 1980), pp. 133–50

SHARMAN, JULIAN, *The Library of Mary Queen of Scots* (London: Elliot Stock, 1889)

SHAW, DUNCAN, 'Adam Bothwell, a Conserver of the Renaissance in Scotland', in *The Renaissance and Reformation in Scotland: Essays in Honour of Gordon Donaldson*, ed. by Ian B. Cowan and Duncan Shaw (Edinburgh: Scottish Academic Press, 1983), pp. 141–69

SHIRE, HELENA MENNIE, *Song, Dance and Poetry of the Court of Scotland under King James VI* (Cambridge: Cambridge University Press, 1969)

SIMONE, FRANCESCO, *Il Rinascimento francese. Studi e ricerche* (Turin: SEI, 1961)

SIMPSON, JAMES, *Reform and Cultural Revolution* (Oxford: Oxford University Press, 2002)

—— 'Subjects of Triumph and Literary History: Dido and Petrarch in Petrarch's *Africa* and *Trionfi*', *Journal of Medieval and Early Modern Studies*, 35 (2005), 489–508

S[PENCER], J[OANNES], *Catalogus Universalis librorum omnium in Bibliotheca Collegii Sionii apud Londinenses* (London: Robert Leybourn, 1650)

STAMATAKIS, CHRIS, *Sir Thomas Wyatt and the Rhetoric of Rewriting: 'Turning the Word'* (Oxford: Oxford University Press, 2012)

STERN, VIRGINIA F., *Gabriel Harvey: His Life, Marginalia and Library* (Oxford: Clarendon Press, 1979)

STOLL, JESSICA, 'Petrarch's De vita solitaria: Samuel Daniel's Translation c. 1610', *Modern Language Review*, 109 (2014), 313–32

STRYPE, JOHN, *The Life of the Learned Sir Thomas Smith Kt. Doctor of the Civil Law; Principal Secretary of State to King Edward the Sixth, and Queen Elizabeth* (London: A. Roper, 1698)

SUMMIT, JENNIFER, 'The arte of a ladies penne: Elizabeth I and the Poetics of Queenship', in *Reading Monarch's Writing: The Poetry of Henry VIII, Mary Stuart, Elizabeth I, and James VI/I*, ed. by Peter C. Herman (Tempe: Arizona Center for Medieval and Renaissance Studies, 2002), pp. 79–108

SUOMELA-HÄRMÄ, ELINA, 'Note sulla prima traduzione francese dei "Trionfi" di Petrarca', *Studi Francesi*, 129 (1999), 545-53

—— 'Stratégies de traduction dans la première version française des "Triomphes" de Pétrarque', *Moyen Français*, 51-53 (2002-2003), 547-58

TAYLOR, KARLA, 'Writers of the Italian Renaissance', in *The Oxford History of Literary Translation in English: Volume I: To 1550*, ed. by Roger Ellis (Oxford: Oxford University Press, 2008), pp. 390-406

THOMSON, PATRICIA TYLER, *Sir Thomas Wyatt and his Background* (London: Routledge & Kegan Paul, 1964)

TRAPP, J. B., *Erasmus, Colet and More: The Early Tudor Humanists and their Books* (London: The British Library, 1991)

—— 'Illustrations of Petrarch's *Trionfi* from Manuscript to Print and Print to Manuscript', in *Incunabula: Studies in Fifteenth-Century Printed Books Presented to Lotte Hellinga*, ed. by Martin Davies (London: The British Library, 1999), pp. 507-47

—— 'More and the Visual Arts', in *Saggi sul Rinascimento*, ed. by Sergio Rossi (Milan: Unicopli, 1984), pp. 27-54

—— 'Petrarch's *Triumph of Death* in Tapestry', in *Studies of Petrarch and his Influence* (London: The Pindar Press, 2003), pp. 171-200

TRILL, SUZANNE, '"In Poesie the mirrois of our Age": The Countess of Pembroke's "Sydnean" Poetics', in *A Companion to Tudor Literature*, ed. by Kent Cartwright (Chichester: Wiley-Blackwell, 2010), pp. 428-43

VAN HEIJNSBERGEN, THEO, 'Coteries, Commendatory Verse and Jacobean Poetics: William Fowler's Trivmphs of Petrarke and its Castalian Circles', in *James VI and I, Literature and Scotland: Tides of Change, 1567-1625*, ed. by David J. Parkinson (Leuven: Peeters, 2013), pp. 45-64

VERWEIJ, SEBASTIAAN, *The Literary Culture of Early Modern Scotland: Manuscript Production and Transmission, 1560-1625* (Oxford: Oxford University Press, 2016)

—— 'The Manuscripts of William Fowler: A Revaluation of *The Tarantula of Love, A Sonnet Sequence*, and *Of Death*', *Scottish Studies Review*, 8 (2007), 9-23

WALKER, GREG, *Writing under Tyranny: English Literature and the Henrician Reformation* (Oxford: Oxford University Press, 2005)

WALLER, GARY F., 'The Countess of Pembroke and Gendered Reading', in *The Renaissance Englishwoman in Print: Counterbalancing the Canon*, ed. by Anne M. Haselkorn and Betty S. Travitsky (Amherst: The University of Massachusetts Press, 1990), pp. 327-45

—— *English Poets of the Sixteenth Century* (Harlow: Longman, 1986)

—— *Mary Sidney, Countess of Pembroke: A Critical Study of her Writing and Literary Milieu* (Salzburg: Institut für Anglistik und Amerikanistik Universität Salzburg, 1979)

—— *The Sidney Family Romance: Mary Wroth, William Herbert, and the Early Modern Construction of Gender* (Detroit: Wayne State University Press, 1993)

WARNER, GEORGE F., *The Library of James VI: 1573-1583, From a Manuscript in the Hand of Peter Young, his Tutor* (Edinburgh: Constable, 1893)

WASWO, RICHARD, 'The Petrarchan Tradition as a Dialectic of Limits', *Studies in the Literary Imagination*, 11 (1978), 1-16

WATKINS, RENEE NEU, 'Petrarch and the Black Death: From Fear to Monuments',

Studies in the Renaissance, 29 (1972), 196–223
WATSON, GEORGE, *The English Petrarchans: A Critical Bibliography of the Canzoniere* (London: The Warburg Institute, 1967)
WHEATLEY, EDWARD, *Mastering Aesop: Medieval Education, Chaucer, and his Followers* (Gainesville: University Press of Florida, 2000)
WILKINS, ERNEST HATCH, 'The Fifteenth-Century Editions of the Italian Poems of Petrarch', *Modern Philology*, 40 (1943), 225–39
—— 'The First Two "Triumphs" of Petrarch', *Italica*, 40 (1963), 7–17
—— 'A General Survey of Renaissance Petrarchism', *Comparative Literature*, 2 (1950), 327–42
—— *The Making of the 'Canzoniere' and other Petrarchan Studies* (Rome: Edizioni di Storia e Letteratura, 1951)
—— 'On the Chronology of the *Triumphs*', in *Studies in the Life and Works of Petrarch* (Cambridge: The Mediaeval Academy of America, 1955), pp. 254–72
—— 'On Petrarch's Rewriting the *Triumph of Fame*', *Speculum*, 39 (1964), 440–43
WOODS, SUSANNE, 'Lord Morley's "Ryding Ryme" and the Origins of Modern English Versification', in *'Triumphs of English': Henry Parker, Lord Morley: Translator to the Tudor Court. New Essays in Interpretation*, ed. by Marie Axton and James P. Carley (London: The British Library, 2000), pp. 201–11
WRIGHT, GILLIAN, 'Mary Sidney Pembroke', in *The Oxford History of Literary Translation in English: Volume 2: 1550–1660*, ed. by Gordon Braden, Robert Cummings and Stuart Gillespie (Oxford: Oxford University Press, 2010), pp. 78–82
WYATT, MICHAEL, *The Italian Encounter with Tudor England: A Cultural Politics of Translation* (Cambridge: Cambridge University Press, 2005)
—— 'Other Petrarchs in Early Modern England', in *Petrarch in Britain: Interpreters, Imitators, and Translators over 700 Years: Proceedings of the British Academy*, ed. by Peter Hainsworth, Martin MacLaughlin and Letizia Panizza (London: The British Academy, 2007), pp. 203–16
YATES, FRANCES A., *Astraea: The Imperial Theme in the Sixteenth Century* (London: Routledge & Kegan Paul, 1975)
—— 'Italian Teachers in Elizabethan England', *Journal of the Warburg Institute*, 1 (1937), 103–16
—— *John Florio: The Life of an Italian in Shakespeare's England* (Cambridge: Cambridge University Press, 1934)
YOUNG, FRANCES BERKELEY, *Mary Sidney, Countess of Pembroke* (London: David Nutt, 1912)
—— 'The Triumphe of Death Translated out of Italian by the Countesse of Pembrooke', *PMLA*, 27 (1912), 52–75

INDEX

Aesop 39
Alighieri, Dante 9, 13, 17–18, 23, 38
Anne of Denmark, wife to James VI/I 40, 63
Ariosto, Ludovico, *Orlando Furioso* 13–14, 37, 45 n. 191, 202
Ascham, Roger, *The Scholemaster* 21, 25

Beaton, Mary 41–42
Bembo, Pietro 5, 7, 13, 15, 16
Boccaccio, Giovanni 8, 13, 14, 18, 23, 38
    Decameron 23
    De casibus virorum illustrium 23
    De claris mulieribus 38
    Amorosa visione 18
Boethius 54, 55
Bonner, Edmund 22
Bothwell, Adam 24–25
Bourgouyn, Simon 27–28, 29, 40
Brucioli, Antonio 5–6
Bruni, Leonardo, *Lives of Dante and Petrarch* 16

Cappel, Guillaume 12
Castiglione, Baldassarre, *Libro del Cortegiano* 15, 16, 22
Catherine of Aragon 10–12, 22–23, 27
Cecil, Sir William 34
Charles d'Orléans 27
Chaucer, Geoffrey 10, 40
    Canterbury Tales 2, 39
    House of Fame 2
    Treatise of the Astrolabe 12
    Troilus and Criseyde 2
Churchyard, Thomas, *Pleasant Conceite* 25
Cicero 38, 69
Cockburn, Richard 43, 74 n. 35
Colville, Alexander 43, 63, 75 n. 42
Constable, Henry 24
Cromwell, Thomas 22

d'India, Sigismondo 34
da Longiano, Fausto 5–6
da Tempo, Antonio 5

Daniel, Samuel 12
Daniello, Bernardino 5, 57
Daunce, Edward 47
de Madrid, Francisco 22
de Mézières, Philippe 22
de Obregon, Antonio 23, 27
de la Forge, Georges 27
Descartes, René 57
Douglas, Elizabeth 43, 63, 72 n. 26
Drummond of Hawthornden, William 25, 55, 63, 68 n. 8
Du Bellay, Joachim 20–21, 34
Du Plessis Mornay, Philippe, *Excellent discours de la vie et de la mort* 48
Dürer, Albrecht 31
Dyer, Edward 47

'E. D.', *Prayse of Nothing* 36, 47, 59, 175
Edward VI, King of England 23
Elizabeth, Princess of Bohemia 56, 57
Elizabeth I, Queen of England 19, 23, 26, 33–34, 36, 45, 47, 49, 51, 52–55, 115 n. 317, 202, 206–07
Erasmus 16, 38

Farley, Robert 188–89
Ferrabosco, Alfonso 34
Filelfo, Francesco 5, 24
Fleming, Jean, Lady Thirlestane 40, 42, 43, 63, 69–70
Florio, John 1, 14 n. 58, 15–16, 36, 50, 51–52, 205
Fowler, William 40–43, 48, 59, 63–64, 68 n. 8, 69–70
    The Tarantula of Love 41, 45, 63
    translation of Machiavelli's *Prince* 41, 42, 45, 46
    translation of *Triumphi* 26, 28, 36, 40–47, 50, 57, 58, 59, 63–65, 72 n. 22
François I, King of France 7

Garnier, Robert, *Marc Antoine* 48
Geddie, John 63–64

Gesualdo, Giovanni Andrea 5, 6, 24, 76 n. 43
Giotto 31
Giovio, Paolo 38
Golding, Arthur 44
Gower, George 33

Harington, John 48, 52, 176, 202
Harvey, Gabriel 2 n. 5, 14
Hawes, Stephen, *Pastime of Pleasure* 33
Henry VIII, King of England 22, 23, 26, 33, 36, 37–38
Henryson, Robert, *Morall Fabillis* 39
Homer 21, 22, 43, 51
Howard, Henry, Earl of Surrey 13–14, 17, 36–37, 52, 202
Hudson, Robert 41, 42, 43, 73 n. 32, 74 n. 38
Hudson, Thomas 41, 42, 43, 74 n. 38
Hume, Anna 19, 28, 36, 47, 55–58, 59, 188–89
Hume of Godscroft, David 55

Ilicino, Bernardo 6, 23, 46

James VI/I, King of Scotland and England 24, 40, 41,42, 43, 44, 45, 56, 63, 65, 69, 72 n. 22, 143 n. 467
Jonson, Ben 25–26

Ketel, Cornelius 33
Kyd, Thomas, *Householder's Philosophy* 25

Leopardi, Giacomo 6
Lumley, John, Lord Lumley 23
Lydgate, John 2–3, 35
    The Fall of Princes 3, 17
    Isopes Fabules 39

Machiavelli, Niccolò 10, 12, 14, 16, 22, 25, 41, 42
Maitland, John 41, 69, 74 n. 35
Mantegna, Andrea 31
Marenzio, Luca 34
Marot, Clément 29, 34
Mary, Queen of Scots 24, 34, 41, 42
Maximilian I, Emperor 31
Meynier, Jean, Baron d'Oppède 29
Minturno, Antonio, *Arte Poetica* 9
Moffett, Thomas, *The Silkewormes and their Flies* 48

Montgomerie, Alexander 41
More, Sir Thomas 33
More, Sir William 23

Nagonius, Johannes Michael 22

Ovid 35, 37, 44

Parker, Henry, Lord Morley 22, 24, 27–28, 36, 37–40, 42, 44, 47, 48, 50, 54, 58, 59, 160
Parr, Catherine 23
Petrarch (Francesco Petrarca)
    Africa 1, 25, 38
    De remediis utriusque fortunae 1–2, 3, 11–12, 22–24, 31, 38, 46
    De viris illustribus 30
    De vita solitaria 12
    Epistolae 25, 38
    Canzoniere 1, 3, 4–5, 6–10, 14, 17, 18, 19, 21, 23, 24, 25, 29, 34, 35–36, 37, 38, 45, 46, 53
    Liber sine nomine 6
    Psalmi Penitentiales 24
    Secretum 24, 39–40
    Triumphi 1, 3, 4–5, 6–10, 13, 14, 16–19, 21–23, 24, 25, 26–37, 38–40, 42–55, 57, 58–60, 63–64, 69–70, 72 n. 22
Phaer, Thomas 44
Philieul, Vasquin 27
Piero della Francesca 31
Plutarch 38
    De tranquillitate animi 10–12
Propertius 43
Puttenham, George, *Art of English Poesy* 13–14

Raleigh, Sir Walter 21, 25
Randolph, Thomas 34
Rizus Novariensis, Bernardinus 30–31
Robertet, Jean 27
Roman de la rose 18
Rouillié, Guillaume 46

Salernitano, Masuccio 38
Saunder, Nicholas 51
Scott, Walter, Laird of Buccleuch 42
Shakespeare, William 26, 104 n. 250

Sidney, Mary, Countess of Pembroke 19, 36, 47–50
    translation of *Triumphus Mortis* 45, 47–50, 58, 59, 176
Sidney, Sir Philip 14, 20, 47, 48, 49, 52
    Astrophil and Stella 20, 50
    Defence of Poesy 2, 20, 42 n. 180
Skelton, John, *Colin Clout* 33
Smith, Sir Thomas 23
Spenser, Edmund 14, 21, 34, 35
Squarzafico, Hieronimo 5
Stewart, Francis, Earl of Bothwell 41, 68 n. 8
Stewart of Baldynneis, John 45 n. 191
Surrey, Earl of, *see* Howard, Henry

Tasso, Torquato 25
Thomas, William, *Historie of Italie* 15
Tilman, Abraham 24
Tiptoft, John 2
Tofte, Robert, *The Blazon of Jealousie* 25
Tottel, Richard, *Songes and Sonettes* 10, 26, 52
Trevisa, John, *Dialogue between a Lord and a Clerk* 13
Twyne, Thomas 12, 160

van der Noot, Jan 34
Vellutello, Alessandro 6–9, 23, 24, 25, 38, 57, 60
Vergerius, Petrus Paulus 6
Virgil, *Aeneid* 18, 22, 34, 43, 44, 51

Walsingham, Sir Francis 40, 59, 64
Watson, Thomas 22 n. 88
    Amyntas 21–22, 43
Wroth, Mary 50
Wyatt, Sir Thomas 3, 10–12, 13, 23, 26, 36, 52, 202

www.ingramcontent.com/pod-product-compliance
Lightning Source LLC
Chambersburg PA
CBHW061441300426
44114CB00014B/1783